Held
in Trust

Held
in Trust

WAQF IN THE ISLAMIC WORLD

Edited by
Pascale Ghazaleh

The American University in Cairo Press
Cairo New York

First published in 2011 by
The American University in Cairo Press
113 Sharia Kasr el Aini, Cairo, Egypt
420 Fifth Avenue, New York, NY 10018
www.aucpress.com

Dar el Kutub No. 2367/10
ISBN 978 977 416 393 7

Dar el Kutub Cataloging-in-Publication Data

Ghazaleh, Pascale
        Held in Trust: Waqf in the Islamic World/ Pascale Ghazaleh.—Cairo: The American
    University in Cairo Press, 2011
        p.   cm.
        ISBN 978 977 416 393 7
        1. Islamic Law   2. Waqf   I. Ghazaleh, Pascale (ed.)   II. Title
        297.14

1 2 3 4 5 6   14 13 12 11

Designed by Fatiha Bouzidi
Printed in Egypt

Contents

Contributors

Introduction: Pious Foundations: From Here to Eternity?   1
Pascale Ghazaleh

1. Dervishes, Waqfs, and Conquest: Notes on Early Ottoman
   Expansion in Thrace   23
   Rıza Yıldırım

2. Piety and Profit: The Haramayn Endowments in Egypt
   (1517–1814)   41
   Husam 'Abd al-Mu'ti

3. The Sadir al-Fuqaha' wa-l-Fuqara' Endowment (Salah al-Din
   al-Ayyubi) in Alexandria during the Eighteenth Century   73
   Nasir Ibrahim

4. Control of Urban Waqfs in al-Salt, Transjordan   103
   Michael J. Reimer

5. Zawiyat Sidi al-Ghazi: Survival of a Traditional
   Religious Institution   121
   John A. Shoup

6. Guild Waqf: Between Religious Law and Common Law   135
   Nelly Hanna

7. Waqfs of Cyrenaica and Italian Colonialism in Libya (1911–41) 155
   Anna Maria Medici

8. The Waqf System: Maintenance, Repair, and Upkeep 179
   Dina Ishak Bakhoum

9. The Role of Waqf in Shaping and Preserving Urban Areas:
   The Historical Commercial Center of Adana 197
   Tuba Akar

Conclusion: Ottoman Waqfs as Acts of Citizenship 209
   Engin F. Isin

Contributors

Husam 'Abd al-Mu'ti is a professor in the Department of History at Beni Sueif University in Egypt. He has published extensively in Arabic. His publications includes *al-'Ilaqat al-misriya al-hijaziya fi-l-qarn al-thamin 'ashar* (1999) and *al-'A'ila wa-l-tharwa: al-buyut al-tijariya al-maghribiya fi Misr al-'uthmaniya* (2009). His research focuses on Ottoman Egypt.

Tuba Akar graduated from the Department of Architecture at Çukurova University and received her MSc and PhD degrees from Middle East Technical University. Her areas of research and interest are conservation of architectural heritage, waqf and conservation, conservation of historical commercial buildings, and the legal, administrative, and financial aspects of conservation. She currently teaches design in restoration and conservation, architectural design, and graphic communication at the Department of Architecture, Mersin University, Turkey.

Dina Ishak Bakhoum is the conservation program manager at the Aga Khan Trust for Culture (AKTC) in Egypt, where she has been working since 2004. She manages and coordinates a number of conservation and restoration projects in al-Darb al-Ahmar. Bakhoum holds an MA in Islamic Art and Architecture and a BSc in Construction Engineering and Management, both from the American University in Cairo, where she currently teaches courses in Islamic architecture and the conservation of the built heritage of Historic Cairo. Before joining AKTC she worked on several conservation projects in Historic Cairo and in the Theban Necropolis (Luxor) with the American Research Center in Egypt (ARCE), the Theban Mapping Project, the Metropolitan Museum of Art, and others.

Pascale Ghazaleh is an assistant professor of Middle East history in the Department of History at the American University in Cairo. She is the author of *Fortunes urbaines et stratégies sociales: Généalogies patrimoniales au Caire, 1780–1830* (2010, 2 vols.). Her research interests include social networks, material culture, and legal praxis.

Nelly Hanna is a professor in the Department of Arab and Islamic Civilizations, American University in Cairo. She has authored and edited a number of works, including *Artisan Entrepreneurs in Cairo and Early Modern Capitalism (1600–1800)* (2011); *In Praise of Books: A Cultural History of Cairo's Middle Class, 16th–18th Centuries* (2003); *Making Big Money in 1600: The Life and Times of Isma'il Abu Taqiyya, Egyptian Merchant* (1998); and *Money, Land and Trade: An Economic History of the Muslim Mediterranean* (ed., 2002). She has done pioneering research on the social, economic, and cultural history of Ottoman Egypt, and played a founding role in the emergence of a new school of Ottoman historiography.

Nasir Ibrahim teaches modern and contemporary history at Cairo University. He has been an active member of the Egyptian Historical Studies Association since 1992 and was active in helping to establish the association's Ottoman history seminar between 1997 and 2009. He has edited five volumes of the seminar's proceedings and has published several other works, including *Social Crises in Egypt in the 17th Century* and *The French in Upper Egypt: The Financial Conflict (1798–1801)*. He is interested in political, social, and economic changes in late eighteenth- and early nineteenth-century Egypt.

Engin F. Isin holds a chair in citizenship and is professor of politics at the Faculty of Social Sciences, the Open University. He is the author of *Cities Without Citizens: Modernity of the City as a Corporation* (1992), *Citizenship and Identity* with Patricia K. Wood (1999), and *Being Political: Genealogies of Citizenship* (2002). He has co-edited with Bryan S. Turner and Peter Nyers, *Citizenship Between Past and Future* (2008) and with Greg Nielsen, *Acts of Citizenship* (2008). His latest book, *Recasting the Social in Citizenship* (2008), is about bridging social and political struggles over citizenship. Professor Isin is the principal investigator of Enacting European Citizenship (ENACT) and Citizenship after Orientalism (OECUMENE), both funded by the European Research Council.

Anna Maria Medici teaches at the University of Urbino, Italy, and is the author of *Città italiane sulla via della Mecca* (2001). She has also edited *Yemen 2010: La crisi e la sicurezza. Informazione e opinione pubblica in Europa e nel Golfo* (2011) and *Mondo arabo. Cittadini e Welfare sociale*, special issue of "Afriche e Orienti," vol. 1 (2008). Her main research interests are Muslim travelers in Italy, Islamic charitable trusts, welfare and social rights, and contemporary Islamic radicalism.

Michael J. Reimer is an associate professor of Middle East history in the Department of History at the American University in Cairo. His ongoing research and teaching interests include the history and historiography of Egypt; municipal administration, waqf foundations, and the dynamics of local politics in Transjordan; and Muslim–Christian relations. Recent publications include "The Quest of the Historical Jesus at the American University in Cairo: A Progress Report," *Islam and Christian-Muslim Relations* 21 (1): 23–28; and "The Mansuri Collection at the Library of Congress: An Underutilized Resource for the Study of Muslim Religious, Intellectual, and Social History," *Review of Middle East Studies* 44 (1): 19–32.

John A. Shoup taught at the American University in Cairo from 1990 to 1996 and has taught at Al Akhawayn University in Ifrane, Morocco from 1996 to the present. He received his BA and MA in Middle Eastern Studies/ Arabic from the University of Utah and his PhD in Cultural Anthropology from Washington University in St. Louis. He has authored and co-authored several articles and book chapters and is the author of *Culture and Customs of Jordan* (2007) and *Culture and Customs of Syria* (2008) and co-author of *Saudi Arabia and Gulf Arab States Today: An Encyclopedia of Life in the Arab States* (2009). He was part of a research team for the Baseline Survey conducted in the Middle Atlas region of Ifrane (2000) and on the impact of tourism in the Atlantic port city of Essaouira (2001–2002), published as *Assessing Tourism in Essaouira* (2002).

Rıza Yıldırım is assistant professor of Ottoman history at TOBB University of Economics and Technology (Turkey). His research concerns the history and religious beliefs and practices of the Alevi/Bektashi community, as well as other religious movements and trends in the Ottoman Empire. He has published research on the early phases of Alevi/Bektashi history and the formation of their religious institutions.

Introduction

Pious Foundations: From Here to Eternity?

Pascale Ghazaleh

For centuries, *waqf*s (endowments or foundations) were a crucial part of the political, economic, and social history of the Arab and Muslim world. As service-providing institutions, waqfs were a major source of education, health care, and employment. As urban landmarks, they shaped the city and contributed to the upkeep of religious edifices.[1] By definition, these endowments were conceived to generate income and therefore played a crucial role in both rural and urban economies, helping channel surplus from the countryside to the cities. Rulers and subjects, Christians, Muslims, and Jews alike, could establish them; their revenue, while ultimately intended for the community as a whole, could be directed toward private beneficiaries as well. Waqfs constituted a major resource and as such were a favorite target in reform efforts undertaken by various rulers: in that regard, their status and such related issues as ownership and entitlement were repeatedly at stake in struggles to impose competing definitions of legitimacy and community. These essays aim to show that waqf should be seen above all as a collection of specific practices that expressed the intentions of a wide variety of users, rather than as a rigid and unchanging institution. These practices were unified by a common structure that created a specific relationship between a property owner, a property, and those who benefited from its revenues. Beyond that, however, waqfs were sufficiently flexible to embrace a very wide variety of uses and fulfill widely diverging intentions.

1

Before commenting further on their founders, beneficiaries, revenue sources, and uses, let us start with a definition of waqfs. Generally speaking, they had to consist of two main elements: first, a source of revenue, such as a building rented out for residential or commercial purposes, agricultural land that generated taxes, a public bath, or a warehouse; and second, a beneficiary, such as a mosque, a hospital, the poor, members of the founder's family, freed slaves, or any other recipient of the founder's choosing. To be valid, a waqf had to consist of an object or objects originally held in full property; the founder had to be of sound mind and body, and able to dedicate the property in question to God (in other words, a waqf could not be established by a bankrupt founder seeking to protect his property from confiscation); and the waqf had to be permanent, which meant that the revenue it generated had to be renewable, the property had to be subject to renewal or renovation, and the founder had to stipulate means of ensuring the perpetuity of the waqf and the continual disbursement of its revenues.

From this definition, it would be easy to conclude that waqfs, once created, immobilized property and hampered the market forces that might otherwise have affected it. The evolution of jurisprudence, however, as well as the real transactions affecting waqfs show that these institutions, contrary to earlier assumptions, neither led to economic stagnation nor froze up real estate. Closer examination of the interplay between law and custom—and, more specifically, of the varying legal, institutional, and practical aspects of waqfs in different regions and communities (for example, cash waqfs in Anatolia and the Arab provinces)[2]—has been necessary to appreciate their dynamism and resilience more fully. Historians have been able to develop an understanding of how waqfs structured the social and physical landscape through the study of waqf deeds—*waqfiyas*—from a macrohistorical perspective, and supplemented by chronicles, biographical dictionaries, and topography. These sources make it possible to estimate the scope of services provided and draw conclusions regarding prices and salaries, the social identity and status of founders and beneficiaries, and the types of real estate or movable goods selected as targets for investment.[3]

Moreover, individual waqf deeds may be examined from a microhistorical perspective with the aim of recovering the social networks that waqfs created, perpetuated, or bypassed, the family loyalties and rivalries they helped consolidate, and the ways in which founders' intentions and beneficiaries' strategies could clash or coincide. A meticulous, nuanced study of the ways people understood and used waqf in various practical contexts is what this volume offers the reader, thereby filling a gap in our knowledge of waqf and its uses. It is the fruit of research brought together in the context of the annual history seminar organized and financed by the Department of Arab and Islamic Civilizations of the American University in Cairo on the pioneering initiative of Nelly Hanna, who saw the potential in bringing together young historians from Egypt and other countries who would not otherwise have had the opportunity to exchange ideas and publish their work together.[4] In 2005, the theme of this seminar was "The Uses of Waqf: Pious Endowments, Founders, and Beneficiaries." Some of the participants went on to develop the papers they had presented, producing a work we feel is coherent and timely, contributing as it does to a burgeoning field of historiography.

In the past thirty years, historians have come to question some aspects of 'Islamic history' (including, indeed, that ahistorical construct itself), often focusing on institutions that had previously been seen as unaffected by time or place. Waqfs are among the practices that have received renewed attention on the part of scholars keen to examine them not simply as examples of an Islamic ideal (or of a reality that, all too often, failed to live up to the ideal and therefore reflected the inevitable corruption and hypocrisy wrought by human beings), but rather as dynamic expression of human practices.[5] Recent research, much of it focused on the social, economic, political, and cultural dynamics of the Ottoman period (with a small number of studies in architectural history and jurisprudence) has taken as its starting point waqf deeds drawn up in the eighteenth and nineteenth centuries in the Ottoman Empire's largest cities. Thanks to the information they yield regarding founders and beneficiaries, these deeds have made it possible to follow the evolution of families and the strategies they used to negotiate the legal constraints regulating the constitution and transmission of wealth.[6] Looking at specific waqf deeds, it is immediately clear that general statements about Qur'anic inheritance rules imposing a certain division of wealth upon individuals, restricting their free will, fragmenting wealth, and preventing accumulation, are utterly unfounded: the deeds represent a trace of individuals' concrete, deliberate strategies for the preservation or transmission of wealth. In this new perspective, waqfs may be examined not in order to measure how far they adhered to or departed from some Qur'anic ideal, but to determine which social groups and individuals used them, and how and why these uses changed over time. I would situate the contributions to the present work firmly within this problematic, as all of them seek to offer insight into the questions of human agency and social dynamics, taking the creation and use of waqfs as their empirical material.[7] All of them also illustrate the flexibility and diversity of waqf.

Despite the efforts and extraordinary findings of a few scholars, there is much to discover about waqfs as institutions and practices in Islamic history, politics, and economics. The present work was conceived as an effort to tackle various aspects of their role in shaping trade relations, urban planning, political power, and religious observance. Studying waqf requires a multifaceted approach. We can look at the identity of waqf founders, the nature of the property they dedicated in waqf, the identity of the beneficiaries, the conditions of access to waqf revenues, and the principles regulating the creation and management of waqf; we can examine the ways in which waqfs shaped the urban fabric, the types of services they offered, and the kinds of activities that coalesced around them. Each of these elements underwent profound changes according to time and place, and tracing these changes allows historians to understand a great deal about how individuals and social groups engaged with, reproduced, or transformed the patrimony they had inherited from their forebears.

Thus, anthropology, sociology, architecture, or law may inform our approach to waqf. Each of these perspectives provides a window onto the ways human agency wrought change over time. One might think that the legalistic perspective would offer evidence of rigid, unchanging principles, yet, as Nelly Hanna's contribution to the present volume shows clearly, there are many examples of how even the legal parameters governing the definition of a valid waqf could change over time. For instance, when the early jurists set out and elaborated the rules that made a waqf valid, they tended to agree that the revenue-generating property had to be characterized by permanence, since the first characteristic of a waqf was its perpetuity, but as some of the contributions to the present volume show, by the seventeenth century people were founding use rights, salaries, cash, and movables such as the equipment in a public bath or a coffee house as waqf.

The social identity and economic class of waqf founders also tended to change over time. For instance, in Egypt, merchants were not among the prominent founders of waqfs during the Mamluk period (1250–1517),[8] but began to appear a little more frequently as founders during the Ottoman period, and especially starting in the seventeenth century.[9] This was due to several factors, among them the saturation of construction and endowment activity in the heart of the capital. In a related process, the conditions of access to property also began to change during this period, as rights pertaining to property (especially, but not exclusively, urban real estate) came to proliferate and overlap, and became fully commoditized.[10] Rather than a single legal relationship uniting an individual with a piece of property in an exclusive manner, this period witnessed the development of many compatible forms of property ownership and use.[11] For instance, a plot of land in the heart of al-Qahira could belong to one person or institution (say, a waqf established during the Mamluk period); that land might then be rented out to an individual, who in turn transformed the rent contract into a waqf; buildings might be constructed on the endowed land, and then made into an additional separate waqf; and so on. In the same way, once stipends and salaries became commodities that could be bought and sold on the market, an individual who was entitled to a stipend (say, in the form of grain rations) could then establish that right as an independent waqf. The availability on the market of such use rights must have meant that new categories of relatively affordable goods began to appear in the seventeenth century and that new classes of individuals began to find creating a waqf to be within their means. At the same time, the fact that the Ottoman state grew more decentralized in the seventeenth and eighteenth centuries, relinquishing more power to local actors, meant that there was more space for the assertion of multiple political, social, and economic interests.

The rise of these local actors, and their increased involvement in founding waqfs and maintaining all the services that waqfs provided, raises questions about the motives of a new class of donors, the identity of waqf beneficiaries, the uses to which these foundations were put, and the impact they had on the organization of urban space. When a Mamluk sultan founded a waqf, he may have done so to increase his legitimacy as a Muslim ruler who did not share his subjects' local identity, or to provide for his freed slaves in order to consolidate their attachment to him. When a local merchant established a foundation, what were his intentions, beyond saving his soul?

Dynasties at stake

It is unlikely that the aim of establishing a waqf was solely to evade taxes; according to S.J. Shaw, waqfs founded by sultans using imperial property were not taxed, but those established by individuals who wanted to donate their private property continued to pay the same taxes as before. If these 'private' waqfs were ultimately absorbed by one of the great public foundations, the latter also had to acquit themselves of their fiscal obligations.[12] One possibility, emphasized by historians, has been that founding one's property as waqf protected it against confiscation by rapacious rulers.[13] Jean-Claude Garcin's hypothesis[14] offers another interpretation: people established pious foundations because property in itself was seen as less important than the stable, regular revenues it was capable of generating. Like life annuities in

Ancien Régime France, waqfs may have offered people the opportunity to secure their savings by turning them into assets that spendthrift heirs could not waste.[15] Indeed, this is the other side of the argument that presents waqfs as a hindrance to economic development.[16] This characteristic of waqf—to wit, that in theory it removed property from the market and therefore guaranteed its security—constituted an inherent constraint imposed by the founder upon the beneficiaries. These suggestions are plausible, but the diversity of clauses included in waqf deeds indicates that no single motive provides a definitive explanation.

In general terms, however, the possibility of securing property from future transactions and directing revenues toward chosen beneficiaries may have been one of the most important motives for those who established waqfs. This must have been especially pressing in times of economic insecurity brought about by inflation, war, or natural causes such as drought. A second incentive was linked more closely to political circumstances: some waqf founders may have seen endowments as a defensive response to a state that did not hesitate to manipulate the law to its advantage. The Maliki school of Sunni law, for instance, gave the central treasury priority if a Muslim left no heirs, or if the Qur'anic shares distributed among existing heirs did not exhaust an inheritance in its entirety.[17] In such cases, a property holder had the option of putting part of what she owned aside while she was still alive and assigning revenues from it to beneficiaries who would not be able to inherit from her after her death—a wet nurse, a cousin, a fellow freedman, or a cherished slave, for example. Waqf could then serve as a means of avoiding inheritance taxes and of providing a livelihood to beneficiaries the founder could choose freely.[18]

Recourse to such dispositions, however, was not standard practice throughout the Ottoman world, or in the pre-Ottoman Islamic lands. In Ottoman Manisa, for example, historians have noted "an inexplicable failure to utilize the option of making a bequest, even when this meant that nearly the whole of the estate would be turned over to the state."[19] Because this option did not occur automatically and was not universally chosen, it seems likely that it was the expression of a specific material culture whose various manifestations must be analyzed as the products of deliberate choice and conscious human agency rather than the default setting of a general construct we might call Islamic civilization.

A third motive for founding waqfs was charitable; indeed, this may have been the most important reason for some founders, and not just those, evoked above, who sought to justify and legitimize their authority when the population did not accept it willingly. For the Mamluk ruling class, many of whose members were converts to Islam, perhaps waqfs fulfilled a tendency to display the new faith conspicuously, providing a personal and emotional incentive for the accumulation and alienation required for the establishment of such foundations. For other founders, as for these sultans and their successors, charity also made it possible to affirm their existence and inscribe their names on the urban landscape. Indeed, one could argue that waqfs founded by members of the ruling class, who had ample means at their disposal and could lavish their largesse on whatever cause they chose, indicated what goals more modest founders could aspire to emulate; if the beneficiaries on whom they bestowed revenues were the 'default' recipients of endowment revenues,[20] this only serves to underline that the simple fact of establishing a waqf, more than any concrete social difference the foundation might make, was the most pressing incentive on the average founder's mind. That a degree of 'conspicuous distribution' was at work is clear when we look at the waqfs established by two descendants of Muhammad 'Ali after they reached power in Egypt: 'Abbas (1853) and Muhammad Sa'id (1857). The material resources of these two founders forced them to deploy an ostentatious measure of generosity, but the two waqfs were dedicated to the mosque that Muhammad 'Ali had built in the Citadel; and Sa'id showed such enthusiasm for erasing 'Abbas's name from the *maqsura* of the mosque,[21] and for dedicating slightly larger amounts than his predecessor to the same pious works, that we are reminded to what extent dynastic and political concerns remained entangled with the spiritual profits engendered by creating a waqf. Nor should we dismiss the possibility that these concerns were shared by private individuals, who could establish a good reputation and project it into the future by creating a waqf, while enforcing their vision of a particular community: that formed by the beneficiaries of their charity. These twin goals could be achieved for a fairly modest price, since one had only to renovate an existing mosque to obtain the religious benefits waqfs conferred.

Chosen families

It appears, then, that the motives for creating a waqf ranged across a broad spectrum wherein pragmatic and worldly concerns were closely intertwined with a desire for salvation. Similarly, the effects of waqf creation were varied and played out on different registers, such as urban topography or the circulation of wealth on a macro level, and the redistribution of wealth within family groups on a micro level.[22] Waqf deeds can encourage us to rethink the forms and modes of transmission characterizing property in the urban context, the relations between lineage, social cohesion, and transfer of wealth, and the forms whereby surplus was extracted and strategies of resistance to expropriation. For our present, less ambitious purposes, however, waqf deeds can yield two types of information: the first type, relative to the identity of individuals and social groups involved in waqf creation, reveals the concrete ties linking the founder to people and institutions that benefited from waqf revenues;[23] the second type, specific to the material base of the waqf, enables us to reconstitute the history of real estate and property forms.[24]

Even on the small scale of the family, the creation of a waqf, chosen over other mechanisms for the transmission of wealth, could have very different consequences. This is clear when we look at the beneficiaries designated by some founders, spanning the gamut that stretched from *khayri* (purely charitable, that is, designating anonymous beneficiaries such as 'the poor') to *ahli* or *dhurri* (benefiting the founder's 'family,' that is, specific individuals named in the waqf deed) foundations. Every waqf is by definition *khayri* in that it must take as its ultimate goal assistance to the poor and vulnerable members of society (widows, orphans, travelers, and so on). 'Family' waqfs, however, interposed the founder's descendants, and their descendants after them, or other beneficiaries of the founder's choice, between the act of constituting the foundation and the Muslim community at large. When the named beneficiaries died out, the waqf's revenues were transferred to anonymous recipients; but this shift could be deferred by clauses allowing the founder's family to transfer their share of the revenue to their children, brothers and sisters, or other beneficiaries, with those closest to the founder often enjoying a priority.[25] There was thus no absolute dichotomy between charitable waqfs and family waqfs: in Ottoman Aleppo, for example, governors sent from Istanbul and members of the local elite used waqfs to provide revenues for their descendants and for official institutions they chose as beneficiaries. Almost half the waqfs created during this period by Ottoman state officials were devoted to the (biological and legal) families of the founders; local founders' waqfs also included provisions relative to pious works and allowances for relatives.[26]

Ahli foundations therefore allowed founders to place some of what they owned in the service of certain individuals or groups, and thereby to modify the distribution of an estate that would later be carried out according to Shari'a.[27] The authors of the *Description de l'Egypte* were well aware of the fact that waqfs allowed individuals to dispose freely of their wealth and indeed made it possible to circumvent restrictions that Hanafi jurisprudence placed on bequests, which were limited to a third of one's property, the rest being subject to distribution through inheritance according to Qur'anic injunctions:[28] "As it is forbidden to give more than a third of what one owns, there is a means of evading the law and disposing of the entirety. This happens only when a man dies *without leaving descendants*: he makes a pious donation of his capital to a mosque, and leaves the usufruct to those he wishes to favor, and even to their descendants and their Mamluks."[29]

It is true that the founders of 'private' waqfs were, in disproportionate numbers, individuals with no legal heirs.[30] The absence of heirs, however, did not mean that one was completely free to dispose of one's wealth. To cite only one example, in fourteenth-century Crete, rich men who had no children were prevented by considerations of status and lineage from leaving all they had to their wives, as more modest benefactors tended to do.[31] Different social constraints prevented wealthy individuals from passing their property and social standing on to their biological children: this was the case, for example, of the Mamluks in fourteenth-century Egypt and Syria, who were generally prohibited from transmitting their military and political achievements (along with the attendant revenues from land grants) to their offspring. In both cases, waqfs provided a means of creating heirs where there were none recognized by law. According to Christian Decobert, in fact, *ahli* or *dhurri* waqfs were created in order to include legatees other than the legal heirs.[32] By creating heirs in this way, and allowing benefactors to make certain choices relative to the distribution of their wealth, it can even be argued that waqfs reveal 'chosen families' that often trumped or replaced biological or legal kinship ties.

As Jean-Claude Garcin and Mustafa Taher argue, then, waqf deeds may allow us to better know the deep motives that guided founders who had no heirs and who sought to establish their group affiliation and recreate ties to a place of origin.[33] Garcin and Taher show how an Ethiopian eunuch, Jawhar al-Lala, tutor to the children of Sultan Barsbay, remained tied to two amirs who had played a role in his life, to his own freedmen, and to his neighborhood—in other words, to an urban identity woven from "almost familial" forms of solidarity.[34] Apart from asserting his identity, Jawhar al-Lala caused the distribution of his wealth to deviate from its default setting and created an alternative to the legal family he lacked. Just as importantly, his waqf enabled him to remove the property he had accumulated from the government's grasp, since the central treasury would have claimed the estate of an individual who died without leaving legal heirs. One of the consequences of establishing a waqf, then, could be the creation of heirs when none existed—at least, none that the founder accepted as legitimate.

Even more interesting than cases where founders had no descendants, however, are cases where legitimate heirs did exist. Why would an individual create a waqf when doing so meant there was a smaller inheritance left over for his progeny? For example, Mahmud Muharram, the leader of the wealthy import–export merchants in Cairo until 1795, had a son, but set aside some of the real estate he owned, assigning its revenues to the maintenance of a mosque he had restored near his palace[35] and to the payment of salaries for its staff.[36] Muharram could have passed his property on to his son in its entirety; the fact that he did not indicates that charitable endeavors, and the salvation they promised, were seen as important in their own right, even when they entailed restricting descendants' access to one's property or to the capital necessary for perpetuating a business enterprise.

Similarly, Ibrahim Jalabi al-Ghazali, a member of the Sharaybi commercial dynasty,[37] allocated part of the revenue from his relatively modest waqf to the recitation of religious texts, which he had also constituted as a nonmaterial waqf. He dedicated the spiritual benefits from this recitation to the Prophet Muhammad, then to the founder during his lifetime, and to his soul after his death. Finally, these benefits were to devolve to the souls of his ancestors, his relatives, his freed slaves, and all dead Muslims. Once the expenses of the recitation had been ensured, the founder also stipulated that, after his death, a yearly stipend be paid to Ghusun bint 'Abd 'Allah al-Samra, his son's freed concubine.[38] Yet Ibrahim Jalabi had heirs—among them a son, whom the waqf deed does not identify as deceased—but gave them no particular privilege. They were merely to receive whatever was left over from the waqf revenues after deduction of the expenses stipulated by the founder until Ghusun died, after which her stipend was to devolve to them. Only after the extinction of these heirs and their descendants were the founder's brother and sister entitled to a share in the waqf revenues.[39] After all the beneficiaries associated with Ibrahim Jalabi's waqf had died, the mosque of al-Husayn and the poor were to receive revenues from the foundation.[40] This deed shows clearly that, if a founder sought to privilege a freed slave, even at the expense of his children and siblings, the waqf offered him or her a means of doing so. The importance of such freed slaves, therefore, was not necessarily proportional to a founder's fears that he would leave no heirs; on the contrary, when Qur'anic heirs or biological relatives did exist, the prioritization of slaves emerges as all the more striking.[41]

Examples from further afield support the hypothesis that waqfs allowed founders to privilege certain beneficiaries at the expense of others—often, in fact, at the expense of legal heirs or biological kin. In Tripoli and Nablus during the nineteenth century, waqfs were systematically used to exclude agnates from the circle of primary beneficiaries and to favor the nuclear family instead. In the rare cases where agnates were included, the deed normally stipulated that they come into their share only after the founder's direct lineage had become extinct. Beshara Doumani sees "this pattern of inclusion and exclusion" as "the strongest evidence we have that the endower's line of descent within the conjugal family in both Tripoli and Nablus is the primary beneficiary of waqf endowments and not the extended patrilineal family."[42]

In his study of sixteenth-century Maliki waqfs in North Africa, David Powers also concludes that "the endowment system reinforced the boundaries of the Muslim nuclear family and contributed to its social reproduction."[43] Isabelle Grangaud makes comparable observations for eighteenth-century Constantine, where "what determined the understanding and practice of family habous [the North African equivalent of waqf] is the fact that lineage was invariably the framework for transmission" (only one deed among the twenty she studied concerned neither the founder nor the members of his family).[44] In Mosul during the same period, the revenues from a waqf created by a member of the Jalili family were reserved for the founder's household; he explicitly excluded his brother's descendants from the group of beneficiaries, whereas, according to the laws of inheritance, the brother and his heirs after him should have had a right to the property set aside as waqf.[45] Finally, in Ottoman Cairo, the 'middle stratum' (which, according to Muhammad 'Afifi, included ulama and religious officials, artisans and merchants, and 'well-off' country folk) tended to found waqfs and designate themselves as beneficiaries during their lifetimes, with revenues devolving to their descendants after them.[46] The waqf deed of 'Abd al-'Aziz Ghurab, who belonged to a merchant family from Sfax that had settled in Cairo in the early eighteenth century, supports these conclusions: the founder attributed the revenues from the waqf to his two sons, who were merchants in Suq al-Sharb, and to their descendants after them.[47]

These examples all show that waqfs allowed their founders to preserve their capital while attributing a regular stipend to individuals or groups they chose freely. This freedom also meant they could deprive relatives of the chance to inherit a larger portion of their estate, shape their families' future as they saw fit, and dispose of their property in ways they determined. In other words, waqf had no intrinsic impact: its consequences depended purely on the uses to which social actors put it.

Another way in which founders could project their wishes into the future and shape the group of beneficiaries receiving waqf revenues was by determining the portions allocated to each class of beneficiaries. For example, the head of the Cairo merchants, who established his waqf in 1825 jointly with his mother,[48] stipulated that his male descendants should receive twice the portion of their female counterparts, in accordance with Qur'anic inheritance regulations *(li-l-dhakar mithl hazz al-unthayayn)*.[49] As its initial beneficiaries, however, the waqf designated non-relatives, whom the deed nevertheless designates as a specific kind of family: *ahl al-waqf* (the people of the waqf, or the waqf family), whose members were the founder's freed slaves. These were also divided into two groups enjoying different conditions of access to waqf revenue: the "white" (Circassian) freed slaves were to receive annual stipends equal to twice those of the "blacks and Ethiopians." Distinction founded on status and ethnic identity thus replaced the gender inequality that regulated access among free beneficiaries.[50] Further differences were introduced by stipulations that allowed some of the beneficiaries to pass on their right to their descendants while preventing others from doing so, or making such a transfer conditional upon certain behavior (for example, refraining from marrying).

Only by studying concrete examples of the uses to which social actors put waqf—uses that were bound by a specific time and place—can we hope to understand the different ways in which the institution functioned: how it served different purposes for state and nonstate actors, expressed a wide range of intentions, and exerted an impact on a broad spectrum of human interactions. This nuanced, concrete understanding is what the present work seeks to bring to the literature, and the significant contribution it aims to make.

The contributors to the present volume cover a wide chronological and geographical spectrum, ranging from the fourteenth to the twentieth century and from Morocco to Jordan, and illustrate the diversity that characterized waqf as an institution. In all the cases examined here, however, the authors have sought to shed light on the uses that historical actors made of waqfs as they endeavored to shape urban space, configure trade patterns, influence political power, and organize social relations. The first chapter, by Rıza Yıldırım, is a case study of waqf as a vector and anchor of expansion in the early years of the Ottoman Empire. By investigating the example of one dervish, and the waqf with which he was associated, Yıldırım shows how closely military and religious imperatives were intertwined during a crucial period of dynamism and change for the fledgling Ottoman dynasty.

The three chapters that follow also concern the sultanate, but at a later stage, when provincial actors had begun to assert themselves in a power struggle where waqfs served as both tools and prizes. In a study of endowments created in Egypt to benefit Mecca and Medina, Husam 'Abd al-Mu'ti shows how the Ottoman sultans relied on these institutions to bolster their legitimacy and therefore found themselves obliged to battle local groups for control of waqf revenue, while taking care not to disrupt relations with Egypt's increasingly autonomous and fractious military commanders. Examining a foundation created by Salah al-Din (Saladin) in Alexandria, Nasir Ibrahim shows how the Ottoman state continuously sought to interfere in the endowment's affairs and fought the beneficiaries for a larger share of endowment revenues. In both cases, the state emerges as a social actor in its own right, fraught with conflicting interests and competing agendas, rather than as a monolithic and univocal entity. In both cases, too, the authors show how rising provincial groups were able to assert themselves against the will of the Ottoman sultans using an array of unconventional weapons to obtain the income to which they felt entitled.

The same ambivalence evidenced in state practices toward waqfs, and the state's limited ability to counter local actors' bids for control over waqf assets, is evident in Michael Reimer's analysis of endowments in the newly created state of Transjordan, where the Ottoman government struggled to supplant the wide range of services provided locally by waqfs. By the twentieth century, however, Ottoman officials were aware that a state's claim to modernity rested at least in part on its ability to offer its citizens a degree of protection. The battle unfolding in al-Salt, then, concerned the state's sphere of action, its rights and responsibilities vis-à-vis the populations under its purview, as much as it did the revenues generated by the waqfs. A similar process is at work in the case examined by John Shoup, where the Moroccan government's support for certain shrines and the ability of rural economies to withstand external pressures have meant the difference between survival and extinction for some waqfs. In some ways, Shoup's chapter shows the reversal of trends noted by 'Abd al-Mu'ti and Ibrahim for the eighteenth century, with an increasingly powerful central state asserting its authority over regional religious centers.

Tension between a waning imperial government and increasingly powerful provincial groups, or between a nation-state and local institutions, was accompanied by conflicts over mutual rights and responsibilities. In times of change, furthermore, various groups—including state actors—attempted to put forth competing definitions of waqf, reshaping its meaning to suit their purposes. In the fascinating cases of guild waqfs examined by Nelly Hanna, artisans made use of waqf as an institution that fulfilled their collective need at a particular moment of uncertainty and economic insecurity.

The way they administered it corresponded to their specific understanding of what waqf was, but not necessarily to what was in the books. Another example of contending definitions of waqf is offered in Anna Maria Medici's look at Cyrenaica under Italian colonial rule, where Muslims (particularly notables, appointed and co-opted by the Italians to work on waqf administration boards) initially attributed the legitimacy of waqf to Qur'anic stipulations, hoping in this way to buttress the security of waqf assets and set up a barrier to colonial economic penetration. As for the Italians, they tried to interpret complex regulations pertaining to waqf in such a way as to take full advantage of resources 'from within.'

The last two chapters, by Dina Bakhoum and Tuba Akar, examine waqfs as instruments of urban planning, mechanisms for preserving the historical fabric of two cities (Cairo and Adana respectively), and poles of attraction that accommodated spontaneous, organic growth while providing a framework that contained it. The authors approach waqf from an architectural and urbanistic perspective and draw prescriptive as well as analytical conclusions from their research.

Finally, in the conclusion to this work, Engin Isin offers a more philosophical appraisal of waqf as an act of citizenship, suggesting that the institution allowed non-Muslims to govern themselves, their relation to the central authorities, and their ties with other subjects—in other words, it allowed different groups to negotiate their differences and similarities. Isin's conclusion is faithful to a work that seeks to respect the variety of waqf while portraying the underlying unity of purpose and design that made these endowments recognizable to members of classes, religious groups, and gender categories. In adopting a thematic approach to the organization of the contributions, we hope to inspire the reader to see new connections and points for comparison across widely differing geographical and chronological contexts. We also hope that this work serves as a starting point for further research into the uses of waqf by historical actors determined to shape the institutions they had inherited in the ways they saw fit.

Notes

1 Parts of this introduction are based on my dissertation research, published in French as *Fortunes urbaines et stratégies sociales*.
2 See Mandaville, "Usurious Piety."
3 Scholars have mined waqf deeds for information on social, economic, architectural, and urban history, with admirable results. No research on waqf should fail to mention the monumental and groundbreaking work of Amin, *al-Awqaf*, a comprehensive study

of foundations in Egypt during the Mamluk period. See also Petry, "A Geniza for Mamluk Studies?"; and 'Abd al-Latif Ibrahim, one of the earliest scholars to recognize the value of waqf deeds, and the author of an unpublished manuscript on the waqf of Sultan al-Ghuri. Scholars have also focused on waqfs founded by members of the ruling class, especially in Mamluk times, and used waqf deeds as a fruitful source for urban history. See for example Fernandes, "The Foundation of Baybars al-Jashankir."

4   I would like to thank Nelly Hanna and Tamer El Leithy for their incisive comments on a draft of the present introduction. They are, of course, innocent of any errors herein. Special recognition is due to Amina Elbendary for her important role in organizing the seminar, and to Marwa Sabry Osman for her patience and administrative skill.

5   Among the authors who look specifically at the identity of waqf founders are Garcin and Taher in "Identité du dédicataire." For very valuable contributions to the field of waqf studies, specifically addressing the social identity and aims of waqf founders, see among others Fay, "Women and Waqf"; contributions to Deguilhem, ed., *Le waqf dans l'espace islamique*; Doumani, "Endowing Family"; Roded, "The Waqf and the Social Elite of Aleppo"; Müller, "A Legal Instrument"; and Powers, "The Maliki Family Endowment."

6   See for example Doumani, "Endowing Family"; Meriwether, *The Kin Who Count*; Roded, "The Waqf and the Social Elite"; Crecelius, "The Incidence of Waqf Cases"; Fay, "Women and Waqf"; and Gerber, "Anthropology and Family History."

7   I am grateful to Michael Reimer for pointing out that I emphasize the secular purposes of waqf and the human agency of its founders, to the detriment of the institution's religious dimensions. He argues that I understate the religious mentality of pre-modern societies, in which "life was short and very uncertain . . . and the supranatural was very real." Reimer makes the provocative assertion that "in the midst of manipulating the bequest of the property through waqf, some founders were thinking of who would be most faithful in praying for their souls, or what kind of foundation would redound most to their spiritual credit." It is true that, in reaction to analyses that make 'Islam' the irreducible and unfathomable cause of very diverse behavior, I have almost entirely disregarded otherworldly motives, which may well have been foremost in the founders' minds. I have chosen instead to focus on the concrete material effects of waqf, which, while occasionally prosaic, seem to spring more clearly from the documents.

8   "One of the most distinctive facts about charity in Mamluk Cairo is the total absence of the merchant class from the endowment deeds. While prominent merchants were called upon to play a role in famine relief in the thirteenth and fourteenth centuries, by the early fifteenth century they no longer appear as important patrons in this area either. The key role in providing charity to the poor was played by the military elite." Sabra, *Poverty and Charity*, 173. Waqf deeds from the Mamluk period do include a few foundations established by merchants; for four examples (further research will surely yield more) see Morisot, "Le patrimoine des commerçants."

9   Tuchscherer, "Evolution du bâti," 70–71; 'Afifi, *al-Awqaf*, 231.

10 See Nelly Hanna's contribution to this volume and Ghazaleh, *Fortunes urbaines*, ch. 5, as well as Kenneth Cuno's important article, "Ideology and Juridical Discourse in Ottoman Egypt." In Mamluk times, one does not find evidence of

waqfs created on the right to rent a shop, for instance, or on a salary or the position of imam at a mosque. Starting in the seventeenth century, such waqfs become fairly commonplace. I should point out that my work on waqf pertains principally to urban property (land, real estate, and use rights within the urban areas); agricultural land, much of which belonged (in theory) to God, represented on earth by the state, was subject to different but no less complex laws and transactions.

11 For an astute analysis of the evolution of property rights in nineteenth-century rural Egypt, see Hakim, "A Multiplicity of Rights." For a fascinating comparative study of property and modernity, see Islamoglu, ed., *Constituting Modernity*. For an incisive exploration of the links between property and state-building, see Mundy and Saumarez Smith, *Governing Property*.

12 Shaw, *Financial and Administrative Organization*, 154. Amin states on the contrary that waqfs were exempted from all kinds of taxes, including *kharaj* on waqf land, but that rulers commonly sought to levy extraordinary sums on them or to expropriate them, especially in times of crisis. Amin, *al-Awqaf*, 92–93.

13 Confiscation is a trope in writings on the Mamluk and Ottoman eras, but is also mentioned by historians working on earlier periods. See for example Petry, *Protectors or Praetorians?*, 167: "This kind of appropriation, which actually reclaimed caliphal allotments made by previous rulers from the royal fisc, had occurred since the early Islamic era and represented no innovation."

14 Garcin, "Le waqf," 106.

15 Hoffman et al., *Des marchés sans prix*, 34.

16 An argument most vocally made by those who sought to dismantle waqfs.

17 Khalil, "Ikhtisasat," 165.

18 Cf. Crecelius, "The Incidence of Waqf Cases," 181.

19 Matthews, "Toward an Isolario," 71.

20 See for example Mubarak, *Khitat*, 164. Among these establishments, to which the revenues of most waqfs eventually devolved after the initial beneficiaries had died out, we may cite the sanctuary of al-Husayn; the tombs of the imams al-Layth and al-Shafi'i; Sayyida Zaynab and Sayyida Nafisa; Sidi Ibrahim al-Dusuqi; Sidi Ahmad al-Badawi, in Tanta; and (less frequently, or receiving lesser sums) Sayyida Sakina, Fatima al-Nabawiya, and Sayyida 'Aysha. The services paid for by beneficiaries typically included reading certain parts of the Qur'an *(rub'a)* or the holy book in its entirety *(khatma)*, as many times as the founder specified; sometimes Hadith classes; and the recitation of works like the *Burda* (a poem praising the Prophet Muhammad, recited on numerous occasions, and especially during funerals (Delanoue, *Moralistes et politiques musulmans*, 591–92)) or *Dala'il al-khayrat* ('The Guide to Good Works'). Finally, foundation deeds often stipulated that bread, water, and—in the case of wealthier founders, meat—be distributed to the poor; that candles and oil be provided to illuminate a mosque or a shrine; and that other provisions be supplied, such as palm fronds and basil to cover graves and incense for burning. These charitable donations, however, seem to have belonged to conventional categories rather than being chosen deliberately by the founders: the authors of the *Description de l'Egypte* mention them among other "expenses for which the sultan is responsible, paid from the myry" (candles for the Qur'an reciter at al-Azhar; cheese and onions distributed to the poor during the mulid of Ahmad al-Badawi . . .): Jomard et al., *Description de l'Egypte*

(herein *DE*), vol. 12, 214. Donations to the poor of Medina were also a widespread form of charity throughout the Muslim world in the fifteenth century (Faroqhi, *Pilgrims and Sultans*, 75).

21 Mubarak, *Khitat*, vol. 5, 192.

22 "Sans doute le procédé préservait-il, en dépit des confiscations, une certaine perpétuation des patrimoines familiaux, mais il n'en menait pas moins, les biens légués devenant inaliénables, à l'immobilisation sous le régime du *vaqf* d'une part croissante des richesses du pays" (Veinstein, "Trésor public," 129).

23 Tawab and Raymond studied the eighteenth-century waqf deed of a wealthy coffee merchant and observed that it enabled them to establish a number of facts concerning the entourage of Mustafa Ja'far ("La *waqfiyya* de Mustafa Ja'far," 180), but simply mentioned the individuals who intervened during the writing of the deed, and the names of the waqf beneficiaries, without analyzing them further.

24 Garcin and Taher, "Enquête sur le financement," 264.

25 *Waqfiya* 903: *fa in lam yakun lahu ikhwa wala ikhwat fa li-aqrab al-tabaqat li-l-mutawaffi min ahl hadha al-waqf*. . . .

26 Roded, "The Waqf and the Social Elite," 83–85.

27 Cf. Grangaud, *La ville imprenable*, 187: waqfs, like bequests and donations, "made it possible to remove at least part of the inheritance from the normal succession process." Some of the Sunni schools of law were more flexible than others, allowing the founder to designate himself or herself as the first beneficiary: this is why those seeking to establish 'family waqfs' in Algeria followed the Hanafi rather than the Maliki school (Saidouni, *Dirasat tarikhiya*, 256; Garcin, "Le waqf," 104).

28 Hanafi jurisprudence imposed this limit: cf. Barbir, "Wealth, Privilege, and Family Structure," 184.

29 *DE*, vol. 18, part 1, 259–60 (author's translation).

30 In his study of litigation relative to several waqfs founded in the eighteenth and nineteenth centuries by freedmen or to the benefit of former slaves, Ron Shaham observes that most of the founders, who were members of the Ottoman–Egyptian elite, were childless or had survived their children. To explain the profile of his sample, he cites a study of slavery in late eighteenth-century Egypt, which pointed out that around 70 percent of the affranchised population of Cairo had no descendants. Shaham, "Masters," 164. The problem of succession, however, was not restricted to slaves or former slaves: very high infant and child mortality rates affected even the ruling class in nineteenth-century Egypt. Of Muhammad 'Ali's thirty children, only five sons and two daughters reached adulthood. Audouard, *Les mystères de l'Egypte dévoilés*, 102 (she counts an inflated total of eighty-four children; I wish to thank Ghislaine Alleaume for providing the correct figure).

31 McKee, "Households," 49.

32 Cited in Denoix, "Fondations pieuses," 26.

33 Garcin and Taher, "Identité du dédicataire," 190.

34 Garcin and Taher, "Identité du dédicataire," 194–95. Among many other examples, we may cite that of Yusuf Agha, who dedicated all he owned to the construction of a public water fountain. Revenues from the waqf he established were assigned to him during his lifetime, to his freed slaves after his death, and finally to the aghas who served the Prophet's Sanctuary in Medina (Mubarak, *Khitat*, vol. 6, 186–87).

35 Muharram renovated the mosque, which had been built in 1540, and it was named after him. Mubarak, *Khitat*, vol. 2, 221. Khedive Isma'il was born in Muharram's palace, which burned down in 1998.
36 Rent from the real estate founded by Mahmud Muharram was projected to cover almost twenty thousand paras in annual expenses. The staff include an imam (preacher); a *khatib* (orator); a person responsible for greeting the faithful on Friday; two muezzins; cleaners and maintenance workers; teachers; and nine pupils who received scholarships of almost 2,500 paras a year in total, for attending hadith classes.
37 He was probably the great-grandson of Muhammad Dada al-Sharaybi (Raymond, "Une famille," 124).
38 *Waqfiya* 254, 18 January 1791.
39 Cf. Raymond, "Une famille," 124.
40 *Waqfiya* 254, 18 January 1791.
41 'Afifi makes this argument: *al-Awqaf*, 226–27.
42 Doumani, "Endowing Family," 20.
43 Powers, "The Maliki Family Endowment," 386. For similar conclusions regarding nineteenth-century Tunis, see Hénia, *Propriété*, 322–33.
44 Grangaud, *La ville imprenable*, 187.
45 Khoury, *State and Provincial Society*, 131.
46 'Afifi, *al-Awqaf*, 228–31.
47 Zouari, "La waqfiyya," 321–22.
48 *Waqfiya* 903, 2 October 1825.
49 This is what the Qur'an stipulates for male and female heirs of equal rank (Surat al-Nisa', Qur'an 4:11).
50 Such discrimination was not infrequent. Sultan Khayrbak, to cite only one example, reserved the supervision of his waqf to his male Turkish freed slaves: see 'Afifi, *al-Awqaf*, 225. Ron Shaham considers that ethnic distinctions expressed two types of concerns, corresponding to two sets of intentions: discriminatory stipulations, according to him, resulted from the founder's wishes alone, while egalitarian modes of distribution expressed an initiative taken by the founder or the judge or scribe who formulated the deed ("Masters," 171–72). I dwell on this point because Shaham's interpretation is arbitrary and, more importantly, evacuates the question of choice, which is precisely what interests us here: the possible variations in stipulations (left up to the founder's discretion) were not simply procedural issues, and scribes or judges were not necessarily bearers and advocates of univocal and homogenous 'Islamic values,' if only because an office does not necessarily create a set of values. Rather, Shaham's conclusion seems to be the natural result of a position that consists of "considering social groups as real objects," in Guerreau's formulation, and therefore of "closing the door to any explanation." See Beunza, "Communauté," 34, n. 11.

Bibliography

Archival Sources

Egyptian Ministry of Endowments, *Waqfiya* no. 254, 18 January 1791.

Egyptian Ministry of Endowments, *Waqfiya* no. 903, 2 October 1825.

Publications and Other Sources

Abdul Tawab, A.-R., and André Raymond. "La *waqfiyya* de Mustafa Ja'far." *Annales Islamologiques* 14 (1978): 177–93.

'Afifi, Muhammad. *al-Awqaf wa-l-hayah al-iqtisadiya fi Misr fi-l-'asr al-'uthmani*. Cairo: General Egyptian Book Organization, 1991

Amin, Muhammad Muhammad. *al-Awqaf wa-l-hayah al-ijtima'iya fi Misr, 648–923 H, 1250–1517 M: dirasa tarikhiya watha'iqiya*. Cairo: Dar al-Nahda al-'Arabiya, 1980.

Audouard, Olympe. *Les mystères de l'Egypte dévoilés*. Paris: Dentu, 1866 (accessed online, June 2010).

Barbir, Karl K. "Wealth, Privilege, and Family Structure: The 'Askaris of 18th Century Damascus According to the Qassam 'Askari Inheritance Records," in T. Philipp, ed., *The Syrian Land in the 18th and 19th Century: The Common and the Specific in the Historical Experience*, 179–95. Stuttgart: Franz Steiner Verlag, 1992.

Beunza, J.M. "Communauté, réseau social, élites: L'armature sociale de l'Ancien Régime," in J.L. Castellano and J.-P. Dedieu, eds., *Réseaux, familles et pouvoirs dans le monde ibérique à la fin de l'Ancien Régime*, 31–66. Paris: CNRS éditions, 1998.

Crecelius, Daniel. "The Incidence of Waqf Cases in Three Cairo Courts: 1640–1802." *Journal of the Economic and Social History of the Orient* 29 (1986): 176–89.

Cuno, Kenneth. "Ideology and Juridical Discourse in Ottoman Egypt: The Uses of the Concept of *Irsad*." *Islamic Law and Society* 6, no. 2 (1999): 136–63.

Deguilhem, Randi, ed. *Le waqf dans l'espace islamique: Outil de pouvoir socio-politique*. Damascus: Institut français de Damas, 1995.

Delanoue, Gilbert. *Moralistes et politiques musulmans dans l'Egypte du XIXe siècle 1798–1882*. 2 vols. Cairo: Institut français d'archéologie orientale, 1982.

Denoix, Sylvie. "Fondations pieuses, fondations économiques, le waqf, un mode d'intervention sur la ville mamelouke," in Denoix et al., eds., *Le Khan al-Khalili*, 19–26.

Denoix, Sylvie, Jean-Charles Depaule, and Michel Tuchscherer, eds. *Le Khan al-Khalili: Un centre commercial et artisanal au Caire du XIIIᵉ au XXᵉ siècle.* Cairo: Institut français d'archéologie orientale, 1999.

Doumani, Beshara. "Endowing Family: Waqf, Property Devolution, and Gender in Greater Syria, 1800 to 1860." *Comparative Studies in Society and History* 40, no. 1 (1998): 3–41.

Faroqhi, Suraiya. *Pilgrims and Sultans: The Hajj under the Ottomans.* London: I.B. Tauris, 1994.

Fay, Mary Ann. "Women and Waqf: Toward a Reconsideration of Women's Place in the Mamluk Household." *International Journal of Middle East Studies* 29, no. 1 (1997): 33–51.

Fernandes, Leonor. "The Foundation of Baybars al-Jashankir: Its Waqf, History, and Architecture." *Muqarnas* 4 (1987): 21–42.

Garcin, Jean-Claude. "Le waqf est-il la transmission d'un patrimoine?" in J. Beaucamp and G. Dagron, eds., *La transmission du patrimoine: Byzance et l'aire méditerranéenne,* 101–109. Paris: De Boccard, 1998.

Garcin, J.-Cl., and M. Taher. "Enquête sur le financement d'un waqf égyptien du XVᵉᵐᵉ siècle: les comptes de Jawhar al-Lala." *Journal of the Economic and Social History of the Orient* 38, no. 3 (1995): 262–304.

————. "Identité du dédicataire, appartenances et propriétés urbaines dans un waqf du XVᵉ siècle," in C. Décobert, ed., *Valeur et distance: Identités et sociétés en Egypte,* 189–97. Paris: Maisonneuve et Larose, 2000.

Gerber, Haim. "Anthropology and Family History: The Ottoman and Turkish Families." *Journal of Family History* 14 (1989): 409–21.

Ghazaleh, Pascale. *Fortunes urbaines et stratégies sociales: Généalogies patrimoniales au Caire, 1780–1830.* Cairo: Institut français d'archéologie orientale, 2010.

Grangaud, Isabelle. *La ville imprenable: Une histoire sociale de Constantine au 18ᵉ siècle.* Paris: Editions de l'EHESS, 2002.

Hakim, Muhammad. "A Multiplicity of Rights: Rural–Urban Contradictions in Early Nineteenth-century Egyptian Land Ownership," in Nelly Hanna, ed., *Money, Land and Trade: An Economic History of the Muslim Mediterranean,* 50–66. London: I.B. Tauris, 2002.

Hénia, Abdelhamid. *Propriété et stratégies sociales à Tunis à l'époque moderne (XVIᵉ–XIXᵉ siècles),* Tunis: Faculté des sciences humaines et sociales de Tunis, 1999.

Hoffman, Philip T., Gilles Postel-Vinay, and Jean-Laurent Rosenthal. *Des marchés sans prix: Une économie politique du crédit à Paris, 1660–1870.* Paris: Editions de l'EHESS, 2001.

Islamoglu, Huri, ed. *Constituting Modernity: Private Property in the East and West*. London: I.B. Tauris, 2004.

Jomard, Edmé-François, et al. *Description de l'Egypte ou Recueil des observations et des recherches qui ont été faites en Egypte pendant l'expédition de l'armée française*. 24 vols. Paris: Imprimerie de C.L.F. Panckoucke, 1829.

Khalil, Hasan. "Ikhtisasat mahkamat al-qisma al-'arabiya," in N. Ibrahim and 'I. Hilal, eds., *al-'Adala bayn al-shari'a wa-l-waqi' fi Misr fi-l-'asr al-'uthmani*, 141–77. Cairo: Cairo University Faculty of Letters, 2002.

Khoury, Dina. *State and Provincial Society in the Ottoman Empire: Mosul, 1540–1834*. Cambridge: Cambridge University Press, 1997.

Mandaville, Jon. "Usurious Piety: The Cash Waqf Controversy in the Ottoman Empire." *International Journal of Middle East Studies* 10 (1979): 289–308.

Matthews, Joyce H. "Toward an Isolario of the Ottoman Inheritance Inventory, with Special Reference to Manisa (ca. 1600–1700)," in D. Quataert, ed., *Consumption Studies and the History of the Ottoman Empire, 1550–1922: An Introduction*, 45–82. Albany: State University of New York Press, 2000.

McKee, Sally. "Households in Fourteenth-Century Venetian Crete." *Speculum* 70, no. 1 (1995): 27–67.

Meriwether, Margaret M. *The Kin Who Count: Family and Society in Ottoman Aleppo, 1770–1840*. Austin: University of Texas Press, 1999.

Morisot, Corinne. "Le patrimoine des commerçants à l'époque mamelouke d'après les archives conservées au Caire." Proceedings of the Eighth Colloquium on the History of Fatimid, Ayyubid and Mamluk Egypt, Leuven, 2001.

Mubarak, 'Ali Pasha. *al-Khitat al-tawfiqiya al-jadida li-Misr al-Qahira wa muduniha wa-biladiha al-qadima wa-l-shahira*. Cairo: General Egyptian Book Organization, 1994.

Müller, Christian. "A Legal Instrument in the Service of People and Institutions: Endowments in Mamluk Jerusalem as Mirrored in the Haram Documents." *Mamluk Studies Review* 12, no. 1 (2008): 173–89.

Mundy, Martha, and Richard Saumarez Smith. *Governing Property, Making the Modern State: Law, Administration and Production in Ottoman Syria*. London: I.B. Tauris, 2007.

Petry, Carl F. "A Geniza for Mamluk Studies? Charitable Trust (Waqf) Documents as a Source for Economic and Social History." *Mamluk Studies Review*, no. 2 (1998): 51–60.

————. *Protectors or Praetorians? The Last Mamluk Sultans and Egypt's Waning as a Great Power.* Albany: State University of New York Press, 1994.

Powers, David. "The Maliki Family Endowment: Legal Norms and Social Practices." *International Journal of Middle East Studies* 25 (1993): 379–406.

Raymond, André. "Une famille de grands négociants en café au Caire dans la première moitié du XVIIIe siècle: Les Sharaybi," in M. Tuchscherer, ed., *Le commerce du café avant l'ère des plantations coloniales: Espaces, réseaux, sociétés (XVe–XIXe siècle)*, 111–24. Cairo: Institut français d'archéologie orientale, 2001.

Roded, Ruth. "The Waqf and the Social Elite of Aleppo in the Eighteenth and Nineteenth Centuries." *Turcica: Revue d'études turques* 20 (1998): 71–91.

Sabra, Adam. *Poverty and Charity in Medieval Islam: Mamluk Egypt, 1250–1517.* Cambridge: Cambridge University Press, 2000.

Saidouni, Nacereddine. *Dirasat tarikhiya fi-l-milkiya wa-l-waqf wa-l-jibaya: al-fatra al-haditha.* Beirut: Dar al-Gharb al-Islami, 2001.

Shaham, Ron. "Masters, Their Freed Slaves, and the Waqf in Egypt (Eighteenth–Twentieth Centuries)." *Journal of the Economic and Social History of the Orient* 43, no. 2 (2000): 162–88.

Shaw, S.J. *The Financial and Administrative Organization and Development of Ottoman Egypt 1517–1798.* Princeton, NJ: Princeton University Press, 1962.

Tuchscherer, Michel. "Evolution du bâti et des fonctions à l'époque ottomane," in S. Denoix et al., eds., *Le Khan al-Khalili*, 67–96.

Veinstein, Gilles. "Trésor public et fortunes privées dans l'Empire ottoman (milieu XVIe–début XIXe siècles)," in *L'argent et la circulation des capitaux dans les pays méditerranéens (XVIe–XXe siècles)*, 121–34. Actes des journées d'études, Bendor, 3–5 May 1979, *Cahiers de la Méditerranée*, Nice, 1981.

Zouari, Ali. "La waqfiyya de 'Abd al-'Aziz Ghurab al-Maghribi al-Safaqusi." *Annales Islamologiques* 17 (1980): 311–32.

1

Dervishes, Waqfs, and Conquest: Notes on Early Ottoman Expansion in Thrace

Rıza Yıldırım

In the medieval Islamic world, many of the services today provided by modern governments and municipalities were left to 'civil agents' such as waqfs and charitable institutions. States were to provide security, against both internal and external threats, and to distribute and maintain justice. Services such as education, health, relief of poverty, public and religious constructions (mosques, ablution pools, cemeteries, baths), and infrastructure projects (water supply, bridges, roads) were all provided by the waqf system. From this point of view, as a modern scholar observed: "it is not an exaggeration to claim that the waqf, or pious endowment created in perpetuity, has provided the foundation for much of what is considered 'Islamic civilization.'"[1]

Occupying such a central position in Islamic civilization, waqf and its associated institutions had social, political, legal, and religious dimensions, and could interact with various social classes on different levels and in diverse contexts. A basic twofold division, however, was always valid for the people connected to a waqf: on the one hand, a person endowed private property on condition of perpetuity; on the other hand, a group of people, which might well include the endower him- or herself, benefited from the revenues of this property. The first group comprised members of ruling dynasties, ruling elites, dignitaries attached to the ruling class, and ordinary people possessing a degree of wealth. The beneficiaries tended principally to be the subjects of the ruling class, although the ruling classes could also benefit from waqf revenues.

In view of the patrimonial nature of Islamic states during medieval times, the process of property appropriation was by no means independent from state control. As the ultimate proprietor of the state, and tacitly of the territory over which the state enjoyed sovereignty, the ruler could always lay claim to land, even as a private possession. As İnalcık points out, all arable lands were considered in principle *miri*, that is, under the state's eminent domain.[2] Hence, private ownership of land seems to have been the exception rather than the norm in the land regime of Islamic states. All kinds of nonstate proprietorship of land, however, could result from bestowal by the ruler. Once a legitimate ruler had granted an asset or piece of land as private property *(milk)*, succeeding sovereigns were supposed to recognize the owner's rights, which thus became hereditary and per-petual. Nevertheless, a patrimonial monarch could intervene to abrogate or confiscate private property; this type of intervention was always valid, and indeed not infrequent.

The method of religious endowment, waqf, appeared as the most efficient way of safeguarding one's property from state interference. This, of course, is not the only reason why a person would bequeath his belongings for the pub-lic good, restricting his or her own rights over his or her (former) property.[3] And one can ask further why a ruler would bestow a part of his *miri* land (or real estate), or some portion of tax revenues generated by land, to individuals or to groups perpetually, when such endowments had the automatic effect of diminishing treasury incomes. There may have been a number of reasons for this. Every attempt to answer this question, however, would immediately recognize the political nature of the issue. From the state's point of view, establishing waqf was above all a method of governance.[4]

Like so many of their predecessors, the Ottomans resorted extensively to waqfs in providing social services and welfare, thereby seeking to keep society governable.[5] This paper, however, focuses on a slightly different and specifically Ottoman use of waqf. During the formative period, the Ottomans employed waqf as a tool of conquest and colonization, especially in Rumelia and the Balkans. The process was quite straightforward. As a first step, a military victory was followed by annexation of a territory. Then the sultan distributed some of the conquered land as private property *(milk)* to Sufi leaders who had taken part in military action. The land grant was legally set down in a royal diploma called *temlikname* (in the Mongol tradition of *soyurgal*).[6] Grants were made to Sufi leaders in recognition of their services to Islam and the early Ottoman dynasty, but also incurred an obligation to fulfill certain public services through hospices to be founded on the newly conquered territories. Sufi hospices supported by revenue-generating religious endowments functioned as a vector of colonization. Sufi leaders usually turned these *milk* lands granted by the sultan into '*evlatlık* waqf,'[7] most probably to safeguard their progeny's beneficiary rights on usufruct from government intervention and to guarantee the perpetuity of Sufi activities in the hospice.

Remnants of myriad hospices, whose origins may be traced back to this process of conquest and colonization during the early period of the empire, are still found in Thrace and the Balkans. One of them, namely the hospice of Seyyid Ali Sultan, is a good example of how the Ottomans successfully employed waqf, a deep-rooted Islamic institution, in their conquest of Rumelia. After a brief overview of the early Ottoman conquest of Thrace and the Balkans, this chapter attempts to locate the role of Seyyid Ali Sultan and his waqf in the bigger picture of early Ottoman conquest and colonization of Eastern Europe.

After crossing the Dardanelles in 1352, the Ottomans expanded very quickly through Thrace and the Balkans. The Ottoman army, under the command of Lala Shahin, captured Adrianople in 1361. In 1372, the despot of the Dobrudja and the king of Bulgaria became Ottoman vassals. In 1389, the Ottomans defeated combined Serbian and Bosnian forces in Kosovo. Soon after this victory, the Ottoman ruler brought Danubian Bulgaria under direct Ottoman rule, installed the Bulgarian king as a vassal prince in Nicopolis, and expelled Mircea from Silistra and Dobrudja. The decisive Ottoman victory of Nicopolis against a crusader army under the leadership of Hungary and Venice in 1396 firmly established Ottoman suzerainty on Thrace and permanently dashed any hope that the Muslims could be kept out of Europe.

The factors behind this lightning-quick success have long been a subject of fierce debate in Ottoman historiography. Although scholars have differed in their explanations, one of the points on which almost all historians agree is that this was not merely a territorial and military expansion, but rather a deep social process that included cultural transformation, colonization, conversion, reforms in land regimes and tax systems, and changes in existing political structures.

Aşıkpaşazade records in his chronicle that, after passing to Gallipoli through the Dardanelles, Süleyman Pasha requested that his father Orhan send Turks from the other side—namely Anatolia—to settle in the newly captured regions.[8] This passage reveals some clues about the Ottoman policy of colonization in Thrace. Contemporary sources suggest that the Ottomans pursued a conscious policy of *istimalet* (the conciliatory policy of tolerance applied in order to gain the favor of the indigenous population for the new regime) toward their new subjects,[9] on the one hand, and impelled Muslim Turkish subjects in Anatolia to migrate toward newly conquered territories, on the other.[10]

It would not be an exaggeration to assert that mystic dervishes and the hospices they founded (*tekke* or *zaviye*) dominated the whole process of Ottoman conquest and colonization in Rumelia. Ömer Lütfi Barkan showed how these dervishes founded their zaviyes (Arabic *zawiya*, pl. *zawaya*), which were economically supported by rich waqfs endowed by Ottoman sultans; how they preached Islam among local Christian laymen; and how the zaviyes turned into economic, social, and cultural centers. Barkan also demonstrated that most of the villages in Thrace and the Balkans can be traced back to a zaviye foundation.[11]

It should be noted that waqf and zaviye were inseparable institutions. Every zaviye accompanied a waqf, which supplied necessary economic–fiscal revenue for the dervishes living in the zaviyes. This revenue also made it possible to provide public services such as temporary accommodation, food service, religious education, and so on. The principal condition in almost all waqf deeds (which determined the rules of a waqf and guaranteed the rights of the beneficiary associated with these early zaviyes was formulated as *"ayende ve revendeye hizmet"*—that is: to serve people coming to and passing through the region.[12]

Waqfs endowed by Ottoman sultans provided financial support for the activities of dervishes lodged in the zaviye. Shaykhs founded the zaviyes and usually received waqf benefits in return for their pious activities and public services. Seyyid Ali Sultan, also known as Kızıldeli, was a shaykh who crossed to Thrace in the army of Süleyman Pasha, the eldest son of Orhan Beg and heir apparent. He fought in the Ottoman army against "the enemies of the religion" with his disciples, and then Sultan Bayezid I[13] endowed a waqf in his name in Dimetoka, where he founded his zaviye. Records of this waqf housed in the Ottoman archives show how the economic, religious, and social conditions of the zaviye evolved in later periods.[14] A hagiography *(velayetname)* of Seyyid Ali Sultan provides more information about his life, although it is flawed as a historical source.[15]

It is worth noting the differences between the early Ottoman conquests of Asia Minor and Thrace and the subsequent Ottoman expansion into Central and Eastern Europe. The early conquests involved a degree of colonization and conversion accompanied by fundamental changes in the cultural and social structures of the region. The later phases, in contrast, were carried out through the annexation of large territories, usually after a decisive military victory, and—at least to begin with—left the social structure on the micro level almost intact.

This second type of Ottoman conquest has been analyzed by Halil İnalcık in his seminal article "Ottoman Methods of Conquest."[16] İnalcık divides the conquest process into two main stages. First the Ottomans established a form of suzerainty over neighboring states; then the central Ottoman state asserted direct control over its new vassals and established the *timar* system (tax grants in return for military service) in these lands. This process also involved some degree of assimilation, but it occurred gradually rather than through forcible conversion. The Ottomans never totally eliminated the indigenous local aristocracy when they set up the timar system in a newly conquered territory; rather, they let the local aristocracy enter the Ottoman system as timar holders without forcing them to convert to Islam.[17] As a result, in parts of the Ottoman Balkans in the fifteenth century, as many as half the timariots were Christian. Being Muslim, however, was always profitable in the Ottoman lands in terms of economic advantages and social prestige, and conversion to Islam eventually became a de facto prerequisite for participation in the Ottoman administrative system, which led to the gradual assimilation of local aristocrats, who held high offices in the apparatus of the Ottoman state. Thus, by the sixteenth century, very few timariots were still Christian—not, apparently, because they had been dispossessed, but rather because, over two or three generations, they had embraced Islam.[18] This was the second phase of Islamization of the Balkans, which took place at the level of the aristocracy. Since this type of conversion was based mainly on worldly interests and never extended beyond a narrow circle in the higher echelons of society, Islam almost disappeared from these territories after the collapse of Ottoman rule.

As noted above, the early Ottoman conquests—which included Bythinia and Rumelia—were carried out very differently. In the absence of a powerful state that could annex large territories in one blow, annexation was rather a gradual and somewhat spontaneous process that included a cultural invasion affecting all strata of the conquered society, not just the higher echelons. Indeed the early phase of Ottoman expansion is a mirror image of the later phase, since it was the lower strata of society that collaborated with the Ottomans and converted, while the aristocracy initially resisted the conquest.

Turkomans who were searching for a new life, and their spiritual leaders (in Turkish called *baba*s and *dede*s), played an important role in Ottoman conquest and colonization during this earlier phase. V.L. Ménage, in "The Islamization of Anatolia," notes that the dominant figure in the life of the Turkish nomads and settled peasantry was not the orthodox *alim* but the Turkish 'holy man' under a variety of names: *şeyh, baba, abdal, ışık, torlak, kalender*.[19] Other prominent historians, such as Frederick W. Hasluck, Fuat Köprülü, Franz Babinger, and Ömer L. Barkan, have also underlined the leading role of Sufi dervishes in the spread of Islam in Anatolia and the Balkans.[20] Barkan, using *tahrir* (tax) registers pertaining to waqf lands bestowed upon dervishes by the Ottoman sultans, reveals the pioneering role dervishes played in turning the newly conquered territories into Muslim-Turkish lands.[21] The case I examine below, that of Seyyid Ali Sultan, shows striking conformity with Barkan's general formulation.

Moreover, the role of dervishes in the early conquests was not confined to military and religious affairs: they were also active in establishing cultural, economic, and even political institutions in the new territories. As Barkan discovered, Sufi dervishes not only provided Muslim warriors for the Ottoman army, but also had very important functions in reshaping the new social and political structure in the conquered lands by spreading religious and social ideas among the masses.[22]

The process would begin with a certain shaykh and his disciples providing services to the ruling dynasty. These services could consist of direct participation in military operations (as in the cases of Seyyid Ali or Geyikli Baba), or of religious works that served to legitimize the Ottoman presence in the eyes of the populace (as in the cases of Kumral Abdal and Edabali). Then the sultan would grant a portion of newly conquered land (which had usually been abandoned by its former inhabitants) to the shaykh through a royal edict *(temlikname)*. Finally, the dervishes would establish their hospice on the endowed land and undertake agricultural, economic, social, and cultural activities within the context of their mystical way of life. The tax revenue generated by the endowed land was to cover the hospice expenditures. In order to safeguard the autonomy and perpetuity of the granted income, shaykhs usually turned their private property into waqf, appointing their progeny as trustees.[23]

However, sultans made gifts of these waqf lands conditional upon the fulfillment of certain public duties. First of all, since most of these lands were abandoned, the dervishes were expected to reclaim them by establishing hospices: they were expected to turn fallow fields into thriving agricultural and economic centers. Village settlements gradually emerged around most of these hospices. In this way, many villages populated predominantly by Muslims came into existence. According to waqf deeds, the state gave the right to administer the waqf to a shaykh and his descendants provided that they served the needs of travelers passing through (*ayende ve revendeye hizmet ideler*, as noted above). If the shaykh or his offspring failed to fulfill their duties, the sultan had the right to take the waqf back and give it to another shaykh.[24]

Another function attributed to these hospices and waqfs is that they were usually made responsible for guard highways *(derbend)*. It is recorded in the survey register dated 1485–86, for example, that one of the villages included in the waqf of Seyyid Ali Sultan was a derbend village. An individual named Gülşehri, presumably a grandson of Seyyid Ali Sultan, was in charge of controlling the waqf income on the authority of a royal decree. It is also recorded that Gülşehri and the dervishes living off the waqf income were responsible for protecting free passage along the highway (from attacks by mobs or bandits).[25]

The lives of Seyyid Ali Sultan and Seyyid Rüstem Ghazi, if we are to believe the *velayetname* (hagiography), are two excellent examples of the procedure described above. These two dervishes first came to Rumelia in order to help the Ottoman sultan in the 'Holy War' against the 'infidels' and to enlarge the realm of Islam. They fought and conquered lands and fortresses. When they won their battles, they were given lands as waqf in a certain region they had conquered in the newly occupied territories. There, they established their hospices. The velayetname states that, for example, Seyyid Rüstem Ghazi founded his hospice in a region bestowed to him by Bayezid I. As time passed, people began to gather around him as his disciples. They established a mill for which the water was provided, according to the velayetname, by a miracle of Seyyid Rüstem Ghazi. The hospice gradually became an economic and social center in the region.[26]

Although the sources do not go into as much detail in the case of Seyyid Ali Sultan, it is reasonable to infer that his situation must have been more or less the same. Seyyid Ali Sultan has long been considered one of the great saints in Bektashi circles. He is also called Kızıldeli, after the river near which he founded his hospice. Ahmet Ocak considers that his hospice—the Kızıldeli Tekkesi, in Dimetoka—is one of the four most important Bektashi zawiyes,[27] while Bedri Noyan rates it among the top five.[28] There are many works in Bektashi literature praising the glory of Seyyid Ali Sultan. He held the second of the traditional twelve stages *(post)* of the Bektashi order: *aşçı postu* (the cook).[29] He is also praised as *"Rum ilinin Gözcüsü Seyyit Ali Sultan"* (the watcher of Rumelia). In sum, he has been a significant figure in the Bektashi order and heterodox circles since at least the sixteenth century and still commands great respect in 'Alawi-Bektashi society.[30]

Despite the important place Seyyid Ali Sultan and his legacy have occupied in the Bektashi order, however, historical information about him is very limited. Fourteenth-century chroniclers such as Aşıkpaşazade, Oruç, Neşri, and Anonim Tevarih remain silent about him. He is, however, mentioned in Ottoman tax registers and in a file titled "Musa Çelebi Dosyası," preserved in the Başbakanlık Arşivi in Istanbul. This file concerns the hospice founded by Seyyid Ali Sultan.[31]

Apart from the Ottoman archival documents, there is a fairly short passage about Seyyid Ali Sultan in a European source: the chronicle of Konstantin the Philosopher, which narrates the life story of the Serbian despot Stefan Lazarevic. Konstantin wrote his book in 1431, only four years after Stefan's death.[32] Konstantin mentioned Seyyid Ali Sultan as 'Seidija' and depicted him as a companion of Süleyman, the grandson of Orhan. He also stressed that Süleyman first crossed the Dardanelles with Seidija and opened the way to the West.[33]

In addition, two hagiographic sources contain information about Seyyid Ali Sultan. One is about him and explains how Rumelia was conquered by forty heroes who had come from Khorasan following a divine order given by the Prophet Muhammad in a dream. In this velayetname, Seyyid Ali Sultan is depicted as a warrior-saint who used his divine power to conquer lands from 'infidels' to broaden the realm of the true religion, Islam—an excellent prototype of gazi-dervishes who were actively involved in early Ottoman expansion into Byzantine lands.[34] The second hagiography that contains information about Seyyid Ali Sultan is the velayetname of Abdal Musa, which mentions Seyyid Ali Sultan as a disciple of Abdal Musa and links him to the conquest of Thrace.[35]

These hagiographic accounts seem at first to be unlikely sources of reliable historical information, due to the obvious anachronisms and narrations of supernatural deeds that characterize such documents. As I have discussed elsewhere,[36] however, if one compares the stories in the velayetnames to events recounted by other sources, it becomes clear that the hagiographies cannot be dismissed as mere fictions. Taken together with the archival records about the hospice and what the chronicles tell us of the conquest of Rumelia, the hagiographies contribute significantly to the elucidation of Seyyid Ali Sultan as a historical figure,[37] including his role and that of his waqf in the conquest and colonization of Thrace.

Of the archival evidence, the Musa Çelebi file provides the most informative account. Six documents in this file are directly related to the Kızıldeli Tekkesi and have been referred to by Wittek,[38] Ménage,[39] Gokbilgin, Barkan, and Beldiceanu. One of those documents is a copy of a survey register established in 1568.[40] The introduction to this document reads: "This is the waqf of Kızıldeli, who passed to Rumelia when it was converted to Islam and upon whom the Village of Büyük Viran, Daru Büki ve Turfillu Virani was bestowed as waqf by Yıldırım Han in AH 804 [1401–1402 CE]."[41] This is the earliest mention of Seyyid Ali Sultan in the archives.

The second document is a *berat*, or edict, by Musa Çelebi, dated AH 815 (1412 CE). This document renews the rights of Kızıldeli's offspring to the waqf lands. At the beginning, it states: "Former *begs* endowed the villages of Shaykh Kızıldeli as waqf." Musa Çelebi was the son of Yıldırım Bayezid and his successor in Thrace during the civil war. The previous survey register mentions an edict by Yıldırım Bayezid dated 1402, and Musa Çelebi's edict employs the plural form of *beg*—indicating that by this time multiple rulers had endorsed Kızıldeli's waqf. It is thus possible to trace the waqf's origin even further back, possibly to the time of Murad I, under whom considerable parts of Thrace and the Balkans were conquered, among them Dimetoka, in which Kızıldeli's hospice was founded.

Keeping in mind these key points derived from archival sources, let us move on to an analysis of the hagiography mentioned earlier.[42] The velayetname poses certain problems as a historical source, shrouding as it does the life of its subject in a dense cloud of legend. The ability to tease out the real life of a historical figure from such a source is thus limited: hagiography can provide only a loose frame that still allows for a fairly large spectrum of possibilities. The Velayetname of Seyyid Ali Sultan tells the story of Seyyid Ali Sultan thus: The saint and his forty companions devoted themselves to prayer in their hospice in Khorasan. At the same time, the Ottoman sultan (Orhan according to the Cairo copy, Bayezid I according to other copies) was deep in thought. He was trying to conquer Rumelia, but could not find any reasonable way to achieve his goal. Sultan and saint both dreamed that the Prophet Muhammad directed them to conquer Rumelia. Seyyid Ali and his forty companions came to Anatolia and, in accordance with the Prophet's directions, went first to the hospice of Hacı Bektash to obtain his approval. Hacı Bektash accepted them and, appointing Seyyid Ali Sultan as the leader of the forty heroes, sent them to the Ottoman sultan Orhan. They met Orhan in his camp, agreed on a plan, and went on to conquer Gallipoli, İpsala, Dimetoka, Edirne, Şumnu, Silistre, and other fortresses across the Balkans.

With the exception of some supernatural acts that Seyyid Ali Sultan and Seyyid Rüstem Ghazi are said to have performed as they conquered these fortresses,[43] the narrative of the hagiographies appears to be compatible with the Ottoman chronicles. The primary difference lies in whom the texts portray as heroes: the hagiographies obviously stress the role of saints, while chroniclers tend to attribute all victories to the Ottoman dynasty.[44]

As mentioned above, there is documentary evidence that Seyyid Ali Sultan was given a waqf by Bayezid I—or more probably by Murad I—in return for the role he played in the conquest of the Balkans. Since his waqf privileges were renewed by Musa Çelebi in 1412, he must have died sometime after 1412. He is described as a disciple of Abdal Musa and joined the campaign of Umur Ghazi upon the order of his shaykh.[45] It is known that Umur Ghazi was killed in 1348 in a war with the papal army. Relying on the hagiography, it is possible to infer that Seyyid Ali Sultan was a disciple of Abdal Musa toward the middle of the fourteenth century. During this time, he is likely to have been between twenty-five and forty-five years old, and thus would have been born in the first quarter of the fourteenth century.[46]

Hagiographic and historical sources agree that Seyyid Ali Sultan played a significant role in the conquest of Rumelia. As indicated above, archival sources clearly trace his connection with the conquest. Another contemporary account supports the idea that he not only took part in the conquest and colonization process but also had a close friendship with the Ottoman sultans:

When the Ismailis[47] came to power and subdued the eastern lands, they also won the people . . . to their hateful beliefs. They forced the other people to accept their beliefs.

After some time, Süleyman, the grandson of Orhan, led the ex-ruler of Ajamiya,[48] whose name was Seidija and who was great-grandson of that monk, into the western countries during the lifetime of Orhan. By that time he had already subdued him and his country. And he promised that he would give him one of every ten conquered cities.

The great-grandson of the emperor dressed in dervish clothes; his evil beliefs are well known and his name was Orhan. His eldest son was

Süleyman. This Süleyman took power during the lifetime of his father and went west, passing to Gallipoli with Seidija and opening the way west for his people. That happened during the time of Emperor Andronikos, who was at war with his brother.[49]

Meanwhile, the hagiography of Abdal Musa relates that he commissioned his disciple, Seyyid Ali Sultan, to conquer Rumelia, while the velayetname of Seyyid Ali Sultan is devoted to narrating how the saint and his forty companions succeeded in this task. There is a striking concordance between the information given in the two hagiographies. Although Seyyid Ali Sultan's place of origin and the person who charged him with his mission are given differently, the core theme—the conquest of Rumelia—is the same. It is unlikely that one of these hagiographies used the other, since they employ completely different narrative frames. The concordance can therefore be taken as strong evidence for the close connection between Seyyid Ali Sultan and the Ottoman conquest of Rumelia. This conclusion is supported by the fact that Umur Ghazi of Aydın launched naval expeditions in the Aegean Sea and raids in the Balkan lands.

The hagiography says that, after a series of conquests, Seyyid Ali Sultan and his companions left the warrior bands to settle in pre-determined places. Their mission was to establish zaviyes and radiate Islam in a mystical form by training disciples and hosting people in these hospices. Seyyid Ali Sultan himself settled somewhere close to Sarıkızıl Pastureland *(yayla)*.[50] Although the hagiographic account stops at that point, it is possible to fill the gap with archival evidence. The tax revenues of some villages around his hospice were bestowed by the Ottoman sultan to provide financial support for activities centered around the zaviye. The tax records reveal that Ottoman sultans bequeathed these sources of revenue to the zaviye partly because of Seyyid Ali's active participation in the conquest of the region.

The process of establishing a zaviye and associated waqf is more clearly explained in the narrative of Seyyid Rüstem Ghazi, who occupies as much space as Seyyid Ali Sultan in the hagiography. Hacı Bektash allegedly appointed him *kadiasker* (judge) of the forty heroes. Seyyid Rüstem not only fought by Seyyid Ali Sultan's side, but also developed war strategies and state policies that were accepted by the Ottoman sultan. According to the velayetname, after a series of conquests under the command of Kızıldeli, the dervishes were permitted to settle and each of them went to a different place. Rüstem left the group and secluded himself in a cave to meditate. After a while he returned to normal life and established a zaviye in a region bestowed upon him by Sultan Yıldırım Bayezid. In time, other devishes gathered around him, and they established a mill near the zaviye. They engaged in agricultural activities as well as religious worship.[51]

To sum up, the hagiographies, read in tandem with archival sources and chronicles, indicate that close links existed between dervishes, warriors, and the Ottoman dynasty in the early period of Ottoman expansion into Europe. Ottomans employed waqf as an efficient device in the conquest and colonization of Rumelia and the Balkans. It is reasonable to infer that the sultan's promise of conquered lands to participants in the *gaza* (holy war) inspired many people, including large groups of Sufis, to join Ottoman ranks. Once a region was captured, however, a bigger question arose: the problem of occupation, or *şenlendirme*.

One should not underestimate Sufis' contribution to the Ottomans' actual military campaigns. The evidence strongly suggests that they played an active role on the battlefield. Their role as spiritual leaders stimulating warriors' emotions, however, was far more influential than their fighting capabilities. Their most valuable contribution came in the second stage of the conquest, that is, during the process of securing the annexed territory by settling inhabitants there. The classical Islamic institution of waqf, combined with the establishment of dervish hospices, played an essential role in this process of Ottoman expansion and consolidation, as illustrated by the cases of Seyyid Ali Sultan and Seyyid Rüstem Ghazi. The waqf–hospice pairing not only provided autonomous spheres for Sufis to develop cultural and economic life in deserted regions, but also helped to anchor the Ottoman regime by consolidating ties between the ruling class and the local masses, to whom the Sufis brought a mystical version of Islam, providing fertile ground for the diffusion of new social, cultural, and religious practices.

Notes

1   Hennigan, *Birth of a Legal Institution*, xiii.
2   İnalcık, "Autonomous Enclaves," 117–18.
3   Scholars have offered some possible reasons. The reader will find various explanations in the present volume. For a summary, see Ghazaleh's introduction in this volume.
4   For a reading on various aspects of the waqf in medieval Islamic societies, see, for example, Baer, "Waqf as a Prop"; Köprülü, "Vakıf Müessesesi ve Vakıf Vesikalarının"; Köprülü, "Vakıf Müessesesinin Hukuki"; Peri, "Waqf and Ottoman Welfare Policy"; Arjomand, "The Law"; Shatzmiller, "Islamic Institutions"; Subtelny, "Socioeconomic Basis of Cultural Patronage"; and Subtelny, "Timurid."
5   See Yediyıldız, "Vakıf Müessesesinin XVIII" and Barnes, *An Introduction*.

6 For a general assessment on the political implications of *temlīk*s, *soyurghal*s, and waqf in Islamic states, see İnalcık, "Autonomous Enclaves." For *soyurghal*s in Timurids, see Subtelny, "Socioeconomic Bases of Cultural Patronage."

7 This means the trustee of the waqf would be chosen from among the offspring of the endower. See Barkan, "Şer'i Miras Hukuku."

8 Aşıkpaşazade, "Tevarih-i Al-i Osman," 124.

9 İnalcık, *The Ottoman Empire*, 5–16.

10 For the Ottoman conquest of Rumelia and the Balkans, see Aktepe, "Osmanlı Türkleri'nin," and Selçuk, "Rumeli'de Osmanlı."

11 Barkan, "Kolonizatör Türk Dervişleri."

12 For example, the waqf records of the Kızıldeli Tekke in the Ottoman Archives frequently underline the duty of the dervishes living in the lodge to serve people staying there or passing through. See Başbakanlık Osmanlı Arşivleri, Istanbul, TD 370, 33.

13 The earliest archival reference to the establishment of the Kızıldeli waqf goes back to the time of Bayezid I. Nevertheless, some phrases in the same documents allude to an earlier time of establishment during the reign of Murad I. For a broader discussion of this issue, see Yıldırım, "History Beneath Clouds of Legend."

14 For a study of the Kızıldeli Tekke based on these records, see Faroqhi, "Agricultural Activities."

15 The whole text of the hagiography is published in Yıldırım, *Seyyid Ali Sultan*. For a study of this hagiography as a source for history, see Yıldırım, "Efsanede Gizli Gerçek."

16 İnalcık, "Ottoman Methods of Conquest."

17 For further reading, see İnalcık, "Ottoman Methods of Conquest."

18 İnalcık, "Ottoman Methods of Conquest," 113–17.

19 Ménage, "Islamization," 60.

20 See Köprülü, "Anadoluda İslamiyet"; Babinger, "Der Islam in Kleinasien"; Hasluck, *Christianity and Islam*; Barkan, "Kolonizatör Türk Dervişleri."

21 See Barkan, "Kolonizatör Türk Dervişleri."

22 Barkan, "Kolonizatör Türk Dervişleri," 283.

23 This process is clearly defined in the Ottoman archival documents. The survey register compiled during the reign of Selim II, for example (dated 1568–69), shows how the waqf of Seyyid Ali Sultan was established. It records that in 1401–1402, Ottoman sultan Bayezid I granted the villages of Büyükviran, Tarubükü, and Tırfılluviranı to Seyyid Ali Sultan as *mülk* and gave him a *mülkname-i şerif*. Seyyid Ali Sultan turned this land into *evlatlık* waqf, which was approved by successive sultans up until Selim II. See Tapu Kadastro Genel Müdürlüğü KKA TD 562, f. 126b.

24 See İnalcık, "Osmanlı Tarihine," 49.

25 See Başbakanlık Osmanlı Arşivleri, TD 20, 265.

26 Yıldırım, *Seyyid Ali Sultan*, 179–84.

27 Ocak, *Bektaşî Menâkıbnâmelerinde*, 13.

28 Noyan, ed., *Seyyit Ali Sultan*, 13.

29 See Birge, *The Bektashi Order*, 178; Mélikoff, *Hacı Bektaş*, 259.

30 For an attempt to capture the Seyyid Ali Sultan picture as drawn by the Bektashi tradition, see Yıldırım, "Bektaşi-Alevi."

31 For an attempt to delineate the historical life of Seyyid Ali Sultan on the basis of these sources, see Yıldırım, "History Beneath Clouds of Legend."

32 I would like to thank Professor Halil İnalcık, who brought the existence of this short passage relating to Kızıldeli to my attention.

33 Konstantin dem Philosophen, *Lebensbeschreibung*.

34 See Yıldırım, *Seyyid Ali Sultan*, 159–84.

35 See Güzel, *Abdal Musa Velayetnamesi*.

36 Yıldırım, "Efsanede Gizli Gerçek."

37 Yıldırım, "History Beneath Clouds of Legend." Before my own study, several scholars were interested in Seyyid Ali Sultan and his waqf. Among modern scholars, it was Birge who first paid attention to Seyyid Ali Sultan in his work on the Bektashi Order (Birge, *The Bektashi Order*). Barkan, using two tax registers, referred to Kızıldeli's hospice in his famous article, "Kolonizatör Türk Dervişleri." Later on, Gökbilgin published relevant archival sources (*XV. ve XVI. Asırlarda Edirne*). The most comprehensive study on Seyyid Ali Sultan is arguably that of Beldiceanu-Steinherr ("Osmanlı Tahrir Defterlerinde"). This article analyzes eight tax registers starting from that of Mehmet II in 1456 and an archival file titled "Musa Çelebi dosyası." Beldiceanu-Steinherr compares and analyzes the information that the tax registers provide about Kızıldeli's hospice and attempts to trace the historical development of the legend of Seyyid Ali Sultan, reaching some conclusions about his historical personality. One should also mention the remarks by Bedri Noyan, a Bektashi dede, in his publication of the velayetname of Seyyid Ali Sultan (Noyan, *Velayetname*).

38 Wittek, "Zu einigen frühosmanichen Urkuden II."

39 Ménage, "Musa Çelebi's Nishan."

40 TT 460 (reign of Selim II).

41 Başbakanlık Osmanlı Arşivleri, Musa Çelebi Dosyası File.

42 The author of the velayetname cannot be identified with certainty. A mention of the name Cezbi in a poem within the text might be a clue, but it is not impossible that this name is a later addition. A linguistic analysis of the text would situate its composition in the fifteenth or the first half of the sixteenth century. Besides this initial difficulty, there are some differences among the extant copies of this velayetname. A copy located in Cairo situates the events narrated in the time of Orhan, who reigned between 1326 and 1362, while all other copies of the manuscript note that the events occurred during the reign of Bayezid I, between 1389 and 1402. Apart from this significant difference in the names of sultans, the texts are more or less the same. As I will show in more detail below, however, the names and events reported in the velayetname clearly belong to Orhan's time, and it is therefore safe to assume that the other manuscripts are mistaken in mentioning Bayezid I. For further analysis of the velayetname as a source for history, see Yıldırım, "Efsanede Gizli Gerçek."

43 Supernatural power *(karamat)* was seen as one of the significant signs of being *veli* among Sufis. One should therefore recognize that the narration of supernatural events was the norm in texts that circulated extensively among dervishes and were read as guidebooks.

44 I would like to draw attention to a distinctive feature of this velayetname. When one considers the story's purpose and style, the velayetname of Seyyid Ali Sultan resembles an archetypal Ottoman historical romance *(destan)*. The heroes, Seyyid Ali Sultan and his companions, are supposed to be saints, show courage on the battlefield, conquer fortresses, strike fear into the hearts of 'infidels,' and convert these 'infidels' by force. During the conquest of the Fortress of Murtad, for instance, Tahir, one

of these forty heroes, fights an infidel. The velayatname tells of Tahir hitting the infidel and knocking him to the ground before sitting on his chest and inviting him to embrace the true religion, Islam. Upon the infidel's acceptance and conversion to Islam, Tahir frees him. These types of events are frequent in the Velayetname of Seyyid Ali Sultan. What this particular story implies is that if this infidel had not agreed to convert, our warrior dervish would have killed him without hesitation. The heroic tone of the velayetname places it in the same category as the *Saltukname, Battalname,* and *Danismendname,* which are dedicated to the heroic life of warriors.

45   The velayetname of Abdal Musa also reports that Abdal Musa met Umur Ghazi and gave Seyyid Ali Sultan a "wooden sword" before sending him with Umur Ghazi to conquer Rumelia. According to this velayatname, Abdal Musa addressed Seyyid Ali Sultan and Umur Ghazi as follows: "Now go directly to Boğaz Hisarı. Lay siege to it; you will take it. After conquering Boğaz Hisarı, I gave you Rumelia. Let nobody stand in your way" (Güzel, *Abdal Musa Velayetnamesi,* 149). Seyyid Ali Sultan does not appear elsewhere in the velayetname. In the end, Abdal Musa sends his prominent disciples to several places. Though the velayetname mentions the names of some *halife*s, including Gaybi (Kaygusuz Abdal), Kızıldeli is not among them (Güzel, *Abdal Musa Velayetnamesi,* 151–52). From this narrative, it appears that Abdal Musa must have left Seyyid Ali Sultan in the campaign of Umur Ghazi.

46   See Yıldırım, "History Beneath Clouds of Legend."

47   Konstantin calls Ottomans 'Ismailis,' although the latter are in fact a branch of Shia who believe that the rightful imam after Imam Ja'far, the sixth imam, was his grandson Ismail. Turkish sources give no information about the Ottomans' relationship with Ismailism. But we know that, as partly explained in this paper, the early Ottoman conquests in Thrace and the Balkans were accompanied by intense religious propaganda. These missionary activities were led by heterodox dervishes, like Seyyid Ali Sultan, who were preaching a mystic and Gnostic perception and interpretation of Islam. This dervish milieu might have some Ismaili beliefs, but this subject requires further investigation.

48   This is another interesting point made by Konstantin. In none of the other sources do we find mention of Kızıldeli being a ruler.

49   Konstantin dem Philosophen, *Lebensbeschreibung.*

50   Yıldırım, *Seyyid Ali Sultan,* 174–79.

51   Yıldırım, *Seyyid Ali Sultan,* 179–83. Seyyid Rüstem Ghazi and his hospice were long absent from modern scholarship. Until recently, the single available source about him was the abovementioned legendary account. As a result, his existence as a historical figure, as well as that of his hospice and waqf, was a subject of dispute. Nevertheless, some recent discoveries, including the ruins of the Seyyid Rüstem Ghazi hospice, buttressed the picture drawn by the velayetname. See Yıldırım, "History Beneath Clouds of Legends," 49–50.

Bibliography

Primary Sources from the Ottoman Archives

Başbakanlık Osmanlı Arşivleri, İstanbul, TD 20, TD 77.

Başbakanlık Osmanlı Arşivleri, İstanbul TD, 370.

Başbakanlık Osmanlı Arşivleri, İstanbul, TT 460.

Başbakanlık Osmanlı Arşivleri, İstanbul, Ali Emiri Fonu, Musa Çelebi Dosyası.

Tapu Kadastro Genel Müdürlüğü, Ankara, KKA TD 562, f. 126b.

Publications and Other Sources

Aktepe, M. Münir. "Osmanlı Türkleri'nin Rumeli'ye Yerleşmeleri." PhD diss., İstanbul Üniversitesi Edebiyat Fakültesi Tarih Bölümü, Istanbul, 1949.

Arjomand, Said Amir. "The Law, Agency, and Policy in Medieval Islamic Society: Development of the Institutions of Learning from the Tenth to the Fifteenth Century." *Comparative Studies in Society and History* 41, no. 2 (1999): 269–93.

Aşıkpaşazade. "Tevarih-i Al-i Osman," in Nihal Atsız, ed., *Osmanlı Tarihleri*, 77–319. Istanbul: Türkiye Yayınevi, 1949.

Babinger, Franz. "Der Islam in Kleinasien, neueu Wege der Islamforschung." *Zeitschrift der Deutschen Morgenlandischen Gesselschaft* 76 (1922): 126–52.

Baer, Gabriel. "The Waqf as a Prop for the Social System (Sixteenth-Twentieth Centuries)." *Islamic Law and Society* 4, no. 3 (1997): 264–97.

Barkan, Ömer Lütfi. "Osmanlı İmparatorluğunda bir İskan ve Kolonizasyon Metodu olarak Vakıflar ve Temlikler: İstila Devirlerinin Kolonizatör Türk Dervişleri ve Zaviyeler." *Vakıflar Dergisi* 2 (1942): 279–304.

———. "Şer'i Miras Hukuku ve Evlatlık Vakıflar," in *Türkiye'de Toprak Meselesi; Toplu Eserler I*, 209–30. Istanbul: Gözlem Yayınları, 1980.

Barnes, John Robert. *An Introduction to Religious Foundations in the Ottoman Empire*. Leiden: E.J. Brill, 1986.

Beldiceanu-Steinherr, Irène. "Osmanlı Tahrir Defterlerinde Seyyit Ali Sultan: Heterodox İslam'ın Trakya'ya Yerleşmesi," in *Sol Kol; Osmanlı Egemenliğinde Via Egnatia*, ed. Elizabeth A. Zachariadou, 50–72. Istanbul: Tarih Vakfı Yurt Yayınları, 1999.

Birge, John Kingsley. *The Bektashi Order*. London: Luzac and Co., 1937.

Faroqhi, Suraiya. "Agricultural Activities in a Bektashi Center: The Tekke of Kızıl Deli, 1750–1830." *Südost-Forschungen* 35 (1976): 69–96.

Gökbilgin, M. *XV. ve XVI. Asırlarda Edirne ve Paşa Livası Vakıflar-Mülkler-Mukataalar.* Istanbul: İşaret Yayınları, 2007.

Güzel, Abdurrahman. *Abdal Musa Velayetnamesi.* Ankara: Türk Tarih Kurumu, 1999.

Hasluck, William. *Christianity and Islam under the Sultans.* Oxford: Oxford University Press, 1929.

Hennigan, Peter C. *The Birth of a Legal Institution: The Formation of the Waqf in Third-Century AH Hanafi Legal Discourse.* Leiden and Boston: Brill, 2004.

İnalcık, Halil. "Autonomous Enclaves in Islamic States: *Temlîks, Soyurghals, Yurdluk-Ocakliks, Mâlikâne-Mukâta'as* and *Awqaf,*" in Judith Pfeiffer and Sholeh A. Quinn, eds., *History and Historiography of Post-Mongol Central Asia and the Middle East: Studies in Honor of John E. Woods,* 112–34. Wiesbaden: Harrassowitz Verlag, 2006.

———. "Osmanlı Tarihine Toplu Bir Bakış," in Güler Eren, ed., *Osmanlı,* 37–116. Ankara: Yeni Türkiye, 1999.

———. *The Ottoman Empire: The Classical Age, 1300–1600.* London: Phoenix, 1973.

———. "Ottoman Methods of Conquest," *Studia Islamica* 2 (1954): 104–29.

Konstantin dem Philosophen. *Lebensbeschreibung des Despoten Stefan Lazarevic.* Göttingen: Maximilian Braun, 1956.

Köprülü, Fuat. "Anadoluda İslamiyet." *Dârülfünûn Edebiyat Fakültesi Mecmuası* 4 (1922–23): 291–303.

———. "Vakıf Müessesesinin Hukuki Mahiyeti ve Tarihi Tekamülü." *Vakıflar Dergisi* 2 (1942): 1–35.

———. "Vakıf Müessesesi ve Vakıf Vesikalarının Tarihi Ehemmiyeti." *Vakıflar Dergisi* 1 (1938): 1–6.

Mélikoff, Irène. *Hacı Bektaş Efsaneden Gerçeğe.* Translated by Turan Alptekin. İstanbul: Cumhuriyet Kitapları, 1999. (The original work is published in French: *Hadji Bektach, un mythe et ses avatars.* Leiden: Brill, 1998.)

Ménage, Victor L. "The Islamization of Anatolia," in Nehemia Levtzion, ed., *Conversion to Islam,* 52–67. New York: Holmes and Meier, 1979.

———. "Musa Çelebi's Nishan of 815/1412." *Bulletin of the School of Oriental and African Studies* 26 (1963): 646–48.

Noyan, Bedri, ed. *Seyyit Ali Sultan Velayetnamesi.* Ankara: Ayyıldız Yayınları, 1999.

Ocak, Ahmet Yaşar. *Bektaşî Menâkıbnâmelerinde İslam Öncesi İnanç Motifleri.* İstanbul: Enderun Kitabevi, 1983.

Peri, Oded. "Waqf and Ottoman Welfare Policy." *Journal of the Economic and Social History of the Orient* 35 (1992): 171–85.

Selçuk, Hava. "Rumeli'de Osmanlı İskan Siyaseti (1299–1481)." PhD diss., Erciyes Üniversitesi Sosyal Bilimler Enstitüsü, Kayseri, 2002.

Shatzmiller, Maya. "Islamic Institutions and Property Rights: The Case of the 'Public Good' Waqf." *Journal of the Economic and Social History of the Orient* 44, no. 1 (2001): 44–74.

Subtelny, Maria Eva. "Socioeconomic Basis of Cultural Patronage under the Later Timurids." *International Journal of Middle East Studies* 20, no. 4 (1988): 479–505.

———. "A Timurid Educational and Charitable Foundation: The Ikhlasiyya Complex of 'Alī Shīr Nava'ī in 15th-Century Herat and Its Endowment." *Journal of the American Oriental Society* 111, no. 1 (1991): 38–61.

Wittek, Paul. "Zu einigen frühosmanichen Urkuden II." *Wiener Zeitschrift für die Kunde des Morgenlandes* 54 (1957): 240–56.

Yediyıldız, Bahaeddin. "Vakıf Müessesinin XVIII. Asır Türk Toplumundaki Rolü." *Vakıflar Dergisi* 14 (1982): 1–27.

Yıldırım, Rıza. "Bektaşi-Alevi Geleneğine Göre Seyyid Ali Sultan." *Türk Kültürü ve Hacı Bektaş Veli Araştırma Dergisi* 53 (2010): 59–87.

———. "Efsanede Gizli Gerçek: Bir Tarih Kaynağı Olarak Seyyid Ali Sultan Velâyetnâmesi." *Tarih ve Toplum: Yeni Yaklaşımlar* 6 (2008): 1–43.

———. "History Beneath Clouds of Legend: Seyyid Ali Sultan and His Place in Early Ottoman History According to Legends, Narratives, and Archival Evidence." *International Journal of Turkish Studies* 15, nos. 1–2 (2009): 21–62.

———. *Seyyid Ali Sultan (Kızıldeli) ve Velayetnamesi.* Ankara: Türk Tarih Kurumu, 2007.

2

Piety and Profit:
The Haramayn Endowments
in Egypt (1517–1814)[1]

Husam 'Abd al-Mu'ti

Long before the Ottoman period, the Hijaz had relied on Egypt's governments to provide it with financial support and grain in exchange for
religious and moral authority, validating Egypt's rulers as leaders of
the Islamic world. When the Ottomans annexed Egypt in 1517, responsibility for protecting Mecca and Medina was transferred from the Mamluk rulers to the Ottoman sultan in his capacity as Guardian of the Two Holy Cities,
strengthening political and economic ties between the Ottomans and the rulers of Mecca. These ties were founded on mutual interests: in exchange for
lavish gifts of money and grain sent each year by the Ottomans from Egypt
to Mecca and Medina, prayers were said for them at the Great Mosque in
Mecca and during the pilgrimage, reinforcing their claim to the religious and
spiritual leadership of the Islamic world. Not content with reforming and
expanding Mamluk religious endowments, the Ottoman sultans endowed
large tracts of agricultural land for Mecca and Medina with a combined
annual yield of around 33,000 *irdabb*, and revenues of five million paras.

The present chapter will examine the waqfs endowed in Egypt for the
benefit of the Two Sanctuaries *(al-Haramayn al-Sharifayn)*. In what follows,

I will attempt to identify the income of the Meccan and Medinan religious endowments endowed in Egypt for Mecca and Medina, map out the holdings and functions of each endowment, and understand the problems they faced in performing the duties assigned them by the Ottoman state. What was the nature of relations between the directors of these endowments, the central bureaucracy in Istanbul, and the local administration in Cairo? How were the villages and properties owned by these endowments administered? What was the relationship between the endowments' directors and their tenants? By posing these questions, the present study seeks to develop the conclusions of existing research on the Haramayn endowments in Egypt during the Ottoman period, in particular the important analyses of Muhammad Fahim Bayyumi[2] and Azza Shahin.[3] I will pose questions that past research has not addressed: for example, until now historians have not asked why these endowments expanded dramatically during the early seventeenth century. I also eschew the idea of continuity or stagnation in the situation of these endowments, arguing rather that waqfs underwent rapid changes triggered by the group that controlled political power in Egypt in late Ottoman times. The local political leadership tried to divert most of the revenues from these foundations to their own pockets in order to develop their households and, ultimately, to carry out their project of achieving independence from the Ottoman state. This process became particularly clear in the eighteenth century.

Before delving into the relations between local and imperial elites, however, we will examine a number of factors that lay behind the desire to create these vast endowments in Mecca and Medina and administer them from Egypt. In Cairo and Istanbul, rulers sought religiously charged political endorsement as guardians of the two holy places. Whoever commanded the loyalties of the Hijaz possessed spiritual authority over the entire Islamic world: 'Guardian of the Two Sanctuaries' was among the sultan's most important titles. These same rulers were careful to supply the Hijaz with the food rations it required to ensure the safe passage of pilgrims and pilgrimage caravans through the region. They also dispensed lavish gifts and funds to cultural and religious institutions such as mosques, hospices, and schools, and to the scholars and Sufis they housed. These donations feature particularly frequently in the records of endowments established by sultans, pashas, and amirs. In a similar fashion, the Ottomans furnished the Hijaz with gifts and provisions from their wealthiest storehouse, Egypt, which at that time enjoyed a large surplus. Delays in the arrival of these annual provisions always resulted in unrest and petitions sent to the sultan from inhabitants of the Hijaz. The Ottoman central government was sensitive to these problems and worked to avoid them by various means.[4]

For all these reasons, the Ottoman state was careful to ensure the timely arrival of allocations to the Hijaz, as evidenced by the fact that the first decree issued by any new ruler of Egypt was to dispatch the allocations of the Two Holy Cities. Indeed, the Sublime Porte required even those governors who had been dismissed from their post to send cash and provisions to the Hijaz before they left the country. In 1724, Muhammad Pasha al-Nishanji received an order to step down as governor of Egypt accompanied by a second order that forbade him from leaving Egypt without first dispatching grain to the Two Holy Cities.[5] The Ottomans had in fact inherited a number of vast endowments, founded in Egypt for the inhabitants of Mecca and Medina. Their task, therefore, was to organize and reform these existing endowments while adding others to reinforce their standing in the Islamic world. Sultan Sulayman al-Qanuni ('The Lawgiver,' known in Europe as Sulayman the Magnificent) had organized these endowments and added many others, using the protection the Ottoman state afforded Islamic religious foundations in Mecca, Medina, and Jerusalem to affirm its hegemony and power.

Here, we should draw attention to the fact that many researchers[6] have erroneously conflated the endowments' payments to the Hijaz with both state expenditures[7] and the *surra rumiya*. This surra comprised monies collected from the state's non-Muslim subjects and salaries taken from Egypt's revenues[8] and sent to institutions in the Hijaz. The administration also set aside a maintenance budget for the upkeep of institutions and public services, such as remuneration for water carriers who brought water to Jedda, and for ascetics who had settled in Mecca and Medina.[9]

The period spanning the late sixteenth and early seventeenth centuries witnessed the greatest expansion in the endowments of Mecca and Medina. Sultan Mehmet III (1594–1603) created a large endowment for the Two Holy Cities, as did Sultan Ahmet I (1603–17), though his endowment was smaller than that of his predecessors. Finally, in 1626, the mother of Sultan Murad III also founded an endowment for the Two Holy Cities. The question here is why such a large group of endowments was created during this period. I propose four explanations that enable us to locate this phenomenon in the broader framework of Ottoman history.

First, during this period the Ottoman state underwent a transformation from a state deriving its influence from formidable military might to one that based its prestige on the symbolic force of religion. In other words, aware that its military power was in decline relative to that of Europe, the state began to exert its religious authority as a tool to further its political influence and control. The Ottomans' awareness of their religious clout was raised when North

African rulers began to place themselves under Ottoman control. The sultans began to portray themselves as protectors of the faith and of Sunni orthodoxy in particular and, by extension, as the guardians of Mecca and Medina.

Second, the value of the Ottoman para began to decline during the last quarter of the sixteenth century as large quantities of New World silver entered the market. This caused drastic inflation, raising the prices of basic commodities and provoking violent unrest throughout the empire.[10] As a consequence of the continuous complaints made by the inhabitants of the Hijaz to the Ottoman authorities and the desire of the sultans to be seen as guardians of Mecca and Medina, sultans Mehmet III and Ahmet I decided to endow vast tracts of land and bestow their revenues on the Two Holy Cities. Furthermore, in order to spare the Hijaz the effects of rampant inflation, they decreed that the bulk of these endowments' income would be paid 'in kind,' in the form of grain and basic necessities.

Third, the sultans were concerned with their role and image as protectors of pilgrims to the Hijaz. The annual pilgrimage was an event the Ottoman state exploited to assert its temporal authority and its role as the paramount Islamic power. Ottoman rulers always displayed concern for the secure and orderly passage of the pilgrimage caravans.[11] The *sharif*s of Mecca imposed substantial levies on pilgrim convoys arriving in the city. In response to pilgrims' repeated complaints over this practice, the sultans asked the sharifs to desist from imposing these levies.[12] When the Meccan rulers began to suffer the effects of inflation, Sultan Murad III created a large endowment for the Two Holy Cities as compensation.

And fourth, in 1569, the Ottoman authorities made the Yemeni port of Mocha the main hub for traffic through the Red Sea. All Indian and European ships were required to put in at this port, where Egyptian and other Arab vessels would load up with Indian goods. Although these vessels would then pass through Jedda to take on water or unload a small part of their cargo, the rulers of Mecca would still force them to pay customs duties on their full cargo. Complaints from traders led Sultan Murad III to exempt all vessels passing through Jedda from paying customs duties.[13] Since the Meccan economy relied heavily on Jedda's customs, Murad provided compensation for these exemptions, a policy continued by his successors, Mehmet III and Ahmad II.[14]

Muslim rulers systematically bestowed endowments on Mecca and Medina, and Ottoman policy was no different. The Ottomans, however, perpetuated or developed existing waqfs as well as endowing new ones. Because endowments operated in perpetuity, many of them—some dating to the Ayyubid and Mamluk periods—continued to generate income. As we shall see, their size also increased markedly under Ottoman rule.[15]

Al-Khubziya

This endowment dated back to the Ayyubid period, when Salah al-Din (Saladin) endowed the villages of Nagada (Qina) and Sindabis (Qalyubiya) and bestowed a portion of their income on certain aghas,[16] who were tasked with guarding and cleaning the Mosque of the Prophet in Medina.

Al-Ayshi claims that Sultan Salah al-Din was the first to donate the services of these aghas, a system maintained by his successors. During the seventeenth and eighteenth centuries there were eighty aghas in total, forty known as the 'seniors,' who performed tasks within the tomb and mosque of the Prophet, and a further forty 'inactive' ones, who were employed in activities outside the Prophet's mosque. Presiding over them was the shaykh of the Prophet's mosque, usually a senior *agha dar al-sa'ada* (eunuch of the sultan's harem). One of the most important figures in Medina in this period, he was, in effect, ruler of the city.[17] A new shaykh was dispatched from Istanbul every year or two and in some years was made responsible for administering the affairs of the endowments of the Two Holy Cities in Egypt.

Throughout most of the Ottoman period, the surra (cash and provisions sent to the endowment's beneficiaries) of this endowment remained fixed at 80,000 paras, of which the village of Nagada, in Qena, provided 57,527 and the village of Sindabis, in Qalyubiya,[18] 22,483. In 1638 CE, to take one year as an example, these sums were divided equally between the forty 'senior' aghas, each of whom received 2,000 paras. In 1703, the purse reached 80,000 paras;[19] in 1782 CE, it decreased to 37,000 paras, perhaps because a portion was now reaching its beneficiaries through a *hawala* (money transfer).[20] The surra subsequently reverted to 80,000 paras.

Al-Dashisha al-Kubra

This waqf incorporated the majority of endowments previously created by members of the Mamluk ruling elite,[21] such as the sultans Jaqmaq[22] and Qaytbay,[23] and the *amira khund* (Fatima, the wife of Sultan Qaytbay).[24] Tracing this process of incorporation tells us that the waqf was originally known as 'al-Dasha'ish al-Sharifa' and was made up of a number of different endowments.

A number of documents clearly confirm this impression. In 1569, the overseer of the Dashisha endowment, Ja'far ibn Abadallah, an amir of the Mutafarriqa military corps, leased out the two villages of al-Safiya and Muniyat al-Hamil in Gharbiya, originally part of the Khund endowment. In 1591, the endowment's supervisor leased out a number of villages from the Qaytbay endowment in Bahnasa for the Two Holy Cities, in exchange for 3,750 irdabb of wheat.[25]

Why did Sultan Sulayman incorporate other endowments—the Khubziya and Barsbay endowments—into the Dashisha Kubra waqf? All three were large endowments serving educational institutions, mosques, and other charitable foundations in Egypt, which, just as with the Sinan Pasha and Iskandar Pasha endowments, sent limited sums of money for projects in the Hijaz. These sums remained fixed throughout the period covered by this study: the Khubziya endowment sent 80,000 paras annually and the Barsbay endowment 30,000, sums that were handed to the commander of the pilgrimage by the endowments' supervisors each year.[26]

It appears that the Ottoman administration placed this group of Mamluk endowments under the control of a single director—known as the director of the Dasha'ish Sharifa endowment—in 1553, the year when Ottoman reorganization and inspections of landholdings, income, and religious endowments reached its peak.[27] Sultan Sulayman subsequently added a number of villages to these endowments,[28] generating revenue of 5,000 irdabb, of which 3,000 were sent to Mecca and the remaining 2,000 to Medina.[29] Sultan Murad III also granted villages to these endowments to increase the quantity of grain dispatched to the Hijaz. The endowment incorporated nearly sixty villages from Bahnasa, Qalyubiya, Giza, Daqhaliya, Gharbiya, Jirja, and Ashmunayn.[30]

When recording the lease of land and villages from the Dasha'ish endowment, the documents initially ascribe properties to their original endowments (that is, Qaytbay, Jaqmaq, and so on). By the beginning of the seventeenth century a gradual change can be seen in the records, which begin to refer to these endowments (and especially the endowment of sultans Murad and Mehmet) collectively as al-Dashisha al-Kubra[31] instead of al-Dasha'ish al-Sharifa, while Sultan Murad's endowment was referred to as al-Dashisha al-Sughra al-Muradiya. By effecting a merger, Sultan Sulayman was trying to unify the administration of all foundations and institutions endowed for the Two Holy Cities, enabling a swifter resolution of administrative complications and problems and improving their efficiency.

The endowment also came into possession of two large ships in the Red Sea,[32] previously the property of the Qaytbay endowment. Since 1583, this waqf had been required to send 10,000 irdabb of grain, a figure that soon rose to 15,820 irdabb when Sultan Murad III (1574–95) added another endowment to the initial holdings. The endowment also owned and rented out a number of properties and foundations in Medina that brought in 12,000 paras annually, raising the endowment's revenues to 416,475 paras.[33] This figure remained fixed for extended periods, only changing when the endowment made an early transfer of cash to the inhabitants of Mecca and Medina through the hawala system, or was forced to pay monetary compensation for shortfalls in its grain provision. However, such shortfalls did not mean that the endowment had dispatched fewer provisions and funds to Mecca and Medina, merely that in response to a request by their inhabitants, the supervisor had sent them a down payment before delivery of the surra.[34]

From 1693, these endowments were sending an annual total of 17,100 irdabb of grain to the Two Holy Cities.[35] More than a mere endowment, al-Dashisha al-Kubra was now a powerful economic foundation with its own Nile fleet to transport grain from the provinces to its granary in Bulaq. In 1727 its then supervisor, Zulfiqar Bey, was able to purchase a vessel worth 42,000 paras just to transport the endowment's grain from its villages in the South of Egypt to Bulaq.[36] The endowment's administration usually paid an advance on transportation costs to the ship's captain upon delivery of his contract, detailing the quantities to be transported, the place of loading, and the official in the village from whom he should receive his cargo.[37] In 1705, for example, the head of the endowment's Nile fleet received 700 paras for transporting 100 irdabb of grain from Jirja to Bulaq.[38] Upon arrival of grain shipments, the endowment's supervisor, his deputy, officials from the Bulaq storehouse, and grain measurers had to inspect the purity of the grain, as many local officials mixed dust and gravel with the shipments.[39]

Bedouin then transported the grain on camelback from the Bulaq granary to Suez. Once it reached the Red Sea, two ships owned by the endowment transported it to Yanbu' and Jedda.[40] The Dashisha Kubra endowment was responsible for providing the hospices of Sultan Jaqmaq in Mecca and Medina with grain, ghee, rice, and other basic provisions. However, from the mid-seventeenth century onward these two hospices appear to have fallen into disuse and no longer appear in the sources. The vast quantities of grain assigned to them were instead distributed to residents of the two cities in kind.[41]

The eighteenth century saw a steady rise in the proportion of the endowment's surra paid in cash rather than in kind. Egypt's administration continued to calculate the price of one irdabb at 50 *nisf* and transportation at 14 nisf per irdabb for most of the late eighteenth century despite a considerable rise in grain prices,[42] in which policy they were followed by the majority of these endowments.[43]

Al-Khaskiya al-Kubra (al-Qadima) endowment[44]

In 1552, the *khaski-sultan*, wife of Sultan Sulayman I, created a large endowment incorporating land from the provinces of Bahnasa and Gharbiya. Approximately 14,766 *feddans* were endowed for the benefit of the inhabitants of the Two Holy Cities. While nine villages in Bahnasa produced grain for the endowment, four villages in Gharbiya were probably rented out for cash.

The endowment's charter stipulates that the khaski-sultan be given ownership of the land by her husband and that large swathes of it be endowed to provide for two *takiya*s (Sufi hospices), one in Mecca and the other in Medina. Each hospice was to be given wheat to make wheat porridge (*dashisha*) and a thousand loaves of bread a day to be distributed to the poor, in addition to ghee, honey, onions, and other foodstuffs needed both for the running of the hospice and for payment in kind to the staff.[45]

Sultan Sulayman's wife ordered the construction of two ships for transporting these provisions from Suez to Jedda and Yanbu. She also set aside an annual budget for the transportation of the provisions from Jedda to Mecca and from Yanbu to Medina. The endowment owned four vessels on the Nile to bring the provisions from its villages to Bulaq.[46]

The takiyas received regular supplies from the waqf throughout most of the eighteenth century.[47] The administration in Istanbul was always quick to come to the aid of the endowment, whose limited income often prevented it from fulfilling its obligations in the Hijaz. The historian al-Hijazi al-Sanjari states that in 1684 the sultan ordered the renovation of the Khaski hospice in Mecca at a cost of 15,000 dinars (1,605,000 paras). The endowment had no way of paying amounts like these without help from Cairo and Istanbul.[48]

Occasionally, the total income from endowed property would exceed the sums paid out to the endowment's beneficiaries (religious institutions or charitable causes). This surplus, referred to as the *dulab*, was set aside as reserve funds, which the endowment would occasionally draw on to purchase and endow new agricultural land or property with the sultan's consent. The funds were further used in the renovation and upkeep of existing holdings, such as the endowment's fleets on the Nile and Red Sea.[49]

The Khaskiya endowment owned granaries in Bulaq and Suez, whence the takiya's provisions were shipped to Yanbu'. By 1677, its cash purse contained 125,000 paras, of which 60,000 went to the inhabitants of Mecca and 65,000 to Medina.[50] This amount remained fixed for most of the eighteenth century, except for those years when part of the purse was diverted to the Holy Cities. From 1776 until the mid-nineteenth century, the purse increased and remained stable at 134,000 paras.[51]

The Muradiya endowment (al-Dashisha al-Sughra)

In 1558 Sultan Murad III (1574–95) created a large endowment incorporating twenty-one villages.[52] Proceeds from this endowment went to fund a school for memorizing the Qur'an and a large *sabil* in Mecca. Additional funds were earmarked for washing the bodies of the dead in Mecca and building and maintaining a large hospice in Medina. According to al-Ishaqi, the endowment's administration in Egypt had to provide the following every year: 2,200 irdabb of grain (subsequently increased to 3,174 irdabb) and 425,000 paras, as well as shipping large quantities of ghee, onions, rice, and lentils to Yanbu' to be sent to the endowment's lodge in Medina.[53] Sultan Murad also ordered that a Red Sea vessel be procured to transport provisions from Suez to Yanbu'. The endowment earmarked 42,000 paras a year for the purchase of honey and ghee and 170,000 for the transport of grain from Bulaq to Suez and from there to Yanbu'.[54] Although the endowment's charter makes no mention of quantities of grain to be paid as salaries to the boats' captains and the Bedouin camel drivers, documents show that some 767 irdabb were earmarked for just this purpose.

The Muradiya endowment gradually expanded, purchasing a large granary in Bulaq to store grain from its villages in Upper Egypt and two granaries in Suez and Yanbu'. In 1675, the Bulaq granary received 3,640 irdabb of wheat and 300 of beans from the endowment's villages in Bahnasa.[55] These large quantities indicate that the endowment's administrative apparatus had expanded to become a major productive economic institution. Instead of returning empty from Yanbu', the endowment's ship would take on traders' wares and pilgrims (at a charge, of course),[56] all of which increased the scale and complexity of the Muradiya's revenues.

The endowment also paid out an annual sum to be spent on its foundations and institutions in Mecca and Medina. As with other endowments, this money was handed over to the *amir al-hajj* who, in exchange for a small payment, would transport it to the inhabitants of the Two Holy Cities. In 1629, the endowment dispatched 420,436 paras in this manner, of which almost 41,000 went to pay salaries at Sultan Murad's school in Mecca and burial costs for those with no other means of support, and 367,096 to Medina to meet the needs of the hospice and pay for the transport of provisions being brought there from Yanbu'.[57]

Toward the beginning of the eighteenth century, the endowment's surra was a mere 420,000 paras, although it rose somewhat by mid-century.[58] During the last quarter of the eighteenth century, the waqf started to fall behind in its provision of grain to Medina. As the shortfalls built up, the endowment began compensating the city's inhabitants in cash, but this seems to have been a slippery slope. At the end of the eighteenth century, the endowment's director paid 166,650 paras compensation for 3,030 irdabb owed by the endowment.[59]

Al-Dashisha al-Muhammadiya

Sultan Mehmet III (1594–1603) founded this endowment during a period of decline in the value of the Ottoman currency. Because of these circumstances, Sultan Mehmet made sure to endow villages that could guarantee an income in kind for the Holy Cities. He endowed various tracts of land in twenty-six villages,[60] founded a hospice in Medina, and distributed grain and other basic goods to the inhabitants of Mecca.[61]

The Muhammadiya endowment dispatched a total of 9,900 irdabb annually, of which 2,624 were sent to Mecca's residents and 7,276 to those in Medina. In Yanbu', an amount was diverted from the Medina provisions for the sharif 'Abd al-Mu'in and his relatives, the Awlad Hijar,[62] while the rest was sent on to the endowment's hospice in Medina. The endowment owned two boats on the Nile to bring grain[63] from the provinces to its granary in Bulaq,[64] whence it was taken on camelback to the waqf granary in Suez in preparation for shipping to the Hijaz.[65] It also possessed a ship in the Red Sea for transporting grain to Yanbu'.[66] The endowment paid all transportation costs, including the expense of moving the grain from Yanbu' to Medina.[67]

The endowment also sent 260,800 paras to the Two Holy Cities every year to cover transportation costs and the hospice's expenses. This surra was disbursed as follows:

- 10,000 paras to the teacher of Hanafi jurisprudence at the tomb of 'Ali bin Abi Talib;
- 252,000 paras to the residents of Medina for grain transportation and to cover costs at the hospice; and
- 83,333 paras to the residents of Mecca, either used to pay for transporting grain from Jedda to Mecca or given to the owners of the grain in cash if they took control of the shipment in Jedda.[68]

Delays in the provision of grain, due partly to occasional low flood levels on the Nile, but mostly to Mamluk greed, meant that the endowment constantly owed large quantities of grain to the Two Holy Cities—debts it often paid off in cash. The monetary compensation to residents of Mecca and Medina tended to rise over time and, in consequence, ever larger sums of money were dispatched with the amir al-hajj.[69]

The price of an irdabb of grain, as calculated by the endowment's administrators, remained fixed at 50 paras, to which transportation costs of 14 nisf per irdabb were added, while the average price on the local market throughout the 1780s was 100 paras per irdabb.[70] In 1795, an irdabb of wheat cost 222 nisf on the Egyptian market,[71] while the endowments continued to calculate wheat at 64 nisf per irdabb.[72] By selling their grain on the local market, or exporting it to Mediterranean countries whose need for grain was greater than Egypt's, the endowments' directors were able to make a healthy profit.

The Muhammadiya endowment became a major economic institution, employing porters, measurers, and security guards at its Bulaq and Suez granaries in addition to the crews of its Nile and Red Sea fleets. As they gained control of political affairs in Egypt during the course of the eighteenth century, the Mamluk rulers turned their attention to the administration of this vast endowment.

Al-Ahmadiya

Sultan Ahmad I (1603–17) founded this endowment for the purpose of sending sums of money (rather than grain or other provisions) to the Holy Cities.[73]

Year (AD/AH)	To Mecca	To Medina	Total (paras)
1638/1048	n/a	n/a	219,640
1643/1053	145,080	79,960	225,040
1677/1088	n/a	n/a	223,224
1700/1112	145,080	79,960	225,040
1704/1116	145,080	79,960	225,040
1741/1154	145,080	79,960	225,040
1783/1198	0	55,000	55,000
1795/1210	145,080	79,960	225,040
1798/1212	145,080	79,960	225,040

Sources: Dasht, reg. 162, p. 724; Bab 'Ali, reg. 163, p. 167, doc. 599; reg. 184, p. 273, doc. 1038; reg. 187, p. 173, doc. 706; Diwan 'Ali, reg. 1, p. 94, doc. 193; reg. 2, p. 301, doc. 481.

The table above shows consistency in the amount of this endowment's surra, with variations for some years (that is, 1638), apparently due to the transfer of funds to individuals in the Hijaz. The sizeable reduction in 1783 was due to the Mamluk amirs who oversaw the endowment's lands defaulting on their payments. One of these military leaders owed some 60,000 paras, which he only paid in 1796.[74] These delays in payment forced inhabitants of the Holy Cities to dispatch emissaries to claim the amounts owed.

Due to its comparatively modest size, the Ahmadiya endowment escaped the attentions of the Mamluk beys and was, for the majority of the period under consideration, directly controlled by the eunuchs of the sultan's harem.

Al-Khaskiya al-Sughra

In 1628, the mother of Sultan Murad III endowed 478 feddans of land in the provinces of Qalyubiya and Giza to benefit the Two Holy Cities. This waqf was named 'al-Khaskiya al-Sughra' (the lesser Khaskiya) due to its small size. During the seventeenth century its annual consignments to the Hijaz never exceeded 19,000 paras and 490 irdabb of grain.[75] The endowment's income and its distribution are described as follows in the foundation deed:

Destination	Amount in paras	Further notes
Consignment to Mecca	9,500	
Consignment to Medina	9,500	
Director of the endowment	1,800	
Secretary of the endowment	730	
Notary public (shahid) of the endowment	730	
Revenue officer of the endowment	540	
Fee for the Qadi 'Askar Afandi	300	In charge of public oversight and recording the endowment's contracts
Cost of transporting the endowment's surra	300	Paid to the amir al-hajj
Total income	36,580	
Total expenditure	34,080	
Wheat	490 irdabb	

Source: Deed for the waqf founded by the mother of Sultan Murad, Turki 907.

The endowment remained operational throughout the Ottoman period. Most years it dispatched a small sum to cover the cost of transporting and distributing the grain, and although this relatively small surra is not found in the records for some years, the endowment never fell into disuse. For most of its existence its director was an *agha dar al-sa'ada*.

Al-Khaskiya al-Mustajadda endowment

The wife of Sultan Muhammad IV (1648–87) created a large endowment incorporating land from villages in Munufiya, Gharbiya, and Jirja. Because the endowment's charter is no longer extant, we know little about the size of the endowed villages or their annual grain consignment. A number of hospices from the Muradiya, Muhammadiya, and Khaskiya endowments were located in Medina and supplied its residents with food and shelter. In Mecca, however, there was only one hospice belonging to the Khaskiya endowment, and the city's inhabitants sent a number of complaints to the Ottoman authorities about the weakness of their hospice system. It seems that the endowment was founded in response to the drought and severe food shortages that afflicted Mecca in 1668, a disastrous year when locals were forced to eat dogs and cadavers.[76] Sultan Mehmet was quick to respond: his wife and the mother of Sultan Ahmad II founded a large endowment for the construction and maintenance of a hospice named Dar al-Shifa' and a hospital in Mecca.[77] The endowment charter also earmarked a sum to be paid to the aghas who cared for the Prophet's tomb. In Egypt, the endowment was called al-Khaskiya al-Mustajadda to distinguish it from al-Khaskiya al-Qadima or al-Kubra (the older endowment set up by Sultan Sulayman's wife) and al-Khaskiya al-Sughra (the smaller endowment established by Sultan Murad III's mother).

Wages for the construction of the hospice and hospital cost the endowment 200,256 paras. The authorities in Egypt sent 139 artisans, and Istanbul shipped large quantities of wood, iron, lead, and brass pots and pans from Egypt to the Hijaz. The Egyptian provincial rulers also sent wheat, barley, lentils, chickpeas, and sugar as provisions for workmen constructing the Dar al-Shifa' hospice in Mecca.[78]

The hospice overseers commissioned the construction of a ship in Suez to transport grain, rice, and ghee to Jedda,[79] as well as four Nile boats for transporting the endowment's grain to Bulaq.[80] The greater part of the endowment's surra was set aside to provision the Mecca hospice.[81] Dar al-Shifa' was Mecca's largest and most important hospice. When it closed for twenty days in 1723, an uprising broke out in the city. The poor gathered in front of the courthouse and chanted slogans against the judge before making their way to Dar al-Sa'ada, where they denounced the sharif of Mecca, refusing to be placated until he had supplied the hospice with grain from his own storehouses to be cooked and distributed to the needy. He further ordered that the hospice's supervisor be investigated. The supervisor was then removed from his position, and his personal wealth confiscated and given to the hospice. Management was handed over to the commander of the janissaries.[82] During the eighteenth century the endowment's ever-increasing revenues attracted the attention of the Mamluk elite, who began trading on behalf of the endowment to their personal advantage.

Al-Muhammadiya

This endowment was founded by Sultan Mehmet I (1730–54) in 1753, and incorporated a number of villages in Munufiya.[83] The proceeds were to fund an academy of Islamic jurisprudence and religious studies in addition to paying for the construction of one sabil in Mecca and another in Medina.[84] In 1741, the endowment's surra totaled 135,000 paras, of which 45,000 were given to the residents of Mecca and 9,000 to Medina.[85] As it absorbed other endowments, its surra increased, and some of the additional money was set aside for *mulid al-nabi* festivities (celebrations marking the Prophet Muhammad's birthday) in Mecca.[86]

The Sultan Mustafa III endowment

Sultan Mustafa III created a small endowment that sent an annual sum of 36,900 paras to the Hijaz, of which 5,060 paras went to Mecca and 31,900 paras to Medina. This sum remained unchanged throughout the eighteenth century.[87]

Al-Haramayn al-Sharifayn

In founding this endowment, the Ottomans sought to create an administrative umbrella incorporating private endowments created to benefit the descendants of their founders. When the line of these descendants reached extinction, or as a direct gift to the inhabitants of the Hijaz, waqf revenues were redirected to the Two Holy Places. In their charters, founders of such endowments would usually make over the title deeds of their endowments to a foundation whose continuity was assured. Because no family lasts forever, and because endowments must be bestowed in perpetuity in order to be legally valid, the endowment had to be made over to a permanent institution as its ultimate beneficiary, like Mecca and Medina, Jerusalem, or various mosques and schools in Egypt. The Haramayn (Two Sanctuaries) benefited frequently from such bequests. The Ottoman courts were full of cases where the supervisor of the Haramayn endowment would protest the confiscation of property whose initial beneficiaries had disappeared, and which was supposed to revert to the benefit of the Sanctuaries.[88] In other cases, the incorporation of other foundations was unproblematic, and was simply registered in court: thus, in 1718, revenues from a large waqf in Alexandria were transferred to the Haramayn endowment following the cessation of the founder's family line;[89] in 1736, an endowment in Damietta was integrated to the Haramayn endowment after the last descendant of the original founder died.[90]

Private endowments grew increasingly popular in the course of the Ottoman period. A well-founded fear of the authorities' greed prompted people to endow real estate and other property for the benefit of their descendants. Afraid that these descendants would squander the wealth, however, the founder would ensure that the endowment was made out first to himself and his family, before reverting to a charitable body such as those in Mecca, Medina, and Jerusalem. Besides concerns related to human greed, the prevalence of plagues and other illnesses in the Ottoman period meant that many family lines did indeed die out, and endowment overseers spent a good deal of time trying to save endowed property due to revert to the Haramayn from the depredations of powerful individuals.[91] Furthermore, many high-ranking Ottoman officials endowed large tracts of land and designated themselves and their clients as beneficiaries, with the title deeds reverting to the Haramayn endowment[92] when these initial recipients died out. The Ottoman court records are full of documents testifying to conflicts between claimants and waqf supervisors.[93] Transfers to the Haramayn were particularly rapid when the officials in question were eunuchs.[94] This explains the sheer diversity of the Haramayn holdings, which included oil presses, agricultural land,[95] real estate,[96] and ships[97] all over Egypt. It also explains the continual growth of the endowment despite the sticky fingers of its Mamluk supervisors: the purse increased from around 233,000 paras in 1677[98] to around 455,000 in 1704[99], 456,000 in 1741[100], and 465,000 in 1797. A little over 500,000 of this amount was sent to Mecca and Medina, while the remainder was distributed to beneficiaries in Egypt.[101]

Endowments of pashas and amirs
Many pashas and princes in Egypt founded endowments for the benefit of mosques, prayer rooms, hospices, schools, and other charitable institutions. Some of these endowments were extremely large, such as that of Sinan Pasha, which included properties in Bulaq, Suez, Rosetta, and Alexandria. Part of the proceeds of these endowments were set aside as a surra (either as cash or goods in kind), placed in the care of the amir al-hajj, and sent

to residents of the Two Holy Cities. Whether cash or goods, these sums remained fairly constant throughout the period under study. The endowment of essential goods such as oil was of more use than money to religious institutions in Mecca and Medina: as the currency depreciated, the quantities of these goods remained fixed.

Following is a list of some of these endowments:

1. The Sulayman Pasha endowment
Sulayman Pasha created a large endowment in Egypt for a mosque, a school, and other charitable institutions. Each year, the endowment sent 22,000 paras to the residents of the Two Holy Cities: 10,000 to Mecca and 12,000 to Medina. The money funded thirty Qur'an reciters and provided each city with fifty jugs of water. Sulayman further ordered that lamp oil be dispatched each year at the endowment's expense to light the mosques of Mecca and Medina.[102]

2. The 'Ali Pasha al-Subki endowment (1553–56)
In the records this endowment is referred to as al-Subkiya. Each year 'Ali Pasha would set aside 20,000 paras to fund the burial of destitute Muslims who died in Mecca and to pay a number of Qur'an reciters.[103] Between 1638[104] and 1803[105] the size of this surra remained fixed.

3. The Iskandar Pasha endowment (1556–59)
Iskandar Pasha created a large endowment in Egypt for the benefit of a mosque, a hospice, and a Qur'anic school,[106] with an annual surra of 21,600 paras for the inhabitants of the Hijaz. This sum paid for thirty Qur'an reciters in the Prophet's mosque and the Sacred Mosque, and for water in the Holy Cities.[107] This surra also remained fixed during the eighteenth century.

4. The Sinan Pasha endowment[108]
In the charter of his endowment (founded 1581), which incorporated a number of properties and supported his mosque in Bulaq and other charitable foundations, Sinan Pasha stipulated that an annual sum of 23,080 paras be sent to the residents of the Two Holy Places.[109]

5. The Bashir Agha endowment
In 1729, Bashir Agha, chief palace eunuch, endowed a mill, a bathhouse, and a number of residential buildings in Cairo for the benefit of a

Qur'anic school. From the proceeds of this endowment, Bashir Agha also set aside 150,675 paras to be sent to Medina and distributed among the aghas of the Prophet's tomb, the doormen and servants at the zawiya of Shaykh Anbar al-Mihrashi, and those working at his endowment's school in Medina, among others. Toward the middle of the eighteenth century, this surra increased,[110] and it remained fixed thereafter until the French Expedition of 1798–1801.

The Mamluk amirs also earmarked large sums of money from their Egyptian endowments to be sent to the Two Holy Cities. Amir Radwan Bey Abu-l-Shawarib, for instance, bought and restored a drinking well near Medina, which he endowed for the residents of that city as well as funding Qur'an reciters and the provision of water for Mecca and Medina.[111] Ayub Bey purchased the title to salaries paid to residents of Medina and endowed these for a number of Qur'an reciters in the Prophet's mosque.[112] In 1745, Muhammad Bey Qitas founded a large endowment in Egypt and set aside part of its revenue to supply water to the mosques of Mecca and Medina.[113] Abd al-Rahman Katkhuda established a large endowment for the benefit of al-Azhar University, setting aside 45,580 paras of its revenues to provide water for the Holy Cities and to pay for a Qur'an reciter and attendants at the tomb of al-Hibr Abdallah Bin Abbas in Ta'if.[114]

The administrative apparatus: Imperial harem eunuchs versus Mamluk amirs

A number of employees, including a head clerk, a revenue collector, a witness, and a treasurer, supported the overseer of each waqf.[115] Most of the endowments we have mentioned also employed a second set of officials who worked in the granaries in Bulaq and Suez, including guards, grain measurers, sifters, and the like. The overseer, however, was the most important figure in the waqf administration. In the early stages of an endowment's existence, the founder would appoint a supervisor and lay down conditions for the transfer of this individual's responsibilities. Sultan Murad, for instance, stipulated that the director of his endowment be either Sinan Pasha or the governor of Egypt. Inevitably, circumstance would conspire against the founders' wishes: rulers would grant directorships to relatives and favorites,[116] and, as the grip of the Ottoman central administration weakened, powerful and influential amirs would often monopolize waqf supervision.[117]

Most of the endowments created by sultans had two overseers: one in Egypt and the other in the Hijaz. The director-general of the endowment was always stationed in Egypt, while the director in the Hijaz was responsible for supervising and administering the endowment's hospices and other minor properties in the region. The endowment's founder would determine the salary and responsibilities of its supervisor. Sultan Murad required that his endowment's director receive a certain monthly salary,[118] as did Sultan Sulayman's wife (a slightly smaller amount).[119] Though these were considerable sums in the first half of the seventeenth century, the steady decline in value of the Ottoman currency devalued salaries considerably. Most sultans were fully aware of this and ensured that at least part of the salary was paid in grain or other goods. As we shall see, however, these directors and their subordinates abused their positions endlessly.

Among the duties of the *nazir* or supervisor were the upkeep and renovation of buildings owned by the endowment, to ensure that the properties and land that constituted the economic basis of the endowment's existence remained productive and that the institutions it supported were in good condition. The director oversaw the collection of revenues, disbursed them to beneficiaries listed in the founding charter, and worked with other officials to verify the endowment's annual accounts. Furthermore, he or she was the official representative of the endowment in dealings with the *wali*, the courts, and the endowment's tenants. This last duty—as the endowment's representative in dealings with a second party—is particularly evident in legal disputes or cases involving economic exploitation of endowed properties and state oversight of the endowment and its accounts. As their duties and responsibilities proliferated, some directors were forced to employ one or more deputies to relieve the burden.

Because of the importance of the position, the sultan, the grand vizier, or the wali appointed directors of Haramayn endowments. Judges played little part in the process. The central administration in Istanbul (and, less thoroughly, the chief judge in Egypt) usually carried out the vetting process for these supervisors. There were no fixed guidelines for this appointment process and, in the sixteenth century at least, directorships tended to be given to favored amirs and relatives of pashas: witness the appointment of janissaries[120] and Mamluk and Circassian amirs.[121] Yet the period also witnessed a move in the opposite direction: the first appointment of the *agha dar al-sa'ada* as director of an endowment. The founding charter of the waqf established by Sulayman the Magnificent's wife, drawn up in 1552, stipulated that the chief eunuch of the imperial harem be appointed director for as long as he remained in his post.[122] It also stipulated that excess revenue from the endowment be given to this official and stored in his private treasury, perhaps the first instance of what came to be known as the *dulabi* al-Haramayn al-Sharifayn (treasurers of the Two Holy Cities). I believe this appointment led to the monopoly subsequently imposed by these powerful eunuchs on supervision of endowments for the Two Holy Cities. In 1586, oversight of the endowments' administration became their exclusive responsibility.[123] The state tended to put great trust in these aghas due to their long service at the imperial court in Istanbul, their status as eunuchs (which ensured that their loyalties and wealth would remain untouched by marriage or procreation), and the fact that their property reverted to the state on their death. The additional income this position brought the aghas undoubtedly served to enhance their position in Istanbul. The chief agha thus became the third most important figure in the palace.

However, the trust the central administration had in the harem eunuchs was often misplaced. The endowments were subject to depredations by the aghas on numerous occasions. During the reforms of Ibrahim Pasha (1670), it was discovered that they owed five million paras to the endowments they supervised. The Sublime Porte ordered their dismissal, transferring directorship of several endowments to military men of the janissary and Azaban corps.[124] This abrupt reversal in the fortunes of the imperial harem eunuchs should also be understood in the context of a power struggle that was taking place in Istanbul. The Grand Vizir, Ahmad Pasha Köprülü (1661–76) was then at the height of his powers and endeavoring to establish absolute control at the palace.[125] To weaken his opponents at court, he needed first to reduce the influence of the chief eunuch. By dismissing the aghas, he struck at their economic power. Ahmad Pasha refused to follow the state's traditional policy of appointing an *agha dar al-sa'ada* to the position of shaykh of the Prophet's mosque, instead installing Hajj Muhammad Pasha, formerly a plenipotentiary representative of the Sublime Porte.[126] In the wake of this appointment, members of the janissary corps began to fill positions in the administrations of these endowments.

All too soon, however, these new administrators were exploiting and plundering the endowments, whose directors owed large sums of money. Members of the janissary corps increasingly took over positions in the administration of various endowments, and levels of theft and fraud rose dramatically. In 1691 the Ottoman administration issued orders that the endowments' oversight be removed from the janissaries' hands, but corps members were still able to retain directorship of the Haramayn endowment throughout the eighteenth century.[127] The Ottoman government was trying to prevent the janissaries, who possessed their own treasury, from obtaining the wealth accrued by the endowments' directors.[128]

From the early eighteenth century onward, following the decline of the janissary corps in the wake of the Ifranj Ahmad crisis (1709), the Mamluk beys were able to consolidate their hold on power and transfer directorship of these endowments to their followers, using the waqf administration as an additional weapon in their struggle for power.[129]

During the eighteenth century, the state and the wali lost their grip on the administration of the endowments. The Ottoman state no longer had any say in the appointment of supervisors; sole control rested with the beys who emerged triumphant from the political turmoil besetting Egypt[130] and appropriated positions in the waqf administration from each other.[131] When the figure of the *shaykh al-balad* came to dominate Egypt, whoever managed to assert his supremacy and take over this position also took over endowments, distributing the benefits among his followers.[132] The endowments were a prize fought over by the Mamluk houses competing for power in Egypt, each seeking to increase their revenue and military strength.[133]

Until the Ottoman central administration sought to reassert control over the increasingly autonomous military leaders who had taken over Egypt at the end of the eighteenth century, then, the endowments were not monopolized by the *agha*s of *dar al-sa'ada* alone. The Mamluks struggled to control the endowments for their own personal profit, and it was only after the French had left Egypt in 1801 that the Ottoman administration was able to reassert itself and appoint the aghas to the directorships of the endowments once again.[134]

The multiple opportunities for profit opened up to those who were able to appropriate positions in the administration of various endowments—and especially those established for the Holy Cities, to which generations of benefactors contributed—were partly due to the relative autonomy of this administration from the central government's oversight. By appointing their followers to minor positions in the waqf administration, and obtaining the chief judge's approval of these appointments, members of the military elite that ruled Egypt during the eighteenth century were able to consolidate their hold on power and confer an aura of legitimacy upon it.[135] The sources give us an idea of the profits and gains available even to minor administrative personnel employed by these endowments. Ahmad Shalabi ibn 'Abd al-Ghani, a chronicler, wrote of a saddler who had been appointed revenue collector for endowments benefiting the Holy Cities and became a truly wealthy man who eventually dominated the janissary faction.[136]

During the sixteenth century and first half of the seventeenth century, the endowments' supervisors personally oversaw the leasing out of villages whose tax revenues poured into the coffers of the Haramayn endowments.[137]

This system continued unchanged until the mid-seventeenth century, when the Ottoman rulers sought to reverse the damage being done under this system. The directors' monopoly over the land leasing process led to a rash of bribes from tenants looking to gain possession of more villages. As a result, a sizeable portion of the endowment's revenues were lost, especially when many amirs and soldiers were using the endowments as means of enrichment. The endowment system placed vast tracts of agricultural land and other property in the hands of a single institution, and it was therefore inevitable that members of the political and military elite would exploit their positions by renting out land and property to increase their own wealth at the expense of the endowment.[138] When the Mamluks took control of the directorships, these leases were distributed to friends and followers at a discount. In 1612, Dawud Agha, director of the Dashisha Muhammadiya endowment, leased out a village for 87,000 paras, yet in 1638 the very same village fetched only 82,000, even though the rent should have increased due to inflation. In 1629, Abidin Bey, director of the Dashisha Kubra endowment, leased out five villages for one year in return for 3,500 irdabb of grain and 850 paras, while the same villages were leased out in 1638 for 3,000 irdabb of grain and 850 paras. Where did the missing 500 irdabb go? There had been no famine in the intervening years and Nile flood levels had remained constant.[139]

The Sublime Porte attempted to address this problem by taking the leasing process out of the hands of the directors and making it part of the central financial administration (Ruznama), which leased land through public auction. This led to a notable improvement in the endowments' grain and cash revenue. In addition, usufruct rights to land could now be inherited in exchange for a sum of money *(hulwan)* equivalent to a year's rent.[140] These annual down payments became an important source of funds to which the endowments could turn when they faced a shortfall in revenues or their boats sank in the Red Sea. As the sharifs of Mecca increased their demand for grain, and complained repeatedly to the Sublime Porte, the Ottoman sultan published an edict ascribing the surplus to them.[141]

When the Mamluk amirs took over the endowments in the eighteenth century they channeled the surplus revenue into their own pockets.[142] By the end of their tenure, they owed vast sums of grain and cash.[143] At the time of his death in 1707, Amir Ismail, the financial administrator of Egypt, owed the Haramayn Sharifayn endowment 722,487 paras, and the Dashisha Kubra endowment (of which he had been director) some 3.5 million.[144] The director of the Muhammadiya endowment, a Mamluk amir, owed the state treasury and the endowment a combined total of 22,500,000 paras in 1730.[145] The

Ottoman governors made a number of futile attempts to curb the Mamluks' excesses,[146] but the only way for the endowments to recoup their losses was for the administrator to die and the arrears to be recouped from his estate.[147]

Due to the Mamluk incursions into the sources of their revenue during the eighteenth century, the endowments had great trouble delivering supplies of grain and cash to the inhabitants of the Hijaz. In 1748, they failed to deliver a total of 13,000 irdabb of grain to the Hijaz, or 22.8 percent of the total amount they were required to send each year.[148] After 1779, the Mamluks appropriated the majority of the grain and cash due to Mecca and Medina. They stood to make vast profits by paying monetary compensation to beneficiaries in the Holy Cities and selling the grain in Rosetta and Alexandria, where Egyptian wheat commanded very high prices. France in particular was suffering from food shortages; by sending the Hijaz's wheat quotas to Europe, the Mamluk elites put their own interests ahead of those of the Ottoman Empire.

The Mamluk amirs also used their positions to commit outright theft, further straining the endowments' coffers. The director of one endowment complained to the sultan that he had given the commander of the pilgrimage a large sum of money to purchase a vessel for the endowment, but the commander had instead bought a smaller vessel and pocketed the difference. Not only had he refused to return the money, he then continued to defraud the endowment on a regular basis for the next ten years, prompting the director to raise the case before the sultan.[149]

These were not the only difficulties the endowments suffered at the hands of their administrators. The practice of renting out waqf land[150] for ninety-year periods[151] in exchange for a fixed rent also had a severe impact on their revenues. The problem was rendered more acute by the devaluation of the para. For example, while the Khaskiya endowment's surra to the Hijaz was 125,000 paras in 1704 and 1794,[152] the para itself had lost 300 percent of its value over that period.[153]

Apart from the actions of individuals whose greed could leave the Haramayn endowments' coffers empty (the practice of mixing grain with gravel and dust before delivering it to the endowments' granaries was also widespread),[154] natural disasters also affected these waqfs, leaving little revenue for the perpetuation of the founders' pledges in favor of the Holy Cities. Low Nile flood levels were a constant source of problems, as agricultural production was the cornerstone of the endowments' economic strength and of their role as suppliers of grain to the Holy Cities. Drought always created enormous complications for the endowments. Egypt was repeatedly ravaged by severe famine, and the endowments were unable to send grain consignments to the Hijaz. The

Sublime Porte would then compel the waqf administrators to pay monetary compensation. In turn, the revenue-producing villages would have to provide an explanation of why they were unable to deliver their consignments of grain to the waqf. This involved obtaining a deposition by the local qadi detailing the extent of agricultural land covered by the floodwaters.

Other natural events also hampered the endowments' performance. In 1726, silos belonging to the Muhammadiya and Dashisha Kubra endowments were flooded, destroying the grain stored inside.[155] Another source of problems was the transportation of grain from granaries in Bulaq to Suez: the Bedouin who were responsible for conveying it to Suez often stole the cargo before it reached its destination.[156] Shipwrecks on the Red Sea were yet another serious hindrance. The state would often fund the purchase of new vessels for the endowments, either through loans or gifts of money.[157] Weather conditions, the coral reefs that lay off most of the Red Sea shoreline, and the high temperatures and humidity made sailing difficult. In addition, ships were the targets of Bedouin raids when they put in to replenish their water supplies from wells or weighed anchor at night.

Despite these many obstacles, however, endowments for the benefit of the Holy Cities became vast economic institutions employing large numbers of officials and workers in Egypt, and owning ships on the Nile and the Red Sea as well as granaries in Bulaq and Suez.[158] They developed large administrations, whose scale can be measured by the sums deducted from their revenues to pay the wages of clerks and other officials. The total income of the Muradiya endowment, for instance, was over two million paras.[159] In 1796, half a million was sent to the Hijaz. Much the same was true of the Dashisha Kubra endowment.[160] This means that approximately two thirds of revenue from these endowments went toward salaries in Egypt, while the remaining third made up the surra for the Hijaz.[161]

Conclusion

This study has sought to show how Egypt, through the Haramayn endowments, supplied provisions to the inhabitants of the Hijaz, a population in great need of such aid. The existence of vast Egyptian endowments for Mecca and Medina allowed the Ottoman sultan to impose his sovereignty on the Hijaz and receive in exchange the title of Guardian of the Two Sanctuaries. Because the Hijaz had closer ties with Egypt than with Istanbul, however, the Ottomans had to rely on Egypt to further their policy in the region. So long as Istanbul retained a strong grip on Egypt, the endowments performed their obligations to the Two Holy Cities efficiently, providing educational and social institutions with the funding they needed. Yet with the breakdown of Ottoman rule in Egypt in the eighteenth century, the endowments came under the sway of the Mamluk amirs, who began diverting this income into their own coffers, using the endowments to serve their own interests at the expense of the Ottoman state. Before and after the French invasion, attempts by Istanbul to regain control in Egypt and do away with the Mamluks proved futile. The amirs' independent projects, however, were hampered by the same obstacle Muhammad 'Ali was later to encounter: the need to accumulate considerable local financial resources. Egypt's revenues were completely taken up by general administrative expenses, with the remainder divided between the Hijaz's requirements and the tribute sent to Istanbul every year. The Mamluk amirs sought to withhold payments to Istanbul and to the Hijaz, when circumstances allowed them to do so, and attempted to keep the Haramayn endowments firmly under their control, diverting most of the revenues to their goal of splitting from the Empire. Thus, they kept back grain that was owed to the Sanctuaries and sold it to Europe instead, receiving weapons in return. Muhammad 'Ali was more fortunate than the amirs, reaching power just as the Wahhabis were taking over the Hijaz. He was thus able to channel money and grain from the Haramayn endowments into his own coffers. He also refrained from sending tribute to Istanbul for many years, thus accumulating sufficient funds to break away from the Ottoman fold.

Notes

1   Translated from the Arabic by Robin Moger.
2   Bayyumi, *Mukhassasat*, 2001.
3   Shahin, "Khadamat al-hajij."
4   'Afifi, "al-Awqaf wa-l-milaha," 87–88.
5   Ibn 'Abd al-Ghani, *Awdah al-isharat*, 534.
6   'Umar, *Imarat al-hajj*, 336.
7   After the Ottomans incorporated Egypt into the sultanate, they began sending large quantities of Egyptian grain to the Holy Cities every year. These supplies were stored in state granaries in Coptic Cairo. Sultan Selim set aside 7,000 irdabb of grain for Mecca and Medina, and his successors increased the amount, which reached 36,000 irdabb in 1665 and around 41,500 in 1723. Transporting this grain cost the Egyptian treasury over a million paras in 1723 (Bab 'Ali, reg. 133, p. 448, doc. 1986; *Ruznama, Daftar waridat wa masarif khazina 'Amira mahrusat Misr humiyat 'an al-afat*, 5648, 1723).
8   Tuchscherer, "Approvisionnement," 80.
9   I made this mistake in my master's thesis. See 'Abd al-Mu'ti, *al-'Ilaqat al-misriya*, 270; 'Umar, *Imarat al-Hajj*, 336.

10   Ruznama, Daftar surra rumiya ahali Haramayn Sharifayn.

11   Raymond, *al-Hirafiyyun*, vol. 1, 130–31.

12   Raymond, *al-Mudun al-'arabiya*, 39.

13   al-Nahrawani, "Ibtihaj," 13.

14   al-Nahrawani, "Ibtihaj," 22.

15   al-'Isami, *Samt al-nujum*, 102–103.

16   Bayyumi, *Mukhassasat*, 61.

17   The aghas were slave eunuchs, mainly from sub-Saharan Africa, although some
     were captured or purchased in the Caucasus. Starting in the 'Abbasid period, sultans
     employed them to guard the imperial harem, but they became particularly influential
     in the Ottoman court, where the *kizlar aghasi*, a high-ranking state official, was
     appointed from among them. The term agha was also used to designate the com-
     manders of the Ottoman military corps. See Sulayman, *Ta'sil*, 168.

18   Nasr, "al-Aghawat," 36.

19   Bayyumi, *Mukhassasat*, 63.

20   Bab 'Ali, reg. 187, p. 174, doc. 713, 1703.

21   Diwan 'Ali, reg. 1, p. 231, doc. 196, 1782.

22   The Mamluk sultan al-Zahir Jaqmaq (r. 1438–53) commissioned the construction of
     two hospices in Mecca and Medina, funding them with revenues generated by large
     waqfs in Egypt and Syria. See 'Ashur, *Misr wa-l-Sham*, 179.

23   Qaytbay, one of the Burji Mamluk sultans, ruled from 1468 to 1496 and established
     many educational and charitable institutions in the Hijaz, as well as rebuilding the
     sanctuaries in Mecca and Medina. He dedicated revenue from several villages in
     waqf to the upkeep of these pious works, as well as two Red Sea vessels for the
     transport of the grain to the Holy Cities. These endowments were all incorporated
     in the Dashisha al-Kubra. See al-Nahrawani, *al-I'lam*, 152–53; al-Ishaqi, *Akhbar
     al-uwal*, 159.

24   *Khund* is a title similar to *khatun*, designating nobility or dignity. Khund Fatima,
     Qaytbay's wife, endowed vast properties including agricultural land to the benefit of
     the Two Holy Sanctuaries. Sultan Qansuh al-Ghuri purchased or confiscated most of
     what she owned, to the exclusion of this waqf, and used them to found his own large
     endowment. See Amin, *Fihrist watha'iq al-Qahira*, 195–99.

25   These villages were part of the province of Beni Sueif. Ramzi, *al-Qamus al-jughrafi*,
     vol. 3, part 2, 34.

26   Bab 'Ali, reg. 57, p. 13, doc. 49, 1591.

27   Dasht, reg. 162, p. 723, 1643.

28   'Afifi, *al-Awqaf*, 78.

29   Bab 'Ali, reg. 49, p. 356, doc. 1965, 1584.

30   al-Nahrawani, *al-I'lam*, 225.

31   For an exhaustive list of these villages, see al-Ishaqi, *Akhbar al-uwal,* 159–60;
     'Umar, *Imarat al-Hajj*, 274–78.

32   Bab 'Ali, reg. 49, p. 436, doc. 2363, 1584.

33   On the distribution of salaries in Mecca and Medina drawn from the waqf revenues,
     see Ibrahim, "Watha'iq al-waqf," 252.

34   Dasht, reg. 150, p. 734, 1632.

35   Dasht, reg. 162, p. 722, 1643.

36   Shaw, *Financial*, 269.

37 Bulaq, reg. 66, p. 63, doc. 168, 1727.
38 Bab 'Ali, reg. 160, p. 144, doc. 553, 1675.
39 Bulaq, reg. 61, p. 76, doc. 263, 1705.
40 Bulaq, reg. 66, p. 164, doc. 1705, 1726.
41 'Afifi, "al-Awqaf wa-l-milaha," 94.
42 In 1702, the delivery of 9,333 irdabb of grain (that is, 54.5 percent of the total provisions sent annually to the Two Holy Cities by the endowment) was delayed; in 1743 the endowment failed to deliver 7,946 irdabb of grain, or fifty percent of the provisions it was required to send to the Hijaz (al-Ansari, *Tuhfat al-muhibbin*, 69; al-'Isami, *Samt al-nujum*, 82; Bab 'Ali, reg. 187, p. 172, doc. 705, 1702).
43 An outstanding payment of 4,566 irdabb from 1739 at a value of 292,224 paras was added to the endowment's monetary surra of 1741, raising it to 455,842 paras. Diwan 'Ali, reg. 1, p. 94, doc. 194, 1739.
44 The women of the sultan's harem were referred to as *khaski*, the senior wife being known as the *khaski-sultan*. Unlike other members of the imperial household, they did not receive salaries but received title to revenues from villages or lands belonging to the sultan. The sultan's personal bodyguard was also referred to as khaski, as were a number of agents who were responsible for secret missions. Sultan Sulayman's wife was known as Roxelana in Europe. See Sulayman, *Ta'sil*, 81–85.
45 Egyptian National Library, Deed for the waqf established by the mother of the great sultans, 35.
46 Bulaq, reg. 63, p. 159, doc. 483, 1714.
47 al-Ansari, *Tuhfat al-muhibbin*, 401–409.
48 al-Sinjari, "Mana'ih al-karam," 416.
49 Egyptian National Library, Deed for the waqf established by the mother of the great sultans, 21.
50 Bab 'Ali, reg. 163, p. 166, doc. 587, 1677.
51 Diwan 'Ali, reg. 2, p. 297, doc. 463, 1794.
52 Villages in Qalyubiya, Gharbiya, Daqahliya, Buhayra, Munufiya, Giza, Bahnasa are mentioned in the waqf deed, but not those in Bahnasawiya; it appears that changes were made in the deed. See al-Ishaqi, *Akhbar al-uwal*, 160; Ministry of Endowments, Waqf deed of Sultan Murad.
53 al-Ishaqi, *Akhbar al-uwal*, 160–61.
54 Ministry of Endowments, Waqf deed of Sultan Murad.
55 Salihiya Najmiya, reg. 495, p. 343, doc. 1408, 1629.
56 'Afifi, "al-Awqaf wa-l-milaha," 95.
57 Salihiya Najmiya, reg. 495, p. 343, doc. 1408, 1629.
58 Diwan 'Ali, reg. 1, p. 92, doc. 189, 1741.
59 Diwan 'Ali, reg. 2, p. 304, doc. 489, 1789.
60 al-Ishaqi, *Akhbar al-uwal*, 161.
61 al-Rashidi, *Husn al-safa*, 19–20.
62 Bab 'Ali, reg. 191, p. 258, doc. 112, 1709; Diwan 'Ali, reg. 2, p. 352, doc. 573, 1801.
63 Bulaq, reg. 63, p. 161, doc. 489, 1715.
64 Salihiya Najmiya, reg. 508, p. 120, doc. 400, 1695.
65 Bulaq, reg. 68, p. 192, doc. 71, 1677.
66 Salihiya Najmiya, reg. 508, p. 120, doc. 400, 1598.

67 Bab 'Ali, reg. 163, p. 61, doc. 215, 1677.
68 Bab 'Ali, reg. 184, p. 279, doc. 1050, 1702.
69 Diwan 'Ali, reg. 1, p. 91, doc. 190, 1741.
70 Qisma 'Askariya, reg. 204, p. 78, doc. 100, 1779.
71 Qisma 'Askariya, reg. 224, p. 232, doc. 259, 1795.
72 Diwan 'Ali, reg. 2, p. 301, doc. 483, 1795.
73 Husayn Afandi al-Ruznamji, *Tartib al-diyar*, 46; al-Ishaqi, *Akhbar al-uwal*, 162; Shaw, *Financial*, 270.
74 Diwan 'Ali, reg. 2, p. 302, doc. 478, 1796.
75 Ministry of Endowments, Deed for the waqf founded by the mother of Sultan Murad, Turki 907.
76 Dahlan, *Khulasat al-kalam, 83.*
77 Dahlan, *Khulasat al-kalam*, 93.
78 Bab 'Ali, reg. 158, p. 356, doc. 1254; p. 383, doc. 1268, 1674.
79 Ibn 'Abd al-Ghani, *Awdah al-isharat*, 176.
80 Bulaq, reg. 63, p. 159, doc. 483, 1714.
81 Bab 'Ali, reg. 187, p. 572, doc. 703, 1704.
82 al-Tabari al-Makki, *Tarikh Makka*, 247–84.
83 Ministry of Endowments, Waqf deed of Sultan Mahmud.
84 Diwan 'Ali, reg. 1, p. 91, doc. 189, 1741.
85 Diwan 'Ali, reg. 1, p. 91, doc. 189, 1741.
86 Diwan 'Ali, reg. 2, p. 297, doc. 462, 1795.
87 Diwan 'Ali, reg. 2, p. 298, doc. 467, 1795.
88 Bab 'Ali, reg. 191, p. 377, doc. 145, 1709.
89 Alexandria, reg. 65, p. 301, doc. 539, 1718.
90 Bab 'Ali, reg. 172, p. 290, doc. 522, 1736.
91 'Umar, *Imarat al-Hajj*, 360.
92 Bab 'Ali, reg. 197, p. 61, doc. 216, 1716.
93 Bab 'Ali, reg. 227, p. 128, doc. 269, 1743; reg. 209, p. 28, doc. 112, 1728; reg. 247, p. 127, doc. 264, 1752.
94 Ministry of Endowments, Waqf deed 914.
95 Ministry of Endowments, Waqf deed 541.
96 Bab 'Ali, reg. 247, p. 479, doc. 843, 1753.
97 Bab 'Ali, reg. 184, p. 165, doc. 586, 1677.
98 Bab 'Ali, reg 184, p. 165, doc. 586, 1677.
99 Bab 'Ali, reg. 187, p. 235, doc. 1027, 1704.
100 Diwan 'Ali, reg. 1, p. 93, doc. 191, 1741.
101 Diwan 'Ali, reg. 2, p. 302, doc. 480, 1797.
102 Ministry of Endowments, waqf deed of Sulayman Pasha, 1074.
103 Bab 'Ali, reg. 163, p. 168, doc. 594, 1677; Diwan 'Ali, reg. 1, p. 95, doc. 198, 1754; al-Ishaqi, *Akhbar al-uwal*, 163.
104 Bab 'Ali, reg. 119, p. 236, doc. 1219, 1638.
105 Diwan 'Ali, reg. 2, p. 370, doc. 609, 1803.
106 'Amir, "Watha'iq," 368–69.
107 Diwan 'Ali, reg. 1, p. 94-95, doc. 197, 1739.
108 Sinan Pasha was twice Ottoman governor of Egypt, once from 1571 to 1573 and again from 1584 to 1585. See Ahmad, *al-Idara fi Misr*, 432.

109 Diwan 'Ali, reg. 2, p. 296, doc. 460, 1796.
110 Diwan 'Ali, reg. 1, p. 131, doc. 477, 1741.
111 Ministry of Endowments, Waqf deed of Radwan Bey, 996.
112 Bab 'Ali, reg. 317, p. 50, doc. 116, 1794.
113 Qisma 'Askariya, reg. 154, p. 180, doc. 300, 1745.
114 Qisma 'Askariya, reg. 170, p. 180, doc. 300, 1759; Bab 'Ali, reg. 285, p. 4, doc. 6, 1775.
115 'Afifi, "al-Awqaf wa-l-milaha," 86–100.
116 Qisma 'Askariya, reg. 224, p. 786, doc. 657, 1794.
117 Qisma 'Askariya, reg. 224, p. 786, doc. 657, 1794.
118 Ministry of Endowments, Waqf deed of Sultan Murad, 34.
119 Ministry of Endowments, Deed for the waqf founded by the mother of the sultans, p. 21.
120 Salihiya Najmiya, reg. 455, p. 357, doc. 1281, 1569.
121 Bab 'Ali, reg. 41, p. 54, doc. 226, 1578.
122 Ministry of Endowments, Deed for the waqf founded by the mother of the sultans, 21.
123 Bayyumi, *Mukhassasat*, 139.
124 al-Mallawani, *Tuhfat al-ahbab*, 171.
125 İnalcık, *Tarikh al-dawla,* 159.
126 Haridi, *Tarikh Shibh al-Jazira*, 26.
127 Diwan 'Ali, reg. 1, p. 230, doc. 474, 1742; reg. 2, p. 180, doc. 254, 1776.
128 Qisma 'Askariya, reg. 130, p. 268, doc. 455, 1727.
129 al-Mallawani, *Tuhfat al-ahbab*, 398.
130 al-Mallawani, *Tuhfat al-ahbab*, 200.
131 Thus, when the Fiqariya faction routed Muhammad Bey Jarkas, members of the victorious faction took over posts in the administration of this waqf. Diwan 'Ali, reg. 1, p. 58, doc. 115, 1741.
132 Shaw, *Financial*, 270.
133 Qisma 'Askariya, reg. 143, p. 230, doc. 502, 1736.
134 al-Jabarti, *'Aja'ib al-athar*, vol. 3, 351.
135 Bab 'Ali, reg. 198, p. 536, doc. 1478, 1716.
136 Ibn 'Abd al-Ghani, *Awdah al-isharat*, 430.
137 Salihiya Najmiya, reg. 495, p. 345, doc. 1416, 1629.
138 'Afifi, *al-Awqaf,* 323.
139 Ibrahim, *al-Azamat*, 304–305.
140 Qisma 'Askariya, reg. 183, p. 64, doc. 87, 1768.
141 Ruznama, "Daftar Bast," Egyptian National Archives.
142 al-Jabarti, *'Aja'ib al-athar,* vol. 1, 45; Ibn 'Abd al-Ghani, *Awdah al-isharat*, 187.
143 Shaw, *Financial*, 270.
144 Qisma 'Askariya, reg. 100, p. 28, doc. 321, 1707.
145 Qisma 'Askariya, reg. 145, p. 14, doc. 18, 1736.
146 Ibn 'Abd al-Ghani, *Awdah al-isharat*, 590.
147 Qisma 'Askariya, reg. 91, p. 55, doc. 65, 1694.
148 Ruznama, "Sijillat Surra Rumiya," Egyptian National Archives.
149 'Afifi, "al-Awqaf wa-l-milaha," 98.
150 According to the practice of *hikr*, which designates a rent contract allowing the lessor to construct buildings or plant crops on land rented from a waqf. The buildings may in turn be established as endowments, separate from the endowed land on which they stand ('Afifi, *al-Awqaf*, 16).

151 Qisma 'Askariya, reg. 82, p. 2, doc. 10, 1689; Bab 'Ali, reg. 327, p. 110 doc. 213, 1743.
152 Bab 'Ali, reg. 187, p. 174, doc. 710, 1704.
153 The pataque, a currency in use throughout the Ottoman lands, was worth 30 paras at the beginning of the eighteenth century; by the last quarter of the century, it was worth 90. See Raymond, *al-Hirafiyyun*, vol. 1, 130–31.
154 Bulaq, reg. 61, p. 339, doc. 732, 1705.
155 Ibn 'Abd al-Ghani, *Awdah al-isharat*, 500.
156 Bab 'Ali, reg. 163, p. 61, doc. 215, 1677.
157 'Afifi, "al-Awqaf wa-l-milaha," 95.
158 Bab 'Ali, reg. 237, p. 282, doc. 387, 1748; Bab 'Ali, reg. 291, p. 333, doc. 533, 1796.
159 "Husayn Afandi al-Ruznamji," *Tartib al-diyar*, 46.
160 Diwan 'Ali, reg. 2, p. 304, doc. 491, 1796; p. 304, doc. 489, 1796.
161 Ramadan, "Watha'iq mukhassasat," 264.

Bibliography

Archival Sources
Ottoman Legal Records
Alexandria, reg. 65
Bab 'Ali, reg. 41, 49, 57, 119, 133, 158, 160, 163, 172, 184, 187, 191, 197, 198, 207, 209, 227, 237, 247, 285, 291, 317, and 327.
Bulaq, reg. 61, 63, 66, and 68.
Dasht, reg. 150 and 162.
Diwan 'Ali, reg. 1 and 2.
Qisma 'Askariya, reg. 82, 91, 100, 130, 143, 145, 154, 170, 183, 204, and 224.
Salihiya Najmiya, reg. 455, 495, and 508.

Ottoman Financial Administration
Egyptian National Archives, Ruznama, "Daftar bast wa tatbiq waridat wa masarif khazina 'amira mahrusat Misr humiyat min al-afat wa-l-adrar," reg. 5647, 1705.
Egyptian National Archives, Ruznama, "Sijillat surra rumiya ahali al-Haramayn al-Sharifayn 'an Wajib 1136H," reg. 5530/2087, 1723.
Egyptian National Archives, Ruznama, "Daftar Surra Rumiya Ahali Haramayn Sharifayn," reg. 5661, no 5938.
Egyptian National Archives, Ruznama, "Daftar Waridat wa Masarif Khazina 'Amira Mahrusat Misr Humiyat 'an al-Afat," reg. 5648, 1723.

Waqf Deeds
Egyptian National Library, deed for the waqf established by the mother of the great sultans, ms. 3280 History, 1552.
Egyptian Ministry of Endowments, Waqfiyas 541, 914.
Egyptian Ministry of Endowments, deed for the waqf founded by the mother of Sultan Murad, Turki 907.
Egyptian Ministry of Endowments, Waqfiya of Radwan Bey, 996.
Egyptian Ministry of Endowments, Waqfiya of Sulayman Pasha, 1074.
Egyptian Ministry of Endowments, Waqfiya of Sultan Mahmud, 908.
Egyptian Ministry of Endowments, Waqfiya of Sultan Murad, 906.

Publications and Other Sources
'Abd al-Mu'ti, Husam. *al-'Ilaqat al-misriya al-hijaziya fi-l-qarn al-thamin 'ashr*. Cairo: General Egyptian Book Organization, 1998.
'Afifi, Muhammad. 1991. *al-Awqaf wa-l-hayah al-iqtisadiya fi Misr fi-l-'asr al-'uthmani*. Cairo: General Egyptian Book Organization.
———. "al-Awqaf wa-l-milaha al-bahriya fi Misr fi-l-'asr al-'uthmani," in R. Deguilhem, ed., *Le waqf dans l'espace islamique: Outil de pouvoir socio-politique*, 87–100. Damascus: Institut français de Damas, 1995.
Ahmad, Layla 'Abd al-Latif. *al-Idara fi Misr fi-l-'asr al-'uthmani*. Cairo: Ain Shams University Press, 1978.
Amin, Muhammad M. *Fihrist watha'iq al-Qahira hatta nihayat 'asr al-salatin al-mamalik, AH 239–922/853–1516 CE*. Cairo: Institut français d'archéologie orientale, 1981.
'Amir, Madiha. "Watha'iq Iskandar Basha fi Misr." PhD diss., Faculty of Letters, Department of Documentation and Library Science, Cairo University, 1991.
al-Ansari, 'Abd al-Rahman. *Tuhfat al-muhibbin wa-l-ashab fi ma'rifat ma li-l-madaniyyin min al-ansab*. Edited by M. al-'Arusi al-Matwi. Tunis: al-Maktaba al-'Atiqa, 1970.
'Ashur, Sa'id 'Abd al-Fattah. *Misr wa-l-Sham fi-l-'asr al-mamluki*. Cairo: Anglo, 1994.
Bayyumi, Muhammad Fahim. *Mukhassasat al-Haramayn al-Sharifayn fi Misr ibban al-'asr al-'uthmani (AH 923–1220/1517–1805 CE)*. Cairo: Dar al-Qahira li-l-Kitab, 2001.
Dahlan, Ahmad ibn Zayni. *Khulasat al-kalam fi bayan umara' al-balad al-haram*. Cairo: Matba'at al-Kulliyyat al-Azhariya, AH 1305.
Haridi, Muhammad 'Abd al-Latif. *Tarikh Shibh al-Jazira al-'Arabiya min al-masadir al-turkiya*. Cairo: Dar al-Zahra' li-l-Nashr, 1989.

Husayn Afandi al-Ruznamji. "Tartib al-diyar al-misriya fi 'ahd al-dawla al-'uthmaniya: Misr fi muftaraq al-turuq," in Shafiq Ghurbal, ed., *Misr 'inda muftaraq al-turuq (1798–1801)*, special issue of the *Cairo University Journal of the Faculty of Letters*, vol. 4, part 1, May 1936.

Ibn 'Abd al-Ghani, Ahmad Shalabi. *Awdah al-isharat fi man tawalla Misr al-Qahira min al-wuzara' wa-l-bashawat*. Edited by 'A. Abd al-Rahim. Cairo: Maktabat al-Khanqi, 1987.

Ibrahim, 'Abd al-Latif. *Watha'iq al-waqf 'ala-l-amakin al-muqaddasa*. Proceedings of the First International Conference on the History of the Arabian Peninsula, vol. 2. Riyadh: Matbu'at Jami'at al-Riyadh, 1979.

Ibrahim, Nasir. *al-Azamat al-ijtima'iya fi Misr fi-l-qarn al-sabi' 'ashr*. Cairo: Dar al-Afaq al-'Arabiya, 1998.

İnalcık, Halil. *Tarikh al-dawla al-'uthmaniya min al-nushu' ila al-inhidar*. Translated by Muhammad al-Arna'ut. Tripoli: Dar al-Madar al-Islami, 2002. (Arabic translation based on *The Ottoman Empire, the Classical Age, 1300–1600*. Translated by Norman Itzkowitz and Colin Imber. London: Weidenfeld and Nicolson, 1973.)

al-'Isami, 'Abd al-Malik ibn Husayn ibn 'Abd al-Malik. *Samt al-nujum al-'awali anba' al-awa'il wa-l-tawali*. Cairo: al-Matba'a al-Salafiya, n.d.

al-Ishaqi. *Akhbar al-uwal fi man tasarrafa fi Misr min arbab al-duwal*. Cairo: al-Matba'a al-'Uthmaniya, AH 1304.

al-Jabarti, 'Abd al-Rahman. *'Aja'ib al-athar fi-l-tarajim wa-l-akhbar*. Edited by 'A. 'Abd al-Rahim. Cairo: Dar al-Kutub wa-l-Watha'iq al-Qawmiya, 2003.

al-Mallawani, Yusuf. *Tuhfat al-ahbab bi man malaka Misr min al-muluk wa-l-nuwwab*. Edited by 'Imad Ahmad Hilal and 'Abd al-Raziq 'Abd al-Raziq 'Isa. Cairo: al-'Arabi li-l-Nashr, 2000.

al-Nahrawani, Muhammad ibn Qutb al-Din. "Ibtihaj al-insan fi-l-ihsan al-wasil min al-Yaman li-l-Haramayn." Egyptian National Library, ms. 79 (History), 1887.

al-Nahrawani, Qutb al-Din. *al-I'lam bi a'lam bayt Allah al-haram*. Cairo: al-Matba'a al-Khayriya, 1887

Nasr, Ahmad 'Abd al-Rahim. "al-Aghawat, dirasa tarikhiya muqarana li aghawat al-Masjid al-Haram bi Makka wa-l-Masjid al-Nabawi bi-l-Madina." African and Asian Studies Institute, special journal, Khartoum University, 1986.

Ramadan, Mustafa Muhammad. "Watha'iq mukhassasat al-Haramayn al-Sharifayn fi Misr ibban al-'asr al-'uthmani." Proceedings of the Congress on Sources for the History of the Arabian Peninsula, Riyadh University, 1979.

Ramzi, Muhammad. *al-Qamus al-jughrafi li-l-bilad al-misriya min 'ahd qudama' al-Misriyyin ila sanat 1945*. Cairo: General Egyptian Book Organization, 1994.

al-Rashidi, Ahmad. *Husn al-safa wa-l-ibtihaj bi dhikr man wuliya imarat al-Hajj*. Edited by Layla 'Abd al-Latif Ahmad. Cairo: Maktabat al-Khanji, 1980.

Raymond, André. *al-Hirafiyyun wa-l-tujjar fi-l-Qahira fi-l-qarn al-thamin 'ashr (Artisans et commerçants au Caire au XVIII* siècle)*. 2 vols. Translated by Nasir Ahmad Ibrahim and Patsy Jamal al-Din. Cairo: Supreme Council for Culture, 2005.

———. *al-Mudun al-'arabiya al-kubra fi-l-'asr al-'uthmani (Grandes villes arabes à l'époque ottomane)*. Translated by L. Faraj. Cairo: Dar al-Fikr li-l-Dirasat wa-l-Nashr wa-l-Tawzi', 1991.

Shahin, Azza. "Khadamat al-hajij fi-l-Hijaz fi-l-'asr al-'uthmani 1517/1798." Master's thesis, History Department, Faculty of Letters, Mansura University, 1995.

Shaw, Stanford J. *The Financial and Administrative Organization and Development of Ottoman Egypt, 1517–1798*. Princeton, NJ: Princeton University Press, 1962.

al-Sinjari, Taqiy al-Din ibn Yahya ibn Isma'il ibn 'Abd al-Rahman al-Makki. "Mana'ih al-karam fi akhbar Makka wa wulat al-Haram." Unpublished manuscript. Arab League Manuscript Institute, 831 History, n.d.

Sulayman, Ahmad al-Sa'id. *Ta'sil ma warada fi tarikh al-Jabarti min al-dakhil*. Cairo: Dar al-Ma'arif, 1979.

al-Tabari al-Makki, Muhammad ibn 'Ali ibn Fadl. *Tarikh Makka ithaf fudala' al-zaman bi-tarikh wilayat Bani al-Hasan*. Edited and annotated by Muhsin Muahmmad Hasan Silim. Cairo: Dar al-Kitab al-Jami'i, 1993.

Tuchscherer, Michel. "Approvisionnement des villes saintes d'Arabie en blé d'Egypte, d'après des documents ottomans des années 1670." *Anatolia Moderna* 5 (1994): 79–99.

'Umar, Samira Fahmi. *Imarat al-Hajj fi Misr al-'uthmaniya*. Cairo: General Egyptian Book Organization, 2001.

3

The Sadir al-Fuqaha' wa-l-Fuqara' Endowment (Salah al-Din al-Ayyubi) in Alexandria during the Eighteenth Century[1]

Nasir Ibrahim

Waqfs, religious endowments, have played an important role in the lives of individuals and society in general at various times in the history of the Middle East. For most of the Ottoman period, these endowments, and the foundations they supported, were the sole providers of crucial basic services like education, health, utilities, and public works, as well as scholarly, religious, and social institutions, which fell outside the state's remit. Because the state depended on such endowments for the provision of services to society, the institution came to play an influential role in ordering relations between state and society.

Among the numerous forms of endowment was one whose function was to provide *jamikiyyat* or *jawamik* (salaries, livelihood, or pensions)[2] to particular social groups whose subsistence was nominally the responsibility of the state, either because they had no one to provide for them (that is, orphans and widows or marginalized groups such as beggars; those who would in modern times receive welfare or retirement benefits), or because they were members of groups that performed a social or scholarly/religious role that left them unable to earn a living wage.[3] Profits from an endowment or the state treasury were set aside as sustenance for these groups, allowing them to perform their allotted social function.

Jawamik predated the Ottoman era. When Sultan Selim I occupied Egypt, he not only endorsed the disbursement of jawamik, he also increased the sums set aside for that purpose in the state treasury. A significant portion of the poorer classes' income came from these 'pensions.'[4] Ulama and *fuqaha'* (jurists), especially those who had no other form of income to support them—and whom the chronicler Abd al-Rahman al-Jabarti described as "idle scholars whom the poor man considers richer than is decent"[5]—benefited most from the jawamik system. To compensate these individuals for providing a religious education, overseeing and caring for their students, and producing new generations of scholars and teachers, it was necessary to set aside monies from the sultan's treasury or from endowments to furnish them with material aid.[6] This point was clearly expressed by the Hanafi jurist Hasan al-Shurumbullali when he provided the following definition of the *jamakiya* that the fuqaha' received: "It is not a fee, as there is no skill hired out, nor alms, because those are given by the rich, but rather a recompense for their devotion to learning."[7]

However, this does not mean that beneficiaries of the jawamik were exclusively poor scholars and jurists or those of limited income: the right to these pensions was guaranteed for all designated beneficiaries, whether rich or poor.[8] Indeed, the community regarded all jawamik, whether paid by endowments or taken as a sum from the sultan's treasury, as being due to the ulama and not a gift donated by the sultan. Shaykh Mar'i ibn Yusuf had the following to say on the subject: "For an endowment to be legally valid the *waqif* (founder), not the sultan, must own the endowed property." From this point, he concluded that the sums set aside in these endowments were merely means to facilitate the scholars receiving their due; the sultan had no right to abolish these funds or prevent their distribution.[9]

Such a way of seeing these donations was fundamentally at odds with the state's perception and formed the basis of a struggle between the two parties that lasted throughout the Ottoman period. This chapter approaches the problem through a study of one of the better-known endowments, the *Sadir al-Fuqaha' wa-l-Fuqara'* in Alexandria. The state made continuous attempts to interfere in the endowment's affairs, take it over, and challenge the legality of its existence (this last by demanding that the endowment's founding deed be closely examined and that the provisions the founder had set out be reviewed). This sort of investigation into a religious foundation's charter must be understood as part of a wider struggle between the state and its subjects over endowment incomes. Establishing the accuracy of documentation and deeds related to the Sadir endowment and registered in court enabled the ulama and jurists to resist the state's attempts to gain control of its income. This paper is therefore concerned in equal measure with the significance of documentation and the reasons for which the endowment's charter was registered anew at different points in time. The corpus of archival material relating to the Sultan Salah al-Din endowment is particularly rich, and this analysis of the endowment's charter will take that into account.

One aim of the present study is to understand various dimensions of the state's social policy toward provincial populations during the eighteenth century by examining this endowment, one of the largest providers of official pensions and salaries to ulama, jurists, and orphans in Alexandria. Far from being fixed, this policy was influenced and altered by material circumstances and the various problems facing the Ottoman state during the eighteenth century. A study of this endowment constitutes an entry point that allows us to understand at least some aspects of relations between the state and its subjects and the direction of social policy at various times. The chapter is also concerned with analyzing the reactions of the shaykhs and ulama (representatives of a dynamic social group with considerable social and cultural weight) to the policies and directives issued by the state. In contextualizing these reactions, we must take into account the group's awareness of its rights and its ability to defend its privileged status by exerting social influence and formulating of its position in terms of religious law and jurisprudence (that is, by establishing the illegality of the Ottoman state's attempts to extend its influence and increase the income it derived from Egypt at the expense of the ulama and their interests).

Definition of the Sadir endowment

The endowment we will focus on here was connected to a large and long-standing charitable foundation created by Sultan Salah al-Din al-Ayyubi in 1174. The endowment's income was assigned to the "poor and *fuqaha'* of Alexandria." Indeed, the endowment appears in the records as *sadir al-fuqaha' wa-l-fuqara' fi-l-thaghr al-sakandari*, the name of its beneficiaries replacing that of its founder. It is likely that the preference for this title reflects a desire on the part of the local population to bestow an exceptional status on the endowment and make it the focus of special care and attention. Exhortations to care for the weak, poor, and needy as well as orphans and ulama were contained in the majority of Ottoman decrees and edicts, and they formed a major component of the religious/ideological discourse of the state (and, by extension, its local administrations).[10] Any move to bring charitable endowments under state control would involve this particular endowment so long as it concerned itself with the protection and care of any groups that constituted a priority in the state's socio-religious discourse. In their day-to-day conversations, the inhabitants of Alexandria referred to the endowment as *Sadir al-fuqaha' wa-l-fuqara'*. The name of the founder, Salah al-Din, is only found when the endowment's full title was written out in the records.

The term *sadir* refers to the endowment's most important source of income: the sadir ('export') customs duty levied on all goods leaving Alexandria port. In Salah al-Din al-Ayyubi's time, this tax was referred to as the 'Frankish export'[11] or the 'fifth,' the latter title referring to the value of the tax. Al-Qalqashandi notes that at one time, Frankish traders were required to pay one-fifth of the value of the goods they were transporting.[12] Subsequently, this tax was levied on all goods exported from Alexandria to countries bordering the Mediterranean. A clear distinction developed between the revenue received from Eastern Mediterranean merchants *(sadir al-khums al-rumi)* and that received from European merchants *(rasm sadir al-bahr)*.[13]

Not only was Salah al-Din the first to endow proceeds from the public coffers to the ulama, but, as Mar'i ibn Yusuf states, his endowment was also the oldest charitable institution established for the benefit of this social group in Alexandria.[14]

Archival material concerning the Sadir endowment

This endowment, of course, is significant because of its connection with the name of Sultan Salah al-Din and its status as the oldest and largest charitable foundation dedicated to the service of ulama and *fuqaha'* in Alexandria. The Alexandria court registers also contain a vast and varied body of documents associated with this endowment. Indeed, it would be no exaggeration to state that its records are richer and more valuable than those of any other endowment registered in the Alexandria court. The records are like a window through which we can glimpse people's interactions with the endowment. They shed light on the central authorities' relations with the endowment, and the extent to which the port city's residents were aware of the state's every effort to reduce their jawamik and salaries. The records contain a good deal of important data that help us understand what "benefiting from the endowment's income" meant to the beneficiaries (who seem to have equated their status with absolute ownership). The records also provide more general information on the ways in which the endowment generated revenue, and on the ulama, shaykhs, and fuqaha' who were its principal beneficiaries. On the basis of these records, it is possible to compile a comprehensive list of the beneficiaries' names, identify the senior members of this social group, and observe how this elite was able to monopolize the greater part of the endowment's revenues, thereby further enhancing its privileged position.[15] Finally, it offers insight into how this group perceived and positioned itself within Alexandria's social hierarchy.

Furthermore, the data about social groups contained in the records are not restricted to the fuqaha' and ulama. These records reveal as well information about the poor and needy of Alexandria, a social class usually ignored in contemporary sources. This archival trove really deserves a separate study: it constitutes a unique and authentic source of the city's social history.

From the last quarter of the nineteenth century onward, there is a marked increase in the documentation of dealings concerning the Sadir endowment. In 1663, the central administration in Istanbul made Alexandria's chief judge *(qadi al-thaghr)* responsible for overseeing the endowment's affairs, as part of its wider efforts to extend control over the endowments. The state took as its pretext the fact that the family to which the endowment's founding charter had granted directorship in perpetuity had died out. In such circumstances, it argued, responsibility for overseeing the endowment would fall to Alexandria's legitimate governor.[16] The true significance of this decree lies in the state's efforts to place the Sadir endowment under its control, since Alexandria's chief judges were ultimately representatives of the authority of the Sublime Porte: they were directly appointed by Istanbul and their salaries were second only to those of Egypt's chief judges *(qadi 'askar wilayat Misr).*[17] While it is true that copies of the endowment's records had been kept in the Alexandria court since the sixteenth century, this decree intensified the process of documenting dealings involving the endowment. These documents include records of rental contracts involving the endowment's properties and assets; a copy of the *daftar al-taqsim* (a list of the endowment's salaried staff and details of the way its annual revenues were to be distributed among these beneficiaries); all instances of names on this list being invalidated or removed for various reasons; and difficulties faced by the endowment with those renting out its assets and property. The quantity and diversity of these records grew exponentially and came to include a great amount of detailed information about the lives of Alexandria's inhabitants through their dealings with the endowment. Indeed, subsequent to this date (1663 CE/AH 1074), there is scarcely a single document that is not related to the endowment in some capacity or other.

Nevertheless, this does not mean that the chief judge now had the final say in the administration of the endowment and its accounts. Over time, the ulama were able to confine the judge's role to the process of documenting the endowment's business dealings, alongside his duty to ensure that the conditions of the endowment's charter were being met. The power to appoint the director, manager, and clerks, the organization of the endowment's finances, and the distribution of revenues to its beneficiaries remained the sole preserve of a limited number of ulama and fuqaha'. The judge did little more than ratify their collective will.[18] This is just another instance of the subversion that Alexandria's inhabitants manifested in their dealings with the state. It also reflects the desire of the ulama to retain their privileges and shows their skillful use of legal and religious mechanisms to preserve the endowment's independence. Furthermore, it demonstrates their ability to organize and mobilize themselves as a coherent social group or faction. For instance, they created the position of a leader or chief representative, known as "the shaykh of the fuqaha' in Alexandria," whose job it was to supervise the interests of Alexandria's ulama and fuqaha', including those that related to the Sadir endowment. The ulama had the authority to remove this shaykh from his position if his actions were deemed inappropriate.[19]

The unique character of Alexandria's ulama and fuqaha' becomes particularly evident when we compare this appointment system with that employed by their contemporaries in other port areas. For instance, the *Diwan 'Ali* (Supreme Council) in Cairo would appoint a shaykh from Cairo to head the ulama in Damietta.[20] The internal cohesion and group dynamic of Alexandria's shaykhs ensured they were an influential social force, fully capable of protecting their specific interests.

In addition to this dense body of archival material, we have another set of sources—left to us by a number of contemporary observers, who collated the various imperial orders and decrees issued by the sultan, and reflecting Istanbul's desire to abolish the jawamik and *'ulufat* (originally, salaries paid to soldiers, but by this period many merchants and craftsmen[21] had used various means, including bribery, to enter their names on the salary rolls). While these contemporary observers with their lists of decrees reflected the perspective of the state, the Sadir endowment's documents and other chronicles and petitions authored by ulama leaders express a more grassroots perspective—in other words, the views of wider society toward the decrees and commands of state authorities that would regularly stage unsolicited interventions in their lives.

The Sadir endowment, therefore, can be considered as a dynamic reflection of the social reality in which the relationship between the state and its subjects evolved in the course of the eighteenth century.

Legal status and function of copies of the endowment's charter

The authorities failed to preserve the original founding deed of Sultan Salah al-Din's endowment, and this lent the copies preserved in the Alexandria court archives a particular importance. The court registers contain a number of such documents copied from the original charter, allowing us to compare between them and determine which of these 'alternatives'[22] might provide us with the most complete picture of the original. For instance, the three surviving copies all contain the following information, which is essential to any endowment's founding deed: the founder's name, a detailed topographical description of the property being endowed, criteria identifying the beneficiaries, and a list of the original witnesses. The court clerks were careful to record—within the text itself—that the document was an exact copy of the original.[23]

Further supporting the idea that these copies were faithful duplicates of an original deed is the fact that all of them were taken from the same source. The text is almost identical in all three documents, and they all employ phrases and terminology current at the time of the endowment's foundation. It is hard to disagree with the testimony of those who announced to Alexandria's chief judge that the documents were completely faithful copies of the original charter.

A third argument in favor of their accuracy relates to the historical circumstances in which these copies were produced. It has been established that all three were made in response to certain difficulties then facing the endowment. In each case, the chief judge had demanded a return to the original document, mainly because the state was a party to these problems. The copy we are interested in here was produced in response to an order issued by the Diwan 'Ali that "the charter be read and entered into the court's records."[24] Thus we see that this concern to review the original was generated in part by the struggle for control of the endowment. The reproduction of the complete text of the original foundation charter and its entry into the court records lent veracity to other documents and legal arguments. The pile of documents concerning the endowment also provided validation as it increased in volume, thus supporting the idea of the endowment's perpetuity (a concept referred to in the documents as *isal al-waqf*),[25] and legitimizing the beneficiaries' claim that the salaries and pensions disbursed to them through the waqf had been a recognized and uncontested right for centuries.

Those responsible for monitoring the endowment's legal affairs took advantage of their positions of authority to assert that the copies of the endowment deed corresponded exactly to the original,[26] as had been established before qualified judges on a number of occasions. This was particularly clear in the case of the second copy (1744), which mentioned the date of the oldest copy made in the Ottoman period—some two centuries previously, in 1540.[27] This early copy is especially important as it was made during the time of Dawud Pasha (1538–49), who was in charge of examining and reviewing all endowments and charitable institutions and issuing *ifrajat* (permits, sing. *ifraj*) from the diwan that bestowed the sultan's imprimatur upon those he found to be legitimate. Throughout the Ottoman period, Dawud Pasha's ifrajat were a principal point of reference when attempting to establish the legal validity of a particular endowment or charitable institution. Along with the original founding charter, the document containing Dawud Pasha's ifraj was therefore one of the most important resources available to Alexandria's residents as they sought to prove the legality of the Sadir endowment.[28]

The ongoing process of documentation in the Alexandria court archives also had an important role to play in forestalling any claims that the conditions set down by Sultan Salah al-Din had fallen into abeyance, abrogating the basis for the endowment's perpetuity and legality. Furthermore, this constant re-recording of the original charter indicates that those responsible for the endowment's affairs were very keen to make full use of all available legal tools enabling them to confront the state in court and establish possession over real estate and other property belonging to the endowment.

What lends these alternative charter documents even greater importance is the fact that contemporaries, and in particular senior Ottoman officials, treated the copies as the legal equivalent of the original charter. The diwan of Hassn Pasha Qapudan, commander of the Ottoman navy, issued a decree demanding all documents relating to the endowment contained in the court registers in order to resolve a dispute between the Venetian consul and the Sadir endowment.[29] This demonstrates that in the eighteenth century, the Ottoman authorities in Cairo were treating copies of the charter kept in the court records as the legal equivalent of the original charter.

The importance of the 1744 copy

The three extant copies of the founding charter that have been preserved in the court records all date to the seventeenth and eighteenth centuries. The first was registered in 1663, the second some eighty years later in 1744, and the third in 1787. A comparison between the three reveals that the second and third copies are more accurate, and therefore more valuable, than the first, in which the copyist failed to include the opening formulations common to all endowment charters. Instead the copyist proceeds directly to the charter's content, with the statement:

This is what Sultan Salah al-Din endowed for the benefit of the fuqaha' of Alexandria, the ulama, the imams, the *murabitun* [fighters for the faith] and those Arabs of good descent . . . .[30]

Although the second and third copies are almost identical in form and content, there is one fundamental difference, resulting from the Diwan 'Ali's desire to examine the original document before entering a copy onto the court records. The text of the second copy (1744) mentions that the document was a duplicate of "the original document written on parchment . . . ." This indicates that in the mid-eighteenth century the original charter was still in the hands of the endowment's archivists. It also shows that judges in Alexandria, like their contemporaries elsewhere,[31] would not permit a duplicate to be entered on the court records unless the original was available for verification.

Following the actual text of the charter there was further confirmation that the copy was based on a number of valid documents and was an exact duplicate of the original: "This was taken from various copies and compared to the original from which it was taken, line by line and letter by letter, with nothing added or taken away."

This claim is supported by a number of witnesses: "*al-akabir wa-l-a'yan wa ahl al-ma'rifa wa-l-khibra wa-l-wuquf*"—men of high standing, notables, knowledgeable men, and experts in the community. The document reflects an awareness of the need to meet the conditions laid out in classical jurisprudence for validating witness statements, by ensuring that each witness signed his name under an identical phrase: "This was compared to the original from which it was taken and found to be an exact copy."[32]

Although this 'comparison formula'[33] (as it was known) was important because it established that the copy was an exact duplicate of the stated intentions of the legal founder, and free from any alternations or omissions, it is missing from the 1787 copy. Furthermore, the presence of the chief judge of the Alexandria court among the witnesses named at the end of the 1744 copy gives this document a special evidential and legal force: "[The chief judge] has approved and undersigned [this document] and required that it be used without alteration in phrase and meaning, the above having been corroborated by witnesses."[34]

The charter is then bound in "this excellent new register, to be a support and reference for all students of the religious sciences and masters of jurisprudence, a source of their livelihood, a storehouse for their provisions, and a means to drive off those who would challenge and oppose them."

This clearly shows that the standards of documentation, precision, and accuracy of transmission are considerably higher in the 1744 charter than in the 1787 charter. As the most important and accurate extant copy of the original charter, the 1744 document is therefore clearly the most deserving of study and publication.

Historical context: State intervention and the registration of the 1744 copy

What are the historical circumstances that led to the inhabitants of Alexandria registering copies of the foundation's charter in court? What is the connection between their action and the state's intervention, which took the form of the sultan's decree pertaining to the Sadir endowment,[35] entered immediately after the foundation charter in the court register? The two documents are linked, we believe, by more than their proximity in the register: theirs is a causal relationship, founded on the stance of the central administration in Istanbul toward the Sadir endowment, and more generally toward the jawamik salaries paid by a number of endowments out of the imperial treasury. These salaries, according to the Ottoman state, placed unbearable pressure on an already strained budget.

In 1744, the endowment encountered a problem with Jewish tenants who were delaying their rent payments. This rent made up part of the revenues disbursed to the beneficiaries of the endowment. It seems that the problem was connected to the Jewish tenants' attempts to raise money for a recently introduced tax known as the *mal al-diwan*, which the ulama and fuqaha' regarded as a grave injustice. Indeed, they petitioned the Diwan 'Ali in Cairo regarding the payment of this tax on two occasions: during the reigns of Ali Pasha al-Hakim (1740–41) and Yahya Pasha (1741–43). Both of these Ottoman governors informed Istanbul of the problem, which soon became a pretext for state intervention in the endowment's affairs. We are concerned here less with the details of this legal problem than with the consequences of the dispute, the significance of the state's decision to intervene in the endowment's affairs when it did, and finally the request that the original text of the charter be reviewed before it was registered in court.

The sultan's decree reveals that the state was intensifying its efforts to expose mismanagement of the foundation's accounts by its supervisors.

It seems to have been unconcerned with the payment of mal al-diwan or the postponed rent payments (which after all were the original problem).[36] Instead, the state authorities blamed the endowment's difficulties on its supervisors. The sultan's decree described them as "rotten" and accused them of abusing their positions to enrich themselves at the endowment's expense. The state, always careful to safeguard the ulama and fuqaha' (its responsibility toward this group, indeed, constituted a main theme of official ideological discourse), claimed it could not permit such flagrant transgressions to harm those under its protection, thus legitimizing its intervention. Such an argument had the additional benefit of allowing the state access to the endowment's accounts. In other words, the state was able to manipulate a legal argument to serve its own goals. In reality, misuse of the endowment's funds by its supervisors was a trivial issue that could have been resolved internally among the ulama. This is evident from the records, which show the conditions required for valid dismissal of a supervisor. A given number of ulama and fuqaha' had to appear before the chief judge and announce their decision to dismiss the director. Unable to block or challenge this consensus, the judge would ratify their decision, leaving them free to "choose whoever they wanted to be their overseer."[37]

In short, although the problem of corrupt management was merely hypothetical, the state nevertheless exaggerated and manipulated it as a pretext for intervention in the endowment's affairs. In consequence, a new supervisor (al-Jamali Abdallah) and overseer (Shaykh Hasan bin 'Awad) were appointed directly by Istanbul. Their mission as described in the decree was to conduct a thorough examination of the endowment's finances, especially those revenues generated by the Sadir tariff. Furthermore, "every charitable donation, no matter how small, must be examined, explained, and noted." The decree also included a list of the goods exported from Alexandria and the customs duties liable on each, enabling these new appointees to review the balance sheets for previous years and draw up a "detailed register of this, arranged by year, type of goods, and quantity."[38]

The state, of course, had no intention of showing that its ultimate objective was to take control of the endowment. It focused its discourse on defending its poor subjects and the ulama and expressing discontent with the current state of the endowment. The imperial decree took a strongly disapproving tone, with the chief judge adding his own censure to the overall picture painted by Istanbul: he emphasized that the state would never allow "the livelihoods of the scholars of Prophet Muhammad's nation" to be dependent on Jewish tenants (whom he termed "enemies of the faith"). Obviously the state was using a religious discourse both to soften the anger of the ulama at its intervention in the endowment's affairs and to conceal its true intentions.

Nevertheless, the text of the decree is unusually explicit about the state's intentions. Not only was Istanbul aiming to obtain and scrutinize the endowment's accounts, it was also attempting to discover which of the endowment's properties had fallen into disrepair or collapsed as a further pretext for bringing the foundation as a whole under state control. The decree talks in general terms about the state of collapse and ruin said to characterize much of the endowment: "Most of it is destroyed, collapsed and leveled and what remains is falling down." It proposes a comprehensive topographical survey of the endowment and its property:

> Homes, bathhouses, ovens, mills, property, shops, hostels, and other holdings. Inhabited and standing properties should be recorded separately. The rent and annual revenue from each building should be recorded, alongside the name of the building's owner and the name of the rent collector, the manner of its collection and by what authority he carries out this task.

The Sublime Porte further asked that the report include a list of those properties that could not be restored or rebuilt, or those that were on the point of collapse. Significantly, the decree contained no order to repair any damaged or neglected properties. It should be noted that during the Ottoman period it was common to exploit damage to property by confiscating it and converting it to *ard hikr* (land requiring no more than the payment of ground rent). Whoever assumed responsibility for repairing property on this land was granted full rights and use of the property. Many of the properties and buildings endowed by Salah al-Din in Cairo were subject to this conversion, notably properties belonging to the Khanqah endowment. These properties, which had fallen into a state of disrepair, were rented out by the vizir, Iskandar Pasha (1568–71), who paid *hikr* (ground rent) for the land they stood on. He then renovated some of the properties and incorporated them into his own endowment.[39] They were later confiscated from Iskandar Pasha in turn, and the jawamik reverted to the sultan's treasury.[40]

That is not to say that things went as the Sublime Porte had planned. Those who examined the court's records came up empty handed, although the judge was a key party to the investigation. Furthermore, we find no reference to al-Jamali Abdallah or Shaykh Hasan Bin Awad in this connection; in fact, the ulama and fuqaha' seem to have appointed an individual called 'Umar al-Kharrat as their director, and it was this man who managed the endowment's accounts in 1744. An important document from the same year records the judge's affirmation of the founder's requirement that "the director shall be chosen among them [that is, the fuqaha'] alone and with their consent."[41] It seems unlikely, therefore, that this imperial decree was ever implemented in full: the ulama and fuqaha' seem to have brushed aside the various legal arguments deployed by the Sublime Porte. Ultimately, the whole matter seems to have been confined to the recording of the endowment's charter. The decision by the ulama and fuqaha' to dismiss 'Umar al-Kharrat from his post that same year could be read as a deliberate demonstration of their ability to exercise their right to appoint and dismiss the endowment's director.[42]

It is clear that the ulama were conscious of the dangers facing them and the need to act quickly to preserve the endowment's independence. Nevertheless, the situation ended up playing into their hands more than they could have anticipated: the sultan's decree gave them a legal document containing, albeit implicitly, the state's recognition of the importance of the endowment and their jawamik and, consequently, the need to safeguard its cohesion and continuity. Thus we see that the historical backdrop to the charter's duplication is the authorities' attempt to place the endowment under centralized control.

What, then, were the objective factors preventing the Sublime Porte from imposing its will as described in the sultan's decree? Did local actors (that is, the ulama and jurists) really possess the authority and influence required to protect their interests and privileges from the depredations of the state? At the heart of this question lies the issue of the Ottoman state's views on jawamik and pensions. Those views were expressed through a general policy for dealing with all endowments that disbursed monies in this form, not just Salah al-Din's endowment. It is worth examining this issue from a more comprehensive perspective. We shall take a quick overview of the issue, especially its social dimension, before looking at the directions in which it developed and the wider debate it occasioned between the central authorities and Egyptian society. This last point is of vital significance: it demonstrates that the ulama and fuqaha' did not stand alone in confronting the state's desire to appropriate their livelihoods: it was a struggle that took place across Egypt. The ulama of Alexandria made efforts to reassert the validity of the Sadir endowment only in response to the orders and decrees that Istanbul sent to the Diwan 'Ali in Cairo.

High-ranking ulama throughout Egypt, who were beneficiaries of the major endowments in Cairo, Alexandria, and elsewhere, participated in this struggle with the state over jawamik. As in Alexandria, they sought to protect their privileges and force a retreat over the policy that threatened to cut off their livelihood. This struggle has received insufficient attention in the field of Ottoman studies, which tends to portray the relationship between local ulama and the central state as a peaceful one.[43] The reality was a tug-of-war relationship governed, on one hand, by developments pertaining to Egypt as a province and, on the other, by the state's financial and economic position, political circumstances, and the foreign wars that placed unusual pressures on internal political dynamics throughout the Ottoman Empire as a whole.

The historical context for the development of the state's stance on jawamik

The dates on which all three copies of the Sadir endowment's charter were entered in the Alexandrian court registers coincide with the arrival of public orders from the sultan at the Diwan 'Ali in Cairo to abolish the payment of jawamik. In each case, however, it seems that Alexandria's ulama acted in parallel to the responses mounted by their counterparts in Cairo, a dynamic clearly shown in the accounts of contemporary observers (for example, Ahmad Shalabi ibn Abd al-Ghani, Yusuf al-Mallawani, 'Abd al-Rahman al-Jabarti, and so on). The united front presented by the ulama in both cities proved a powerful tool in preventing the implementation of imperial orders, especially in societies that respected religious learning.[44] In any case, it was no simple matter for the state to disregard the interests of the ulama and fuqaha', who, exercising considerable influence, proved effective intermediaries when the Ottoman rulers wished to communicate with their subjects. The state was also reluctant to reveal the contradictions between its publicly stated desire to protect the agents of religious law and its goal of recovering the privileges and resources previously granted to these same individuals.

While the state was engaged in protracted successive frontier wars with Austria, Persia, and Russia, it attempted repeatedly to secure the status quo in its provinces. This required it to woo influential social forces such as the ulama and the jurists. It was reluctant to clash with these local actors for fear of provoking severe social unrest, which it was ill-equipped to deal with at such a sensitive and difficult time. However, the mounting financial crisis and skyrocketing inflation,[45] exacerbated by the Ottomans' foreign wars, forced the state to make continual efforts to either abolish the jawamik or at the very least to reduce the lists of beneficiaries. The ulama, for their part, were fully aware of these efforts and used all the means at their disposal to prevent attempts to requisition or otherwise encroach on their privileges. A study of the various stages of this struggle over jawamik would enhance an analysis of the Sublime Porte's frequently erratic position on the issue. It would also help us understand the circumstances that enabled the ulama to preserve their interests and the interests of the vulnerable social classes associated with them.

First, the existence of two forms of jawamik (from the sultan's treasury and from the endowments) meant that the conflict evolved in different directions. While the majority of Cairo's ulama drew their jawamik from the sultan's treasury,[46] jawamik in Alexandria tended to be disbursed by endowments. The state pursued a separate policy in each case. In the case of the treasury jawamik, it naturally had the final say over whether to maintain, reduce, or abolish payments. In the case of the endowments' jawamik, it had no such powers: theoretically speaking, the endowment's property and administrative procedures were legally immune from confiscation or invalidation. Thus the state had to find legal pretexts for intervening in the endowment's payments. To this should be added the difference between the composition of influential social forces in Cairo and Alexandria, as well as the status of the ulama and their relationship with these influential and powerful elites. These objective factors had a noticeable influence on the way imperial decrees to suspend jawamik payments were challenged in Cairo and Alexandria respectively.

Because the state began by challenging jawamik drawn from the state treasury, Cairo was the first to experience this confrontation. Over the course of a century (1564–1663), the city witnessed three separate attempts to abolish treasury jawamik. The first attempt was in the time of Iskandar Pasha (1568–71), who is described by contemporary sources as "the one who deprived the ulama of the revenues of the weak, the poor, and the elderly."[47] A clear imbalance appeared in the state's budget, and the abolition of jawamik and pensions was the direct consequence.[48] So severe was the opposition to this move, however (with detractors "railing against it from atop the minarets of al-Azhar Mosque"), that, fearing a revolt, Istanbul rescinded its command and, dismissing Iskandar Pasha from his post, announced that the jawamik would continue to be paid.[49] The second attempt came some thirty years later, during the time of Khidr Pasha (1598–1601), at a time when the shortfall in the state budget had reached unprecedented levels (total revenues of 3,000 *akce* versus total expenditures of 9,000 *akce*),[50] and severe inflation was having serious economic and financial ramifications. In response, Ottoman officials were forced to reexamine the matter of salaries and provisions paid to ulama, orphans, and the poor. Ibn Abu-l-Surur al-Bakri recounts a conversation that took place between his father and the governor of Egypt, who intervened to prevent this decision being ratified. Significantly, the pasha raised the question of the financial situation of the ulama, insisting that they did not deserve these financial gifts as none of them were poor, and many were wealthy traders. However the ulama, led by Shaykh Abu-l-Surur al-Bakri, persuaded the pasha to back down and "authorize the payment of [wheat] to all and sundry."[51] The last attempt, made another thirty years after this, during the time of Musa Pasha (1631), was similarly unsuccessful; the ulama continued to apply pressure until the pasha agreed not to cut off their pensions.[52]

The pressures applied by the ulama on these officials, and their incitement of the population from the pulpits of their mosques, succeeded in provoking the administration, which resolved to delay taking a final decision on the matter until it could be sure of complete success. The rise of the Köprülü vizir dynasty to power in Istanbul and its adoption of a reformist agenda[53] afforded a perfect opportunity to deal decisively with the issue. Istanbul was keen to resolve the matter as part of its wider efforts to reform the empire's shaky finances by locating new sources of revenue and reducing its financial burdens. Egypt was one of the wealthy provinces from which the sultanate was hoping to draw significant income into its treasury. To this end, it dispatched Qurra Ibrahim Pasha (1661–64), an individual noted for his severity, to increase state control of the province's revenues and to restructure the expenditures and financial burdens that weighed so heavily on the treasury.[54] It was against this backdrop that the issue of the jawamik of the ulama, orphans, and poor was reopened.[55] No sooner did new orders and decrees calling for the abolition of jawamik payments begin arriving in Cairo than the ulama of Alexandria sensed the danger. These orders were no longer concerned solely with the treasury jawamik, but also with those disbursed by endowments. The *khatt sharif* (imperial decree) of 1663 suspended the payment of jawamik to "all Arabs," a threat that necessitated rapid action on the part of the ulama of Cairo and Alexandria if they were to block it successfully. This does not imply the existence of any coordination between the two parties' efforts: each acted according to its capabilities.

Cairo's ulama were able to draw on their previous experiences to formulate a strategy of opposition to such decrees: they tended to value the effect of pressure on local authorities and insinuations that they would incite the general population to revolt. The presence of janissaries in their ranks only strengthened their position.

The abolition of jawamik always went hand in hand with attempts to abolish the *'ulufat*. Because the 'ulufat now concerned a wide variety of social classes and groups, they could not be abolished by a simple decree or order. This military connection was a potent tool in the hands of the ulama in their efforts to preserve payment of the jawamik and 'ulufat. The pashas themselves feared the consequences of such an alliance between the ulama, the merchant classes, and the military.

The situation of Alexandria's ulama was completely different. They had no links to, nor did they share interests with, the city's military garrison, which was in fact a tiny contingent of two hundred soldiers stationed in the fortresses of Alexandria and Abu Qir.[56] All the soldiers' daily requirements and salaries were provided from the imperial treasury and disbursed to them at the military bases where they were stationed. Indeed, the contingent had almost no contact with the local population, and the residents themselves preferred that the soldiers remain remote from daily urban life. As al-Jabarti wrote:

Alexandria was a respectable place, where the people stood together and spoke as one. The orders of Egypt's rulers were never carried out here: they never held sway as they did elsewhere; they never confiscated money and property. The *sirdar* appointed by them and the head of the *diwan* could only rule through the known laws.[57]

The scarcity of documents linked to this military presence in the court's records suggests the lack of any real participation in the city's social life by members of the garrison. The threat to the ulama's jawamik was therefore completely irrelevant to them. The ulama and jurists of Alexandria were forced to rely on themselves in a collective effort to frustrate the state's plans to gain control of their longstanding privileges.

The discrepancy between the social influence and power of the ulama in Cairo and Alexandria shows clearly in the approach adopted by each group in its conflict with the imperial representatives. The ulama of Alexandria used legal and religious tools in their dialogue with the authorities, while their colleagues in Cairo used the support of the janissary corps to pressurize the pashas while making reference to the dire consequences of implementing Istanbul's orders: "the suspension of religious ritual, the destruction of mosques, and the starvation of the poor," with clear implications for internal stability. The Cairene shaykhs pursued this policy right up until the nineteenth century.[58]

The authorities were well aware of the challenge that faced them. Inherent in the term 'endowment' are the concepts of inalienability and perpetuity, protecting the endowed property against seizure or efforts to modify or contravene the provisions of the founder. The state had to come up with legal arguments to open a chink in this armor. The Sublime Porte used two avenues of argument to legitimize its appropriation of charitable endowments. The first was to prove that the endowed property was in such a state of disrepair and neglect[59] that it would be impossible to repair or replace it, as a consequence of which its revenues had dwindled to such a degree that it was no longer capable of fulfilling its obligations. The second approach depended on the endowment's administrators having lost the original charters and permits *(ifraj)* issued by the diwan and ratified by the judge on behalf of the sultan. From the state's perspective, the loss or destruction of these original documents invalidated both the founder's provisions and the legal basis for the endowment's right to disburse monies in perpetuity, and allowed the possibility of state confiscation.[60]

As for the strategy deployed by the ulama of Alexandria, it was built on three main pillars. First, they used the courts to protect their rights to the endowment's revenues by producing legal documents ratified by the judicial representatives of the sultan's authority. In other words, they forcibly extracted the state's recognition that they were legally exercising their rights over the Sadir endowment. Second, they used legal argumentation to demonstrate that the founder's provisions were valid, complete, and authenticated by original documents in their possession. Confirming the validity of the founder's provisions was a primary goal of the 'comparison' carried out by the chief judge between the original charter and the copies registered in court. In the 1663 document, the judge made an explicit link between his authorizing the copy and examining the founder's provisions when he wrote:

The content of this document and the set of provisions contained therein have been ratified according to precedent by reading it word for word and scrutinizing it to our satisfaction. We have thus recorded and ratified it in accordance with the orders of the sultan and the pasha concerning these matters.[61]

Third, the ulama sought to prove that the endowment continued to generate revenues that were disbursed to its beneficiaries annually, and therefore that it continued to fulfill its function and provide services. While the judge was keen to emphasize that much of the endowment's real estate and property was dilapidated or had collapsed, he agreed that the Sadir customs continued to generate a stable income, and that the money gathered from these customs duties was distributed to the fuqaha' and the poor, "uncontested, unchallenged, and unobstructed in any way."[62]

It is clear from the respect accorded these procedures and formal regulations that the ulama had ways of blocking the state's attempts to undermine the endowment's operations and the legal basis for its perpetuity. Indeed, they were often prepared to go even further: to modify or interfere with the text of the founding charter in order to deal with the specific problems facing them. In the 1663 copy, for example, we find the following interpolation emphasized in the statement that Sultan Salah al-Din created his endowment for "the fuqaha' of Alexandria, the ulama, the imams, the murabitun and those Arabs whose names were verified . . . ."[63]

This deliberate (and illegal) addition to the text was designed to respond to the Ottoman decree that called for suspending the payment of jawamik and 'ulufat to "Arabs."[64] The ulama and jurists feared that this decree would be extended to target them and their response was this interpolation. The phrase does not appear in the other two copies of the charter.

The ulama of Alexandria were able to safeguard the privileges of the Sadir endowment and obtain the judge's endorsement of the 'valid comparison' and the endowment's perpetuity. Their fellow ulama in Cairo, however, faced more trying circumstances when they were confronted with Ibrahim Pasha's insistence that their names be removed from lists of jawamik and 'ulufat; these payments were to be restricted henceforth to the elderly, orphans, and widows. S.J. Shaw has shown that Ibrahim Pasha was indeed able to reduce the size of the lists by an unprecedented 32 percent[65] The name by which city-dwellers knew him—'The Devil'—may have special significance to those who were affected by his reduction of jawamik and 'ulufat payments.[66]

The ulama of al-Azhar continued to speak directly to Istanbul over the issue, electing Shaykh Ibrahim al-Maymuni al-Shaf'i to write a petition explaining to the Sublime Porte the dangers attendant on cutting off the payment of their pensions and salaries. Contemporary accounts make no mention of the impact this lengthy epistle[67] had on officials in Istanbul. What is known is that the ulama and military corps gradually regained their jawamik privileges, since, only a decade after the death of Ibrahim Pasha, the authorities were once again inspecting the lists. This time, however, the people were unwilling to repeat the experience and they resolved to prevent Ahmad Pasha (1675–76) from touching their jawamik. When Ahmad Pasha refused to bow to pressure on the grounds that "it was not a matter for him to decide, but for the master of the land," they decided to dismiss him and force him to flee the country and proceeded to dispatch letters to Istanbul demanding a new vizir.[68] It was at this point that the Ottoman officials became aware that the situation was slipping out of control and threatening the country's internal security, a particularly grave development since provincial stability was an Ottoman policy priority during wartime.

The state's desire to avoid a local conflagration led it to endorse the continued payment of jawamik and 'ulufat. The concession showed the ulama and the soldiers how important it was to coordinate their efforts to protect their interests. This lesson learned, it took a few short years for them to restore their former privileges and efface all vestiges of the financial reform introduced by Ibrahim Pasha. Shaw shows that expenditure rose and the treasury's income soon fell to pre-1663 levels.[69]

It became clear to officials in Istanbul that the problem of the jawamik was a grave one and unlikely to be resolved by direct means. They devised a more oblique solution: in 1710, an imperial rescript was drawn up prohibiting the inheritance, purchase, or sale of jawamik and 'ulufat, and banning the inclusion of any additional names on the lists of treasury and endowment jawamik.[70] In this way, they hoped to bring an end to all payments in the space of a single generation. The ulama failed to persuade the pasha to retract this order; nor was their petition, escorted by seven officers representing the seven janissary corps and begging the sultan to maintain the current jawamik system unaltered, any more successful. Nevertheless, the Sublime Porte ultimately resolved to allow the jawamik system to continue as before, with the condition that no names be added to the lists.

The Alexandria ulama, for their part, did not really face difficulties related to inheritance of jawamik or changes in the lists of beneficiaries from the Sadir endowment. While Salah al-Din had permitted the ulama and fuqaha' to pass on the endowment's revenues to their descendants, this was conditional on the individual beneficiary's competence, proved by attaining the rank of shaykh.[71] The jurists oversaw the addition of names to the lists. The endowment was also established for the benefit of the poor and needy, so anyone who wished to register as a beneficiary had to go before a judge and swear in the presence of witnesses that he lived in a state of poverty and owned nothing more than the rags on his back. He would receive a certificate recognizing his destitution, which in turn allowed him a share of the endowment's revenues.[72]

It is clear from the court records and the provisions of the founding charter ratified by the judge that the fuqaha' of Alexandria had complete control of these matters and that no one, no matter how influential or powerful, was able to include their names on these lists without their consent. The provisions of the endowment thus protected the lists of beneficiaries from interference by the state. However, it is worth noting that the shaykhs and the destitute beneficiaries followed the example of the Cairo ulama in selling their place on the lists to their dependents or others. This crowded the lists with the names of individuals from outside the narrow circles of shaykhs and ulama. Indeed, so widespread did the practice become that it was regarded almost as a right protected by the founder's provisions. It is significant because it allowed the ulama to pass on their privileges to their sons by simply stating before a judge that they were transferring the right to a salary from the Sadir endowment to their children. The judge would promptly recognize this forfeiture, which was known as al-faragh al-shar'i (legal cession).[73] Indeed, individuals would obtain a legal document ratifying the cession of their rights to their children while they were alive. The records contain the case of an 'alim who died some thirty-seven years after drawing up such a document, only for the judge to approve the inclusion of his children's names on the lists of beneficiaries.[74] There are also cases of children coming forward to demand their father's share without any document of cession or forfeiture to support their claim. In such cases the individual was obliged to prove that he was a scholar.[75] It should come as no surprise, then, when we find families passing down these shares in the endowment's payments from generation to generation for many decades.[76]

Though the transfer of jawamik from the primary beneficiaries to other parties particularly affected the ulama in Cairo, a restricted elite was able to protect its rights and privileges regarding these payments. This is shown by the claim made in a report that Husayn Afandi, Egypt's financial controller, drew up at the end of the eighteenth century.[77] The report stated that the jawamik "continue to be bought and sold and people continue to possess these rights with aid from the treasury." Just as the ulama of Alexandria manipulated the provisions of the founding charter to repel direct interventions by the state, their colleagues in Cairo also developed their own line of legal argumentation. They developed a position that excused and supported their interests and placed their demands in a legal framework. This made it particularly difficult for the Sublime Porte to oppose them without exposing itself to the charge that it was contravening God's laws and calling its own legitimacy into question.[78]

This mode of argumentation, expressive of an anti-authoritarian discourse, gradually took shape through letters and petitions sent to the imperial center between the fifteenth and eighteenth centuries.[79] A wide-ranging study produced by the head of al-Azhar, Shaykh al-Shabrawi, in response to an imperial rescript of 1735 that called for the abolition of the jawamik, gives us a fuller understanding of the ideas held by Egypt's ulama at the time. Although most of what it contained could be found in earlier statements, al-Shabrawi's formulation and presentation of these ideas was more effective and powerful. He was so persuasive, in fact, that calls for the suspension of the jawamik ended and Istanbul became positively supportive of the system in the wake of his work's publication. On one occasion in 1788, the state even justified a war against the Mamluks by claiming that they had cut off the "'ulufat of the poor and the jawamik of the deserving and closed the storehouses."[80] In other words, the Ottoman state made political capital out of the jawamik issue in its struggle with the Mamluk amirs who had stopped sending tribute to the treasury in Istanbul.[81] These developments tended to lend weight to the ulama's case that the system of jawamik, 'ulufat, and salaries should be maintained. Shabrawi's letter was thus the crowning act of a long period during which the ulama and fuqaha' (especially in Cairo and Alexandria) were developing new legal ideas and interpretations that buttressed their material interests and finally coalesced in the form of a powerfully expressed epistle against attempts by the authorities to appropriate their privileges.

Here it would be useful to analyze the content and import of Shabrawi's study, treating it as a public letter through which the ulama and fuqaha' of Alexandria were able, albeit indirectly, to prevent the state from extending control over their jawamik from the Sadir endowment.

Shaykh al-Shabrawi's study of jawamik

Shabrawi's letter paid special attention to three basic aspects of the jawamik issue. The first was the position of ulama, the poor, orphans, and widows. For these groups of beneficiaries, the payment of jawamik (from endowments or other institutions) was the means by which they received treasury money, to which they were entitled. The endowments themselves were no more than a means to obtain this right, especially since it was unrealistic to expect underprivileged beneficiaries to petition the sultans who ruled them. The second aspect was the practical impossibility of reducing the sums allotted to the ulama and students. They were the carriers and practitioners of religious law: thus, suspending their jawamik would destroy the rule of law and the observance of ritual, leading to the downfall of the mosques. The third and last point was that the sheer longevity of these ancient institutions meant that the jawamik and other payments were now cornerstones of the social order.

To remove them would be to threaten this order, and that could only have unpleasant consequences. This point takes the form of a veiled threat: "The populace could rise up, enraged, restless, and violent, because to cut off its livelihood will surely lead to dark deeds and moral laxity." Shabrawi emphasizes that to ignore the needs of the people would unleash chaos in Egypt; the state would find it impossible to contain this social unrest, because the endowments were a central component of the social order. To think of abolishing them was to contemplate destroying this order in its entirety.

Shabrawi implied that he was speaking on behalf of all society, and this authoritative tone undoubtedly strengthened the impact his epistle had on important actors in Istanbul. He depicted the issue of jawamik as a public concern, not the problem of a small social group fighting to protect its own interests. This was undoubtedly a deliberate tactic, a means of insinuating that the ulama would be capable of instigating a mass uprising. By claiming to speak for society, the ulama may well have been sending the Sublime Porte the message that they were the legitimate representatives of that society and that they could manipulate the masses if necessary. Their involvement in local government, especially during the eighteenth century, had cultivated a bond between the ulama and the broader population, and the Mamluks and Ottoman janissary corps always took this special relation into consideration, treating it as political fact to be ignored at the rulers' peril.

Istanbul's speedy response to the letter, its implementation of a considerably softened version of the order banning the jawamik, and the subsequent absence of any orders or decrees suspending the jawamik until the end of the eighteenth century all suggest that this was a watershed moment in a long struggle dating back to the second half of the sixteenth century. In the same vein, when Istanbul tolerated the ulama and fuqaha' of Alexandria refusing to obey the imperial rescript of 1744, which stated that the Sadir endowment should be brought under the control of state administration, this was part of a general social policy that sought to avoid confrontation with influential local social groups. This is why Ottoman policy appeared so changeable and why the Sublime Porte was reluctant to intervene comprehensively in its subjects' lives.[82]

This study has set out to demonstrate that the duplication and registration of the text of the founding charter for the Sadir endowment was not a meaningless or merely procedural act. It should instead be located in the framework of a protracted conflict between the state and its subjects over the revenues from such foundations (especially the older institutions) and the legal basis for perpetual endowments, at a time when the state was seeking effective and permanent ways of increasing its revenues from the provinces.

Because the state based its policy on challenging the validity of ancient endowments, the scholarly community of Alexandria mobilized to establish the legitimacy of its collective claims over the endowment's revenues. By basing their opposition to Ottoman policy on legal grounds, the ulama successfully forced the state to stop trying to cancel their pensions and livelihoods. Indeed, they were able to impose official acceptance of the social status quo, which worked in the interests of the endowment's beneficiaries.

The study also shows that the ulama of Alexandria were not the only social group confronting the state's attempts to abrogate their privileges. The ulama of al-Azhar in Cairo faced the same problem, albeit from a considerably more difficult position. The majority of the Cairene shaykhs drew their jawamik from the state treasury, which the authorities in Istanbul would have been able to abolish easily had the ulama not formulated a powerful and highly effective discourse that eventually forced the state to accept the payment of both forms of jawamik (that is, endowment and treasury). Indeed, the central administration did not return to this issue until the time of Muhammad 'Ali Pasha (r. 1805–48), when its highly centralized policies called for direct intervention in the administration of charitable endowments, placing oversight and management of all income and expenditure under the control of the central administration.

Notes

1   Translated from the Arabic from Robin Moger. The research for this study was carried out within the framework of a group project titled 'The City of Alexandria in the Ottoman Period,' coordinated by five French and Egyptian associations: the Institut de recherches et d'etudes sur le monde arabe et musulman (IREMAM), Aix-en-Provence; Centre d'Etudes Alexandrines (CEA), Alexandria; Institut français d'archéologie orientale (IFAO), Cairo; Centre d'Etudes et de Documentation Economiques, Juridiques et Sociales (CEDEJ), Cairo; and the Egyptian Society for Historical Studies. I was able to use some of the documents from the project's database.

2   *Jamikiya* (pl. *jamikiyyat* or *jawamik*): term designating a monthly payment drawn from waqf revenues, at the same time a salary and a gratuity. See Sulayman, *Ta'sil ma warada*, 59.

3   al-Jabarti, *'Aja'ib al-athar*, vol. 2, 203 (AH 1201/1786 CE).

4   "And he created livelihoods for the elderly, orphans, and foreigners." See Husayn Afandi al-Ruznamji, *Tartib al-diyar*, 64.

5   al-Jabarti, *'Aja'ib al-athar,* vol. 4, 299.

6   In his chronicle, al-Mallawani described two types of jawamik: the first was registered "in the name of children and offspring," in the Orphans' Register; the second was dependent on a waqf. See al-Mallawani, *Tuhfat al-ahbab*, 246.

7   al-Shurumbullali, "Tahqiq al-a'lam," folio 266.

8   During the seventeenth century, some of Egypt's Ottoman governors attempted to prevent the wealthier ulama from continuing to benefit from these jawamik, especially when they were also engaged in commercial activities. See al-Bakri, *al-Tuhfa al-bahiya*, 120. During the eighteenth century, the names of high-ranking ulama and shaykhs in Alexandria, who were renowned for their wealth, nevertheless appeared in the registers listing the beneficiaries of jawamik from the waqf of Salah al-Din. See Alexandria court dossiers, dossier 12, p. 117, doc. 81, 1787.

9   al-Hanbali, *Qala'id al-'iqiyan*, folio 82 (this jurist died in 1632).

10   The Ottoman administration's policy statements to the local population placed particular emphasis on caring for these groups, a concern expressed in almost formulaic terms: "And you must pay the utmost attention to the port of Alexandria and the welfare of the poor and destitute." See for example Alexandria court, dossier 12, p. 147; reg. 107, p. 16, doc. 29; p. 150, doc. 247. When the sultan issued an edict allocating a pension to a member of this social stratum, the recipient was systematically referred to as an orphan. See Egyptian National Archives, Daftar Mawajib al-Aytam, 1794; *Recueil de firmans*, 4.

11   Amin, *al-Awqaf*, 64, note 3.

12   al-Qalqashandi, *Subh al-a'sha*, vol. 3, 463.

13   Alexandria court, reg. 50, p. 37, doc. 88, 1663.

14   al-Hanbali, *Qala'id al-'iqiyan*, folio 82.

15   Alexandria court dossiers, dossier 12, p. 117, doc. 81, 1787.

16   Alexandria court transactions, reg. 50, p. 38, doc. 89.

17   Sulayman, *Tarikh al-mawani' al-misriya*, 88–89.

18   Alexandria court transactions, reg. 78, p. 148, doc. 207; p. 267, doc. 399.

19   Alexandria court transactions, reg. 78, p. 256, doc. 381.

20   Sulayman, *Tarikh al-mawani' al-misriya*, 163–64.

21   For more details on this phenomenon and its various social consequences, see Raymond, *al-Hirafiyyun*, 985–94.

22   For an example of a recent study discussing the importance of this type of document, see al-Misri, "Masadir dirasat al-watha'iq," 25–50.

23   Alexandria court dossiers, dossier 12, p. 125, doc. 86.

24   Alexandria court transactions, reg. 78, p. 303, doc. 495, 1744.

25   'Afifi mentions the existence of an individual appointed to this task, whose title was *muta'ahid kitab al-waqf* (keeper of the waqf book), and who was responsible for renewing permits and keeping track of rulings from the diwan as well as court deeds and correspondence. See 'Afifi, *al-Awqaf*, 101–102.

26   Significantly, the last instance I found of requests for waqf documents to be compared with an old register was dated 1786. See Alexandria court dossiers, dossier 12, p. 125, doc. 85.

27   Alexandria court transactions reg. 78, p. 145, doc. 205.

28   'Afifi, *al-Awqaf*, 41–42.

29   Alexandria court dossiers, dossier 12, p. 111, doc. 80; p. 125, doc. 85, 1787.

30   Alexandria court, reg. 50, p. 37, doc. 88, 1663.

31   On the topic of regulations for the court's notarization of copies of deeds, see Milad, *al-Watha'iq al-'uthmaniya*, 359–66.

32   Ottoman jurists agreed that witness testimony could not be admitted on reports and notarized deeds unless the words of each witness were clearly stated. See Ibn Nujaym, "al-Rasa'il," 269.

33 On validating a copy of a document by comparing it to the original, with mention of the conditions under which this was possible, and the importance of the comparison, see al-Misri, "Masadir," 26–29.

34 Alexandria court transactions, reg. 78, p. 303, doc. 459.

35 Alexandria court transactions, reg. 78, p. 145–46, doc. 206.

36 Note that the qadi's comment, entered in the register, was what clarified the scope of the problem. See the text of this comment by Shukhi Zada on the sultan's edict, Alexandria court transactions, reg. 78, p. 206, doc. 146.

37 Alexandria court transactions, reg. 78, p. 267, doc. 399.

38 Alexandria court transactions, reg. 51, p. 38, doc. 89, 1663.

39 'Afifi, al-Awqaf, 161.

40 al-Bakri, al-Tuhfa al-bahiya, 113.

41 Alexandria court, reg. 78, p. 303, doc. 459, 1745.

42 Alexandria court, reg. 78, p. 267, doc. 399, 1744.

43 Many studies have adopted this perspective. See for example al-Husari, al-Bilad al-'arabiya, 26; 'Azabawi, al-Mu'arrikhun, 209–10.

44 Shaw, Ottoman Egypt, 97.

45 Sugar, Urubba al-'uthmaniya, 212, 217–32.

46 Shaw, Financial, 231–32.

47 al-Bakri, al-Tuhfa al-bahiya, 113.

48 In 1564, revenues reached 1,830 akce, while expenses exceeded 1,890. See Sayyid, Misr fi-l-'asr al-'uthmani, 152.

49 Ibn 'Abd al-Ghani, Awdah al-isharat, 117.

50 Ibn 'Abd al-Ghani, Awdah al-isharat, 117.

51 al-Bakri, al-Tuhfa al-bahiya, 120; Combe, Précis de l'histoire, vol. 3, 27.

52 al-Bakri, al-Tuhfa al-bahiya, 151.

53 Suraiya Faroqhi has discussed this family's efforts to revive the Ottoman Empire, as well as the political and military obstacles they faced: "Crisis and Change 1590–1699," in İnalcık and Quataert, ed., An Economic and Social History, 419–31.

54 Hathaway, Siyasat al-zumur, 265.

55 Anonymous, "Zubdat Ikhtisar," folio 15; Ibn 'Abd al-Ghani, Awdah al-isharat, 156–60; al-Mallawani, Tuhfat al-ahbab, 189.

56 Shaw, Financial, 135.

57 al-Jabarti's Chronicle [Tarikh Muddat] (41 of the Arabic text).

58 al-Jabarti, 'Aja'ib al-athar, vol. 1, 254–55; vol. 4, 229.

59 Çelebi, Siyahatname Misr, 339; the writer estimates that the number of charitable waqfs had decreased in his time to 12,000, from 77,000 at the beginning of the Ottoman period, and ascribes this decrease to the state having incorporated many of them (570).

60 'Afifi, al-Awqaf, 41.

61 Alexandria court transactions, reg. 51, p. 38, doc. 89, 163.

62 Alexandria court transactions, reg. 50, p. 38, doc. 89.

63 Alexandria court transactions, reg. 50, p. 37, doc. 88.

64 Anonymous, "Zubdat Ikhtisar," folio 15; al-Mallawani, Tuhfat al-ahbab, 189.

65 Shaw, Financial, 238.

66 In contrast, Muhammad Pasha was dubbed 'Abu-l-Nur' (roughly, 'Dispenser of Light') because he was merciful and concerned with building mosques, colleges, and

schools for children. He also renovated mosques and other religious edifices. See Ibn
'Abd al-Ghani, *Awdah al-isharat*, 154–55.
67 Manuscript at the Egyptian National Library, microfilm 28747, Tarikh Taymur 1413
(this jurist died in 1668).
68 Ibn 'Abd al-Ghani, *Awdah al-isharat*, 174–75; al-Mallawani, *Tuhfat al-ahbab*, 202.
69 Shaw, *Financial*, 238.
70 Ibn 'Abd al-Ghani, *Awdah al-isharat*, 227–28; al-Mallawani, *Tuhfat al-ahbab*, 246–48.
71 Alexandria court, reg. 78, p. 303, doc. 405.
72 Alexandria court, reg. 34, p. 8, doc. 219; reg. 35, p. 195, doc. 425; p. 369, doc. 759;
reg. 114, p. 41, doc. 58.
73 Alexandria court, reg. 52, p. 420, doc. 834, 1672.
74 Alexandria court, reg. 60, p. 97, doc. 161. The document of cession was dated 1666,
and the scholar died in 1702.
75 Alexandria court, reg. 42, p. 265, doc. 850.
76 Examples include the al-Durri family (during three centuries); the al-Sa'ran family
(starting in the seventeenth century); and the Sulayman Qunayd family (starting in
the second half of the eighteenth century).
77 Husayn Afandi al-Ruznamji, *Tartib al-diyar*, 62.
78 al-Jabarti, *'Aja'ib al-athar*, vol. 1, 254–55.
79 There are four important epistles, which deserve to be studied: in chronological
order, al-Sakandari's *al-Ta'yidat*; al-Maymuni's *Taysir khaliq*; al-Safti's *'Atiyyat
al-rahman*; and al-Shabrawi's *Surat ma istadfa'*.
80 Al-Jabarti, *'Aja'ib al-athar*, vol. 2, 236.
81 Al-Jabarti, *'Aja'ib al-athar*, vol. 2, 236.
82 Sevket Pamuk's study of Ottoman fiscal policies may confirm this result, since
it concludes that Ottoman policy was primarily shaped by influential provincial
groups, which caused that policy to be selective rather than stable. See Pamuk,
al-Tarikh al-mali, 37–44, 405.

Bibliography

Egyptian National Archives
Ottoman Court Records
Alexandria dossiers, dossier 12.
Alexandria transactions, reg. 50, 78.
Alexandria court transactions, reg. 51, p. 38, doc. 89, 1663.
Alexandria Court, reg. 34, 35, 42, 50, 52, 60, 107, and 114.

Ottoman Financial Administration
Egyptian National Archives, Daftar Mawajib al-Aytam, 1794.

Publications and Other Sources
'Afifi, Muhammad. *al-Awqaf wa-l-hayah al-iqtisadiya fi Misr fi-l-'asr
al-'uthmani*. Cairo: General Egyptian Book Organization, 1991.

Amin, Muhammad Muhammad. *al-Awqaf wa-l-hayah al-ijtima'iya fi Misr, 648–923 H, 1250–1517 M: dirasa tarikiya watha'iqiya.* Cairo: Dar al-Nahda al-'Arabiya, 1980.

Anonymous. "Zubdat ikhtisar tarikh muluk Misr al-mahrusa." British Museum Library, Add 9972.

'Azabawi, 'Abd Allah. *al-Mu'arrikhun wa-l-'ulama fi Misr fi-l-qarn al-thamin 'ashr.* Cairo: General Egyptian Book Organization, 1997.

al-Bakri, Muhammad ibn Abi al-Surur. *al-Tuhfa al-bahiya fi tamalluk al-'Uthman al-diyar al-misriya.* Edited by 'Abd al-Rahim 'Abd al-Rahman 'Abd al-Rahim. Cairo: Dar al-Kutub wa-l-Watha'iq bi-l-Qahira, 2005.

Çelebi, Evliya. *Siyahatname Misr.* Translated by Muhammad 'Ali 'Awni. Cairo: Dar al-Kutub wa-l-Watha'iq al-Qawmiya, 2003.

Combe, Etienne. *Précis de l'histoire d'Egypte, par divers historiens et archéologues.* Vol. 3, *L'Egypte ottomane de la conquête par Selim (1517) à l'arrivée de Bonaparte (1798).* Cairo: n.p., 1932.

Egyptian National Library, microfilm 28747, Tarikh Taymur 1413.

al-Hanbali, Mar'i ibn Yusuf. Qala'id al-'iqiyan fi fada'il Al 'Uthman." Manuscript Library, Sohag, ms. 60 History, 1611.

Hathaway, Jane. *Siyasat al-zumur al-hakima fi Misr al-'uthmaniya (The Politics of Households in Ottoman Egypt. The Rise of the Qazdaglis).* Translated by 'Abd al-Rahman 'Abd Allah al-Shaykh. Cairo: Supreme Council for Culture, 2003.

al-Husari, Sati'. *al-Bilad al-'arabiya wa-l-dawla al-'uthmaniya.* Cairo: n.p., 1957

Husayn Afandi al-Ruznamji. "Tartib al-diyar al-misriya fi 'ahd al-dawla al-'uthmaniya: Misr fi muftaraq al-turuq," in Shafiq Ghurbal, ed., *Misr 'inda muftaraq al-turuq (1798–1801).* Special issue of the *Cairo University Journal of the Faculty of Letters*, vol. 4, part 1, May 1936.

Ibn 'Abd al-Ghani, Ahmad Shalabi. *Awdah al-isharat fi man tawalla Misr min al-wuzara wa-l-bashawat.* Edited by 'Abd al-Rahim 'Abd al-Rahman 'Abd al-Rahim. Cairo: al-Khanji, 1978.

Ibn Nujaym. "al-Rasa'il al-zayniya fi madhhab al-hanifiya," in Muhammad Ahmad Siraj and 'Ali Jum'a Muhammad, eds., *Rasa'il Ibn Nujaym al-iqtisadiya.* Cairo: Markaz al-Dirasat al-Fiqhiya wa-l-Iqtisadiya, 1999.

İnalcık, Halil, and Donald Quataert, ed. *An Economic and Social History of the Ottoman Empire.* 2 vols. Cambridge: Cambridge University Press, 1997.

al-Jabarti, 'Abd al-Rahman. *'Aja'ib al-athar fi-l-tarajim wa-l-akhbar.* 4 vols. Edited by 'Abd al-Rahim 'Abd al-Rahman 'Abd al-Rahim. Cairo: Dar al-Kutub al-Misriya, 1998.

————. *al-Jabarti's Chronicle of the French Occupation, 1798: Napoleon in Egypt [Tarikh Muddat al-Faransis bi-Misr]*. Edited and translated by S. Moreh. Leiden: E.J. Brill, 1975.

al-Mallawani, Yusuf. *Tuhfat al-ahbab biman malaka Misr min al-muluk wa-l-nuwwab*. Edited by 'Abd al-Rahim 'Abd al-Rahman 'Abd al-Rahim. Cairo: Dar al-Kitab al-Jami'i, 1998.

al-Maymuni, Ibrahim. *Taysir khaliq al-aradi wa-l-samawat bima fi ard Misr min al-jawamik wa-l-'ulufat*, 17th century, Tarikh Taymur 1413, microfilm 28747.

Milad, Salwa 'Ali. *al-Watha'iq al-'uthmaniya, dirasa arshifiya watha'iqiya li sijillat mahkamat al-Bab al-'Ali*. Alexandria: Dar al-Thaqafa al-'Ilmiya, 2000.

al-Misri, Ahmad Mahmud 'Abd al-Wahhab. "Masadir dirasat al-watha'iq al-'arabiya wa-l-islamiya." *Hawliyat islamiya* 40 (2007): 25–50.

Pamuk, Sevket. *al-Tarikh al-mali li-l-dawla al-'uthmaniya*. Translated by 'Abd al-Latif al-Haris. Beirut: Dar al-Madar al-Islami, 2005.

al-Qalqashandi. *Subh al-a'sha fi sina'at al-insha*, vol. 14. Cairo: n.p., 1913–19.

Raymond, André. *al-Hirafiyyun wa-l-tujjar fi-l-Qahira fi-l-qarn al-thamin 'ashr* (*Artisans et commerçants au Caire au XVIIIᵉ siècle*). 2 vols. Translated by Nasir Ahmad Ibrahim and Patsy Jamal al-Din. Cairo: Supreme Council for Culture, 2005.

Recueil de firmans impériaux ottomans adressés aux valis et aux khedives d'Egypte (1597–1904). Cairo: Institut français d'archéologie orientale, 1934.

al-Safti, 'Isa. *'Atiyat al-rahman fi sihhat irsad al-jawamik wa-l-atyan*. Fiqh Taymur, microfilm 679.

al-Sakandari, Muhammad al-Ghayti. *al-Ta'yidat al-'aliya li-l-awqaf al-misriya*, 16th century, Fiqh Shaf'i 1162, microfilm 42854.

Sayyid, Sayyid Muhammad. *Misr fi-l-'asr al-'uthmani fi-l-qarn al-sadis 'ashr: dirasa watha'iqiya fi-l-nuzum al-idariya wa-l-qada'iya wa-l-maliya wa-l-'askariya*. Cairo: Madbuli, 1997.

al-Shabrawi, 'Abd Allah. *Surat ma istadfa' ahl Misr hadithat ibtal al-murattabat min al-'ulufat lamma amara mawlana al-Sultan Mahmud Khan bi Ibtaliha* (classified with a manuscript titled *Suwar al-faramanat al-sadira min umara' al-Faransiya fi Misr min muddat al-thawra*). Institute for the Revival of Arabic Manuscripts, 100 Tarikh Maktaba, Sohag.

Shaw, S.J. *The Financial and Administrative Organization and Development of Ottoman Egypt, 1517–1798*. Princeton, NJ: Princeton University Press, 1962.

————. *Ottoman Egypt in the Age of the French Revolution*. Cambridge: Harvard University Press, 1964.

al-Shurumbullali al-Wafayi, Hasan ibn 'Ammar ibn Yusuf. "Tahqiq al-a'lam al-waqifin 'ala mafad 'ibarat al-waqifin," in al-Tahqiqat al-qudsiya wa-l-nashat al-rahmaniya fi-l-rasayil al-husayniya li-l-sadat al-hanafiya. Unpublished manuscript dated 1656. Manuscript collection, Hanafi Jurisprudence, no. 1640 (Library of Hasan Jalal Pasha), Egyptian National Archives.

Sugar, Peter. *Urubbat al-'uthmaniya 1354–1804 (Southeastern Europe Under Ottoman Rule, 1354–1804)*. Translated by 'Asim al-Disuqi. Cairo: Dar al-Thaqafa al-Jadida, 1998.

Sulayman, 'Abd al-Hamid. *Tarikh al-mawani' al-misriya fi-l-'asr al-'uthmani*. Tarikh al-Misriyyin Series 89. Cairo: General Egyptian Book Organization, 1995.

Sulayman, Ahmad al-Sa'id. *Ta'sil ma warada fi tarikh al-Jabarti min al-dakhil*. Cairo: Dar al-Ma'arif, 1979.

4

Control of Urban Waqfs in al-Salt, Transjordan

Michael J. Reimer

As has been amply demonstrated by historians of the Middle East, the institution of waqf was essential to the support of religious and social services from the period of the establishment of military patronage states in medieval Islam[1] and on into the high noon of Ottoman hegemony over the region.[2] What is not so often remembered, but which is of significance for the study of the modern era, is that these foundations continued their work during the era of Ottoman reform and even into the post-Ottoman era. Indeed, inasmuch as Ottoman society could not have functioned without endowed properties to support a panoply of communal institutions that would now be considered responsibilities of the bureaucratic state in the Middle East, including the financing of education, hospitals, mosques, even certain infrastructural facilities such as roads, bridges, hostels, and water systems, it is not superfluous to emphasize that, in the uncertainty and turbulence of the immediate post-Ottoman period, the continued operation of charitable foundations was quite as necessary to the normal functioning of society as it had been under Ottoman rule. Of course, as in the study of earlier periods, one must be careful to distinguish among the wide variety of endowments that had been made and continued to be made, as well as the evolving legal framework within which waqfs were established and in which waqf law was interpreted and applied.

The study of waqf in the modern Middle East must therefore begin with the era of unifying and centralizing initiatives of the Ottoman reform movement commonly subsumed under the rubric *Tanzimat*. This era is customarily delimited by the Gülhane Hatt-i Şherifi (The Noble Rescript of the Rose Garden) of Sultan Abdülmecit (1839) and the suspension of the Ottoman parliament, and the subsequent dissolution of parliament by Sultan Abdülhamit II (1878). This periodization is somewhat arbitrary, since centralizing reforms were undertaken by Mahmut II (Abdülmecit's father) well before 1839, and Abdülhamit II's reign witnessed neither a return to the disaggregated system of governance that had existed in the eighteenth century nor a rescission of the most far-reaching enactments of the Tanzimat. Nonetheless, this period is certainly distinguished by a marked acceleration of legislative reform and administrative activism, and most significantly by a shift in the locus of power from the sultans to a reforming bureaucratic elite, or, as it is usually put metonymically, from the Palace to the Sublime Porte.

The original impulse for reform was the overarching need to meet the military challenge of Europe, which Ottoman statesmen realized would require an unprecedented mobilization of the empire's human and material resources. It is not accidental that the three landmark moments of the Tanzimat (the decrees of 1839, 1856, and 1876) occurred in the midst of crises precipitated by war (the Mehmet 'Ali rebellion, the Crimean War, and the Balkan revolts, respectively). As Carter Findley has suggested, an agenda of modernizing reform was grafted onto the traditional regulatory power of the state, which was already acknowledged as legitimate and which was expressed in the sultan's prerogative in promulgating laws or codes of law (*kanun*s or *kanunname*s). Moreover, wherever the center of power happened to be at the moment, whether Palace or Porte, the unquestioned objective of reform was always the same, that is, the maximization of state power.[3] Indeed, it is not too much to assert, as Kemal Karpat has put it, that the reforms of the nineteenth century "changed the very meaning of government as known until then in the Ottoman Empire."[4] In practical terms, this power depended first and foremost upon finance, so it is not surprising to find that among the priorities enunciated in the Gülhane Hatt-i Sherifi was the abolition of tax-farming. Moreover, the Ottoman reformers believed that the establishment of 'justice' (which meant, among other things, the security of property rights) would unleash the energies of society, create new wealth, and generate ever-greater revenues for the state. They were therefore determined to revamp inherited judicial agencies and procedures and to produce new tribunals and codes that would stabilize land tenures and facilitate commercial transactions in particular. Finally, the Tanzimat reformers shared the nineteenth-century's faith in education, not only or primarily as a means of enlightenment, but as a way of training cadres of technical and administrative personnel for new government functions. Public education was also a vehicle for inculcating *Osmalılık* (Ottomanism), itself a controversial notion since it implied that the peoples of the empire should be loyal to an Ottoman national community rather than the sacred person of the sultan.[5]

Given this aggressive agenda of reform, and particularly the concern for increasing the financial resources of the state as rapidly as possible, it was inevitable that the Tanzimat would affect profoundly the institution of waqf. The impact was twofold: waqf property supported functions, like education, over which the state now wished to exercise its supervision and control; and properties held in waqf and their revenues represented an enormous pool of assets shielded, at least theoretically, from the state's administrative and extractive manipulations. Thus, as John Robert Barnes argues in his study of Ottoman waqf, the Tanzimat governments used a great variety of means, including some that Barnes (citing contemporary observers) clearly regards as legally dubious, to reclaim waqf revenues for the state. These included the direct collection of the tithe owed on waqf properties by government tax collectors or farmers (*muhassil*s and *multazim*s), where collection had been formerly in the hands of the waqf administrators (*mutawalli*s). Other means of confiscation were also used, such as takeovers of waqf assets where such assets were constituted as a state monopoly (as with saltworks, for instance); takeovers resulting from the extinction of the family line to whom assets had been dedicated; and takeovers based on accusations of maladministration and/or the ruin of the waqf properties themselves. At all events, the state moved decisively wherever the Tanzimat was applied to reduce the autonomy of the mutawalli or to displace him entirely, and to substitute directors from the Ministry of Evkaf (Religious Endowments) in Istanbul; or, where the mutawalli maintained a tenuous hold over waqf assets, he found himself constrained by agents of the increasingly powerful Ministry of Finance.[6] Increasing state intrusion into the affairs of waqf occurred also by means of accounting and inspection. Barnes notes regarding a regulation concerning waqf enacted in 1843: "An imperial decree had been issued to the effect that all evkaf within the Ottoman dominions were to have their accounts inspected yearly by officials and by the canonical courts, after which they were to have their revenues and signed account registers *(defatir-i mumzaya)* sent to the Imperial Evkaf Treasury."[7] This particular means of bringing waqf into the realm of state regulation and control continued in the post-Ottoman era, as will be studied below. However, it is appropriate to conclude this brief discussion of the history of Ottoman waqf with Barnes's assessment of the overall effect of the Tanzimat on foundations:

> In its attempt to get its hands on the considerable evkaf revenue that existed in all provinces of the empire, the Ottoman government disenfranchised many mütevellis and members of the religious orders of their right to evkaf income. They were required to petition the government frequently for a basic living allowance after their evkaf property had been tithed and taken over by state officials. With the establishment of Tanzimat regulations regarding land tenure in the provinces, the takeover of the business of tax collection by muhassils, and the transfer of administration from the mütevellis to the Imperial Evkaf Ministry, the way was paved for the centralization of all evkaf throughout the empire and the direct control by the state of its revenue. Regrettably, the new arrangement was not to the benefit of the religious foundations.[8]

It is easy to detect parallels between the measures introduced by the Tanzimat reformers throughout the Ottoman Empire and the machinations of colonial states as they sought to reclassify or confiscate the assets of waqf. Such was particularly the case in North Africa, as delineated by Medici in this volume (see chapter 7). The Ottomans possessed however an incomparable advantage over colonial polities in being generally regarded as the legitimate guardians of Muslim identities and interests in an age when these were increasingly jeopardized by non-Muslim aggression. This legitimacy did not preclude local resistance to centralizing measures, but it did mean that the resistance was of a different character and employed different methods, from that of anti-colonial struggles.

However, the long arm of the Tanzimat, with its potentially ominous impact on waqf, was late in reaching the outlying parts of the Ottoman Empire. Our focus here is on the section of southern Syria that became Transjordan, and specifically on its largest town in late Ottoman times, al-Salt. Al-Salt is located in the mountainous but fertile region known as the Balqa and lies twenty-eight kilometers west of modern Amman. Al-Salt's prominence is due not only to its excellent soil and water resources, but also to its command of a strategic pass through the mountains of Transjordan to central Palestine. It was one of the few communities in Transjordan prior to the First World War that can be said to have developed a quasi-urban ethos. Its population in 1913 was estimated at ten thousand souls in 1913, and this is probably an underestimate. In spite of the devastation of many areas in Syria in the latter stages of the war, al-Salt's population in the postwar era remained relatively substantial. Its increasing wealth and sophistication were evidenced by a variety of changes occurring in the appearance and organization of the town. Prewar growth was seen in the construction of imposing multistory limestone houses in and around the town's commercial and administrative center. It was also demonstrated in the establishment of the *baladiya* (municipality) in al-Salt in 1892, which had as its primary task the regulation of the town's increased traffic and the planning and improvement of the street network; a local educational council was set up in 1883, which advised concerning the new Ottoman school, which later became the most prominent secondary school in the entire country. The first new Ottoman school was set up in 1881. The town's growth included the multiplication of *madafa*s, a quasi-public facility that served as both meetinghouse and hostel, which were built for the most prominent families and clans. It was in the madafa of Yusuf al-Sukkar, one of al-Salt's most eminent merchants, that Sir Herbert Samuel met the notables of Transjordan in 1921, prior to the creation of the Emirate.[9]

Eugene Rogan has shown that the Tanzimat's military and bureaucratic machinery arrived in the Balqa in the 1860s and was then gradually able to establish effective Ottoman rule over a notoriously fractious population, which was internally divided into a welter of regional, tribal, and confessional groupings. Nevertheless, by the 1870s one may say with justice that al-Salt and most of the Balqa had been subdued by the Ottomans, and that (to use the terms of local tribal historiography) *zaman al-shuyukh,* the era of the tribal predominance, began to give way to *zaman al-hukuma*, the era of state control.[10] The establishment of some of the institutions noted in the previous paragraph—regulatory, educational, commercial—are again evidence of the relative stability and security that the Ottoman state brought with it. Perhaps the most decisive piece of evidence is also the best known, that is, the building of the Hijaz railway through Transjordan, built in the years 1901–1908. It is not surprising, given this burst of state-directed activity in the late nineteenth century, to find that the Tanzimat had its impact on the position of waqfs in al-Salt as well, though in more ambiguous ways than those described by Barnes, who posits a catastrophic decline precipitated by the government's intervention in the affairs of waqf, "the fleecing of Islam by the state"[11]—an allegation which by the way essentializes both religion and polity and raises a host of questions that will have to remain in abeyance in the present study.

Turning rather to southern Syria/Transjordan, our purpose here is to survey briefly some legal documents related to waqf in al-Salt, which have been located and collected by Jordanian scholars. The major source used herein is a corpus of such documents published by Dr. Mohammad A. Khriesat in 1997 as part of a larger collection of insightful articles on al-Salt. Dr. Khriesat has transcribed and in some cases abridged eighteen documents related to waqf, including endowment deeds, official correspondence, and administrative orders. Some of this material has also been published and/or summarized and discussed in the work of Dr. George Tarif Dawud, in his encyclopedic study entitled *al-Salt wa jiwaruha, 1864–1921* (Amman, 1994).[12]

The method followed in interrogating the documents has been to first categorize the types of property donated and the specific institutions to which the donations were made; then, to examine the provenance and social class of the founders, as far as this can be determined. I have also offered some details concerning the mutawallis that throws light on changes in the social demography of al-Salt. Finally, we will consider the evolving treatment of waqf properties by local administrators and government officials and the legal discourse in which waqf was embedded. I should add that I had begun this study with the additional assumption that waqf constituted a major category of property throughout the period under investigation in al-Salt, as it did in many other Ottoman cities and towns. The evidence for this hypothesis is contradictory: as it will become evident, the documents surveyed from the 1920s indicate that only a small percentage of property in al-Salt was held as waqf dedicated to the maintenance of the two mosques. Dr. George Tarif Dawud has shown, however, that substantial amounts of agricultural property outside the town were also endowed as a kind of waqf, though its legal status was more questionable, since the Ottomans—like other Islamic governments before them—insisted that they held a presumptive right to the land on the basis of its conquest and administration for the benefit of the entire community or *umma*.[13] To muddle the picture yet further, in spite of the seemingly small waqf endowments on behalf of the town's two mosques, the mutawalli of the town's older and larger mosque made substantial loans using waqf revenues—including loans to the municipality—which had accumulated to such an extent that the department of waqfs in al-Salt was threatening to distrain the town's property until it had settled its debts to the account of the waqfs.[14] In addition, there is clear evidence of waqf properties supporting other institutions unrelated to the town's mosques, such as the madafas mentioned above.[15]

We are left with a confused picture of the quantitative value of the waqf in this period. Despite these uncertainties, however, the existing documents remain a useful source for the qualitative study of the categories noted above. In particular, they demonstrate the ambivalence of the state's position vis-à-vis waqf endowments. On the one hand, the legitimacy of the Ottoman state, and that of the Sharifian regimes that succeeded it, rested upon its upholding of the *shari'a*; in practical terms, this meant respect for venerable institutions such as waqf. Thus, the Tanzimat reformers, even at their most radical, avoided contravening what were understood to be clear commands of the shari'a.[16] Moreover, the state remained incapable—even after the implementation of Tanzimat reforms—of replacing the vast network of services and stipends that waqf rendered to urban elements throughout the empire.[17] Against this, however, was the state's quest for revenues that were withheld from it by the very nature of the institution and by the inherent tendency of the mutawallis to guard waqf assets from government impositions and surveillance. These contradictory impulses can be seen working themselves out in both the late Ottoman Empire and in the new state of Transjordan, as elsewhere in the Middle East.

We begin by listing the types of property endowed upon the mosques within the town of al-Salt, of which there were five: the *dukkan* (a shop or store); the *dar* (a house, or residential property); the *tahuna* (a grain or water mill); the *karm* (a vineyard); and the *bustan* or *hakura* (a horticultural garden, usually having fruit trees). In a majority of cases, only sections (*qirat*s) of these properties were given in endowment, that is, they were not donated in their entirety since they comprised fractional legacies owned by the person making the donation. As Barnes has noted, this sort of endowment was particularly vulnerable to impositions by the state, since the property as a whole remained liable to ordinary taxation.[18] In addition, the endowment of fractions of properties must have complicated the work of the mutawalli, who was in principle responsible for leasing out the property; it seems in some cases— especially where the endowment was of little value to begin with—to have rendered the waqf all but useless to its intended beneficiary and may explain why certain diminutive bequests simply disappeared from the records. Since we know that waqfs were sometimes converted into cash through sale of the endowments, it is entirely possible that this explains such disappearances.[19]

As noted above, the documents located and collected by Jordanian scholars are those that detail the endowments made in support of the two mosques of al-Salt, which were known locally as the 'Big Mosque' (al-Jami' al-Kabir) and the 'Small Mosque' (al-Jami' al-Saghir). The Big Mosque had a long history in al-Salt while the Small Mosque was new, having been established only at the end of the Ottoman period (1907) and built with local funds during a period of business expansion that tied al-Salt more closely into broader regional networks of production and trade within greater Syria.[20] A possible explanation for the rather narrow range and modest value of the properties endowed is to be found in the long-standing poverty and paucity of population in the region—thus, none of the endowments we have seen go back to before the 1880s—and the fact that institutions often associated with mosque foundations in other locations, such a schools and medical facilities, were introduced into the region by Catholic or Protestant missionaries or, when the Ottomans began to curtail such activities in the 1880s, by the Ottoman state itself.[21] It is also clear evidence of the shallow roots of urbanism in Transjordan. It was only in the latter half of the nineteenth century that al-Salt's economy began to be invigorated by quantum increases in commerce, as an allogeneous merchant elite began to settle in Transjordan. But, strikingly, these merchants do not seem to have been active in making endowments to expand the town's mosque complexes, preferring perhaps to invest in houses, shops, warehouses, and lands. Certainly the prestige and security offered by agricultural lands made this the most attractive form of investment. Rogan writes concerning Palestinian and Syrian merchants in al-Salt:

> What is certain is that these merchant immigrants emerged over the course of the 1880s and 1890s as some of the largest landholders in the district of Salt; that land tenure represented one of several ways in which merchant immigrants diversified their capital investments in the district; and that the control gained over agricultural properties meant that the great merchant families dominated economic activity in Salt and its district from cultivation through marketing and exportation.[22]

It is also likely that, given the transitory character of many of these "merchant immigrants," they preferred to repatriate their profits to support institutions and foundations in their hometowns. The growing mobility of persons and capital in late-nineteenth-century Syria points incidentally to the historiographical need, still too seldom recognized, to study Syrian society as a whole, even after it was split up into separate states by the establishment of the French and British mandates.[23]

As far as I have been able to ascertain, the persons who did make endowments in al-Salt shared few common characteristics, except of course some sort of connection to the town. Hana' bint Darwish, an Egyptian woman from the town of Bilbays in the Delta, who had lived for a while in al-Salt, donated fractions of some houses and a shop she inherited from her husband, who had apparently acted as the warden *(sajjan)* of the local jail; Muhammad Afandi Abu al-Tuyur, Ottoman district governor *(qa'immaqam)* in al-Salt in the early 1880s, donated three shops; another, unnamed, Turkish officer made over a house, also in the 1880s; a couple of prominent Saltis, one from a Christian family, donated a few shares in local grain mills; another local from one of the most prominent clans in the town, known as *hamulat al-'Awamila*, donated some sections of a garden; and several other persons, probably of local origin, donated six shops, which later came into dispute (a subject to which I will return). There were several other small endowments for which there are no data concerning their origin. It is worth noting again the modest number and value of the endowments; the fact that many of the properties donated were from officials or other non-residents; and the remarkable absence of the immigrant commercial elite from the list of founders of waqf.[24]

We turn now to the administrators, or mutawallis, of the properties endowed upon the Big Mosque in al-Salt. The first two mutawallis whose names and origins are given in our documents are Shaykh Mustafa bin Yusuf bin Zayd al-Qadiri (fl. 1890), whose family hailed from Nablus; his immediate successor was Ibrahim al-Dabsi al-Shami of Damascus.[25] It becomes immediately clear that, while the immigrant elite was not doing much to enlarge the endowments of the town's central mosque, they were keenly interested in controlling the disposal of its revenues. Moreover, the office of mutawalli was not passed on from father to son—another possible indication of the social flux in al-Salt at the time. In addition, the documents offer some tantalizing details about Ibrahim al-Dabsi al-Shami, who was installed as mutawalli of the Big Mosque around 1903. The act of installation confirms him in the right to receive one-tenth of the revenue of the waqfs dedicated to the mosque "in imitation of the administrators of waqf similar to him in Damascus" *(uswatan amthalihi al-nuzzar al-shar'iyyun bi-Dimashq al-Sham)*,[26] suggesting a certain local civic pride in al-Salt by 1903, that allowed its elite to dare the comparison with, and emulation of, the great metropolis to the north—something that would have sounded absurd only a few decades before, when al-Salt was a tiny, insecure provincial settlement and enmeshed in a world of tribal politics. It also suggests that a Damascene mutawalli insisted on the same kind of treatment he would have received at home. Another telling detail is that the character of the mutawalli was attested by persons said to be of local origin or long residence. To be precise, the character witnesses for Ibrahim al-Dabsi al-Shami are called *sukkan al-Salt* (the inhabitants of al-Salt), and were thus probably long-term residents. This may indicate that persons from outside al-Salt (or at least recent immigrants) could not transact important business at court or assume positions of leadership within the town unless they had local or long-resident sponsors. As Rogan points out, consciousness of one's relative identity as 'indigenous' or 'foreign' to al-Salt was strongly marked from at least the 1880s on.[27] At the same time, it also indicates that the power and authority of the immigrant elite had risen sharply, represented here by their control over the local revenues and assets represented by waqf.

Another evocative detail emerges from a record of a quite different transaction in waqf revenues that the new mutawalli conducted soon after his installation.[28] The records show that just after assuming his position as mutawalli al-awqaf, Ibrahim al-Dabsi al-Shami undertook to loan 16,366 piasters from the waqf funds under his control to two Damascenes residing in al-Salt (Abduh Afandi bin Muhammad bin Husayn al-Khatib and Saʻid Afandi bin Muhammad Khayr bin ʻAli Abu Qura), this total incorporating a 'hidden' interest charge by adding a fictive purchase of books totaling 2,727 piasters.[29] The size of this loan is much larger than the average loans of the 1880s and 1890s as ascertained by Rogan; it raises the question as to how such a substantial accumulation of cash occurred, especially since the capital reserve represented by the endowments was small. The data also has an additional use: fixing for us the cost of capital in the local economy at the time, which was almost exactly twenty percent. Moreover, the nearness in time of the two events—his installation and his agreement to issue a substantial loan out of waqf revenues (a controversial practice, frowned upon by some jurists)—leads to the impression that they are linked. Both the lender (on behalf of the waqf) and the borrowers were from Damascus, and the loan is substantial: was Ibrahim al-Dabsi al-Shami's installation an intentional step toward releasing a significant reserve of funds, tied up in al-Salt's provincial economy and by the legal restrictions applied to waqf, into a wider economic sphere of greater Syria? Whether the intention was there, the effect was the reinforcement of a trend documented by Rogan, that is, the incremental integration of Transjordan into regional and Mediterranean markets and the steady monetarization of the area.[30] Of the social impact of this transformation, Rogan writes:

> The changes which occurred in the economic life of Transjordan had direct implications for its society. A greater degree of mixing took place between residents of the different districts of Transjordan, and

Transjordanians interacted more intensely with natives of other parts of Greater Syria. Native speakers of Turkish mixed with Arabs as never before in the villages and steppes of Transjordan, as the local people came to know Ottoman officialdom at first hand. And people were growing used to living with Europeans. Intermarriage and travel also added to this broadening of horizons. Not all such exchanges were beneficial. The social ills which accompany times of rapid change also came to trouble the towns and countryside of Transjordan.[31]

As noted above, among the new institutions set up during this period, which saw the "broadening of horizons" in al-Salt, was a new mosque: the Small Mosque. Its mutawalli in the prewar period was the mufti of al-Salt, Shaykh Muhammad Salih Afandi bin al-Sayyid Khalil Amraysh, who in 1912 was also appointed to become its imam and *khatib*, and to receive fifty piasters annually for his labors, to be paid out of waqf revenues. This was an absolute pittance even for the period, and it raises a question as to why such a derisory sum is even mentioned. In addition, the somewhat insulting term *ujra* (a hired laborer's wage) is used. This is in contrast to the more dignified circumlocution which appears in Ibrahim al-Shami's appointment as mutawalli of the Big Mosque, where the text reads "*udhinat lahu . . . tanawwul 'ushr al-mutahassal*" (it is granted to him to receive a tenth of the revenue). Is this perhaps a semantic pointer of the difference in status between the office of mutawalli and that of an imam or khatib? Nonetheless, he is the mufti of the town and, as we shall see, a formidable figure in regional religious affairs, so it is a strangely abrupt manner of speaking about him for which we have no explanation.[32]

The two mosques of al-Salt and their assets in waqf, and the position of Muhammad Salih Amraysh, feature prominently in another set of documents, this time from the 1920s.[33] After the establishment of the Anglo-Hashemite government in 1921, the new authorities began to seek information about the assets of the territories under their control. Waqf constituted a category of property of some importance; its jurisdiction at the time fell to the supreme judicial authority in Transjordan, *qadi al-qudah*, whose office in 1922 requested full lists and, in particular, financial accounts of the property that had been donated to support the two mosques in al-Salt.[34] The inquiries were naturally made to the mutawallis of the waqfs attached to the two mosques, who were, at this time, Shaykh Muhammad Afandi Manku, and the mufti, Muhammad Salih Amraysh, both of Palestinian origin.[35] The inquiry asked for detailed information to be copied from the ledger books of the waqf, including the type of property held, the donor, the conditions attaching to the donation, the date of donation, the endowment itself, the mutawalli or mutawallis, and the record of receipts and expenditures—precisely the same sort of inspection and regulation the Ottoman government had been seeking to obtain since it issued its decree concerning waqf in 1843.[36]

The instructions of qadi al-qudah may have been somewhat irksome for the mutawallis of waqf in al-Salt, but they are helpful to us in taking stock of the assets that had been deeded to the support of the mosques, which I have cataloged above. Shaykh Muhammad Afandi Manku complied immediately with Qadi al-qudah's request, furnishing a full account of the assets drawn upon by the Big Mosque and its attendants. His cooperation and connections with the emerging judicial establishment in Amman were certainly why, in 1927, he was named by the Amman authorities as the custodian of the imposing foundation of Abi 'Ubayda in the Jordan Valley, whose tangled history and legal status has been examined in painstaking detail by Michael Fischbach.[37]

The mutawalli of the Small Mosque, Muhammad Salih Amraysh, was not nearly so forthcoming. He did finally render a partial account of the mosque's waqf properties, which showed modest holdings in commercial property and a section of a vineyard. According to his report, he undertook his tasks as imam and khatib for God and without remuneration *("majanan wa ihtisaban li-wajh Allah")*.[38] However, the most intriguing aspect of his report is his insistence that the government judiciary had no authority in the matter, that matters of waqf were under the jurisdiction of the mufti. The correspondence on this point reveals a dispute over the application of an Ottoman law passed in 1912 or 1913—that is, just before the war—which apparently designated the mufti the head of local committees *(lijan al-awqaf)* that were given authority for the management of waqf, but which was not implemented by the Arab government, presumably a reference to the brief period of Amir Faysal's rule in Syria, 1918–20.[39] The mufti may have been unusually surly, but his case is made more credible when one considers that he was the author of a law book entitled *Sharh majallat al-ahkam al-'adliya* (Explanation of the Ottoman Legal Code), as well as several other volumes.[40] There was also an element of personal pique in the dispute between the qadi al-qudah and the mufti of al-Salt, which can be illuminated by referring to his biography.[41]

The mufti of al-Salt, Muhammad Salih Amraysh, was a man of considerable religious prestige and learning. He had been born in Nablus around 1860 to a man of modest station (his father is said to have been a grocer). After receiving what Nablus could offer him in the way of education, he traveled to Egypt in 1890, where he studied for a period of ten years and where he came under the influence of Muhammad Abduh and through him the ideas of Jamal al-Din al-Afghani. He returned to Nablus in 1900 after receiving his degree in teaching and jurisprudence. He occupied a variety of educational and legal positions in the district of Nablus until he became the qadi and mufti in the town of al-Salt, and then a teacher and administrator of al-Salt's secondary school, where he appears to have influenced an entire generation of students who were to play an important role in Transjordan and the surrounding areas. At some point he also journeyed to Istanbul and is said to have met Sultan Abd al-Hamid II and Qadi 'Askar Abu al-Huda al-'Ayadi. Later he also journeyed to the Hijaz, met with Sharif Husayn and his family, and seems to have joined with the Arab revolt after its outbreak in 1916. He was appointed qadi al-qudah of the short-lived independent government of al-Salt in 1918. (He died in Nablus in 1945 and was buried there.)

Clearly, Shaykh Muhammad Amraysh was not a man to be trifled with. He had occupied a position equivalent to that of the newly appointed qadi al-qudah and had formidable credentials deriving from his training at al-Azhar, his Ottoman period legal and administrative appointments, his Arab-nationalist activities (he was apparently jailed by the Ottoman authorities at one point), and his service to the postwar Arab government based in Damascus. It seems that he was not about to begin submitting reports to a parvenu, especially when such a requirement contravened what he knew to be Ottoman law, which, in the absence of abrogating legislation, remained in force in Transjordan. In the end, qadi al-qudah received a report based on information gathered by the mutawalli of the Big Mosque, which showed incidentally that the revenues of the Small Mosque were hardly worth bothering about. But the revenues from waqf, small as they were in relative terms, remained important enough to inquire about—one must remember the extremely small dimensions of the Transjordanian government and population at the time. As noted above, the municipality of al-Salt borrowed heavily from these revenues, beginning in the 1920s, and was deep in debt to the town's waqfs by the 1930s.

Before concluding, let us examine one last controversy concerning waqf that takes us back into the Ottoman period but carries us forward into the early history of the Emirate of Transjordan, and thus illustrates very neatly the tug of war between central government (whether in Istanbul or Amman) and local authorities (in this case, in al-Salt) over waqf.[42] The case begins in the 1880s, when the Ottoman ministry of education assumed control over six shops that had been endowed upon the Big Mosque in al-Salt. The mutawalli of the Big Mosque, probably by appealing to the Islamic court, was able to intervene, and revenues reverted for a short time to the mosque, but at some point the ministry was able to regain control of the revenues. Undoubtedly, the logic of the state was that when it assumed responsibilities for tasks previously devolving upon institutions supported by waqf, it also obtained the right to receive revenues from waqf.[43] Interestingly, the same property was still in dispute in the 1920s, when an administrative decision acknowledged the long history of the waqf's claim but awarded the property nonetheless to the new state's department of education. In this case, which was the source of protracted legal and administrative wrangling, we have an example of the ascendancy of state power over the properties and revenues controlled by a hitherto autonomous regime of waqf, a clear legacy of the Tanzimat reforms.

In conclusion, waqf documents from al-Salt offer insights into the creation and control of waqf properties in provinces of the Ottoman Empire, in particular Transjordan, and demonstrate the continuity of this institution in the early history of the emirate. In particular, they show, as I have just suggested, the conflicts generated by the Ottoman state's quest to regulate and appropriate waqf for the benefit of modernizing projects like civil education, which clashed with longstanding conventions concerning waqf property as well as the insistence of local authorities on their right to safeguard such properties from what they perceived as illegitimate uses. Moreover, they show the incoherence of the state despite the centralizing tendencies of the Tanzimat regulation, since—in the last case examined—the courts and sometimes also administrative agents of the state could use their authority to override, at least temporarily, the policy objectives of the state in order to uphold a venerable Islamic principle (here, the inalienability of waqf) and protect the claims of prominent local families. Precisely the same tensions bedeviled the new states which took over from the Ottomans after the collapse of the empire in 1918, as is seen in the government of Transjordan's efforts to collect data concerning waqf and regulate its use, and the resistance of local notables to the state's pretensions.

As an epilogue to this summary, it is perhaps germane to add that governments of Transjordan did not attempt to reform the waqf law inherited from the Ottomans until the issuing of a constitution upon the attainment of independence. Thus, from the standpoint of law and administration pertaining to waqf foundations, the era of the Tanzimat lasted effectively from 1864 until 1946. In the 1946 law, the Transjordanian government recognized in theory the sole authority of Shar'i courts to establish waqfs and to intervene in their internal administration; nonetheless, the autonomy of the Shar'i courts was compromised by the fact that a Supreme Council of Waqfs (al-Majlis al-A'la li-l-Awqaf) was set up, under the direct supervision of the prime minister's office and with members appointed by the prime minister, to oversee the day-to-day administration of waqfs. Moreover, the revenues accruing from the waqf foundations were paid into a central fund out of which all expenditures were to be made. The Supreme Council was also granted the power to set procedures and issue instructions not only to its own employees but to local committees and to mutawallis who remained nominally in charge of waqf foundations in the localities.[44] The concentration of both administrative and fiscal authority in the hands of the Supreme Council of Waqfs was of course precisely the kind of centralizing trajectory that Sayyid Muhammad Amraysh had fought against in the 1920s. It reached a kind of culmination in the 1946 constitution, just in time to supply the state with an instrument for the control not only of the relatively meager assets of religious foundations in Transjordan, but as it happened, over the vast proceeds of the waqfs attached to Jerusalem and other Palestinian institutions after the annexation of the West Bank in 1949, a vast and provocative subject of research that is worthy of a much larger and more deeply documented study.[45]

Notes

1   The term belongs to Hodgson, *Venture of Islam*, vol. 2, 402–408. The passage in question takes the Mongol state as the archetype of the military patronage state, but the Seljuq system, under which the employment of waqf first became widespread, was similar in its political and social structure (51–52).
2   An outstanding study of the latter is 'Afifi, *al-Awqaf*.
3   Findley, "Ottoman Administrative Legacy," 159–60.
4   Karpat, "Transformation," 252.
5   Abu-Manneh, "The Sultan."
6   Barnes, *Introduction*, 118–27.
7   Barnes, *Introduction*, 130.
8   Barnes, *Introduction*, 117.
9   Khriesat, *Dirasat*, 11, 38–42, 44, 50, 58–59, and 91–93. On Samuel's visit to the al-Sukkar madafa, see Wilson, *Abdullah*, 46–47.
10 Rogan, *Frontiers*, ch. 2. Shryock, *Nationalism*, 65. Note however that the late Ottoman period is contained in tribal memory within the 'age of shaykhs,' in spite of clear documentary evidence that Ottoman state authority became increasingly intrusive in the late nineteenth century. In retrospective memory, only with the coming of Emir Abdullah are the tribespeople willing to acknowledge a final and irreversible diminution of shaykhly authority.
11 Barnes, *Introduction*, 127.
12 Khriesat, *Dirasat*, 175–90. I am indebted to Dr. Khriesat, the chairman of the History Department at the University of Jordan, for his personal help in clarifying the text of the documents. See also Dawud, *al-Salt*, 146–47, 474–84.

13   Dawud, *al-Salt*, 474–84; 'Afifi, *al-Awqaf*, 16–17.

14   Khriesat, *Dirasat*, 188–90.

15   Khriesat, *Dirasat*, 58–59.

16   Kramers, "Tanzimat."

17   Barnes, *Introduction*, 118–21.

18   Barnes, *Introduction*, 125.

19   Abraham Marcus' fine study of Ottoman Aleppo confirms what has been established in many other case studies of waqf, that is, the flexibility and pragmatism of mutawallis when dealing with deterioriating or otherwise unprofitable properties, which led them to uses of exchange (*istibdal*), or to the offering of long-term or even perpetual leases on such properties, amounting to the virtual sale of such properties. See his *Middle East on the Eve of Modernity*, 303–13. In the case of fractional legacies of marginal value, one presumes that the cash value of the property was realized as soon as practicable.

20   Rogan, *Frontiers*, 154.

21   Rogan, *Frontiers*, ch. 5.

22   Rogan, *Frontiers*, 112.

23   On the changes occurring in the society of al-Salt after the Ottoman 're-establishment' in the 1860s, see Rogan, *Frontiers*, chs. 4–6; on the thickening web of connections between al-Salt and Nablus in particular, see Doumani, *Rediscovering Palestine*, 23, 47, 125, 192–93, and 203–204. On the underlying unities of *Bilad al-Sham* and their underrepresentation in post-Ottoman historiography, cf. Reimer, "King–Crane," 129–50.

24   Khriesat, *Dirasat*, 177–90.

25   Khriesat, *Dirasat*, 182–85; Dawud, *al-Salt*, 323, 483.

26   Khriesat, *Dirasat*, 185, document dated 4 November 1903.

27   Rogan, *Frontiers*, 119–21.

28   Khriesat, *Dirasat*, 185.

29   Rogan, *Frontiers*, 105.

30   Rogan, *Frontiers*, 166–71.

31   Rogan, *Frontiers*, 170–71.

32   Khriesat, *Dirasat*, 178, 185.

33   Khriesat, *Dirasat*, 178–80.

34   Investing the chief qadi with the authority of a quasi-governmental supervisor of waqf properties, and especially of those properties where the founder or his or her descendants were not entrusted with such oversight, is a practice that dates back centuries. The request for an inventory of such properties was thus within established Ottoman–Hanafi legal tradition, which granted wide latitude to qadis to appoint and remove persons responsible for waqf administration. See 'Afifi, *al-Awqaf*, 19, 70.

35   On al-Shaykh Muhammad Manku, see al-'Amad, *al-Salt, 1928*, 70; and Dawud, *al-Salt*, 577. On al-Shaykh Muhammad Khalil Amraysh, see al-'Amad, *al-Salt, 1927*, 133; and Dawud, *al-Salt*, 392.

36   Khriesat, *Dirasat*, 178 (letter from qadi al-qudah dated 12 August 1922. On the 1843 Ottoman decree, see Barnes, *Introduction*, 104–106.

37   Fischbach, "Britain," 525–44.

38   Khriesat, *Dirasat*, 180 (letter dated 22 August 1923).

39   Khriesat, *Dirasat*, 179–80 (letter dated 24 August 1922).

40   For a list of his books and manuscripts, see Dawud, *al-Salt*, 392.
41   For the following, see al-'Amad, *al-Salt 1927*, 133–34.
42   For the following, see Khriesat, *Dirasat*, 186–87 (reference legal decision dated 16
      September 1896); 185–86 (reference waqf deed dated 19 October 1922); and 181
      (complaint to qadi dated 23 September 1922).
43   Khriesat, *Dirasat*, 86.
44   See: Hashemite Kingdom of Jordan, *Wazarat al-awqaf*, 17–20.
45   On waqf in Ottoman Jerusalem, see Rood, *Sacred Law*; and on Jordanian Jerusalem,
      see Katz, *Jordanian Jerusalem*.

Bibliography

Abu-Manneh, Butrus. "The Sultan and the Bureaucracy: The Anti-Tanzimat
     Concepts of Grand Vizier Mahmud Nedim Paşa." *International Journal
     of Middle East Studies* 22 (1990): 257–74.

'Afifi, Muhammad. *al-Awqaf wa-l-hayah al-iqtisadiya fi Misr fi-l-'asr al-
     'uthmani*. Cairo: General Egyptian Book Organization, 1991.

al-'Amad, Hani. *al-Salt: malamih min al-hayah al-yawmiya li-l-madina min
     khilal sijill al-baladiya li-sanat 1927*. Amman: University of Jordan,
     2001.

———. *al-Salt: malamih min al-hayah al-yawmiya li-l-madina min khilal
     sijill al-baladiya li-sanat 1928*. Amman: University of Jordan, 2002.

Barnes, John Robert. *An Introduction to Religious Foundations in the Otto-
     man Empire*. Leiden: Brill, 1986.

Dawud, George Tarif. *al-Salt wa jiwaruha*. Amman: Business Bank Publica-
     tions, 1994.

Doumani, Beshara. *Rediscovering Palestine: Merchants and Peasants in Jabal
     Nablus, 1700–1900*. Berkeley: University of California Press, 1995

Findley, Carter Vaughn. "The Ottoman Administrative Legacy and the Mod-
     ern Middle East," in L. Carl Brown, ed., *Imperial Legacy: The Ottoman
     Imprint on the Balkans and the Middle East*. New York: Columbia Uni-
     versity Press, 1996.

Fischbach, Michael R. "Britain and the Ghawr Abi 'Ubayda Waqf Contro-
     versy in Transjordan." *International Journal of Middle East Studies* 33,
     no. 4 (2001): 525–44.

Hashemite Kingdom of Jordan, *Wazarat al-awqaf wa-l-shu'un wa-l-muqadd-
     asat al-islamiya: waqi' wa tatallu'at, AH 1320/AD 1999*. Amman: Govern-
     ment of the Hashemite Kingdom of Jordan, 1999.

Hodgson, Marshall. *The Venture of Islam*. 3 vols. Chicago: University of
     Chicago Press, 1974

Karpat, Kemal H. "Transformation of the Ottoman State, 1789–1908." *Inter-
     national Journal of Middle East Studies* 3 (1972): 243–81.

Katz, Kimberly. *Jordanian Jerusalem: Holy Places and National Spaces.* Gainesville: University Press of Florida, 2005

Khriesat, Mohammad A. *Dirasat fi tarikh madinat al-Salt.* Amman: Ministry of Culture, 1997.

Kramers, J.H. "Tanzimat." *Encyclopedia of Islam.* 1st ed., vol. 8, 656–60.

Marcus, Abraham. *The Middle East on the Eve of Modernity: Aleppo in the Eighteenth Century.* New York: Columbia University Press, 1989.

Reimer, Michael. "The King–Crane Commission at the Juncture of Politics and Historiography." *Critique: Critical Middle Eastern Studies* 15, no. 2 (2006): 129–50.

Rogan, Eugene. *Frontiers of the State in the Late Ottoman Empire. Transjordan, 1850–1921.* Cambridge: Cambridge University Press, 1999.

Rood, Judith Mendelsohn. *Sacred Law in the Holy City: The Khedival Challenge to the Ottomans as Seen from Jerusalem, 1829–1841.* Leiden: Brill, 2004.

Shryock, Andrew. *Nationalism and the Genealogical Imagination: Oral History and Textual Authority in Tribal Jordan.* Berkeley: University of California Press, 1997.

Wilson, Mary. *Abdullah, Britain, and the Making of Transjordan.* Cambridge: Cambridge University Press, 1987.

5

Zawiyat Sidi al-Ghazi: Survival of a Traditional Religious Institution

John A. Shoup

The zawiya, or hospice, of Sidi al-Ghazi in the Tafilalt is one of the most important in the western part of the Sahara. It figures among the six most important of those located along the northern fringe of the Sahara, which include Sidi Ma' al-'Aynayn (Tiznit), Sidi Ahmad u-Musa (Iligh), Sidi Sa'id Ahansal (Zawiyat Ahansal), Sidi Muhammad bin Nasir (Tamaghrut), and Sidi Bu Ziyan (Kandasah).[1] The founder of the *zawiya*, Sidi Abu al-Qasim al-Ghazi, was a member of the Sharifian Idrisi family and a direct descendant of the early Idrisi Sufi leader, 'Abd al-Salam ibn Mashish. The Sufi *isnad* (chain of instruction) of the zawiya also stems from 'Abd al-Salam ibn Mashish (d. 1227/8) through his disciple Abu al-Hasan al-Shadhili (1196–1258).[2] The Idrisis or Adarasa trace their line back to Idris I (788–91), founder of the first independent Muslim state in Morocco and a direct descendant of 'Ali ibn Abi Talib and Fatima Zahra bint Muhammad. As such the family of Sidi Abu al-Qasim al-Ghazi was well established as one endowed with religious authority, reputed for piety, and *baraka* (blessings of God). By the nineteenth century, the al-Ghazi family was one of the eight most important religious lineages in the Tafilalt.[3]

Figure 1. Roof of the tomb of Sidi al-'Arabi al-Ghazi (18th century), one of a number of buildings included in the zawiya's property and located in the village of Tabubakart. (Photograph by author.)

Abu al-Qasim al-Ghazi lived in the troubled period of Moroccan history when the Marinid dynasty (1224–1465) had become weak and was replaced by the closely related Wattasids, who ruled in the Marinids' name. In order to try to gain support against the rising power of rural-based Sharifian families such as the Sa'dians, the Marinid/Wattasids revived the cult of Idris I and turned to the Idrisi family for support. The Sa'dians (1524–1659) eventually took power across Morocco, slowly moving from their base in Taroudant in the Sus north and finally defeating the Wattasids in 1537.[4] This was also the time when Portugal and Spain were humiliating the Muslim rulers of Morocco by conquering nearly all of the coastal ports. Local resistance to the Europeans was centered around the Sufi brotherhoods, with many of the new offshoots of the Shadhili or Qadiri orders taking the lead.[5]

Abu al-Qasim al-Ghazi was a contemporary of Muhammad bin Nasir, who lived in the Dra' Valley and founded the Nasiriya order at Tamaghrut.[6] The two men studied together, and each gives credit to the other for much of his learning and understanding of Sufism. Abu al-Qasim al-Ghazi established his zawiya in the extreme southern part of the Tafilalt oasis; ten other *zawaya* (plural of zawiya) were subsequently built in the same area, thus giving the district the

Figure 2. Tomb of Sidi al-Arabi al-Ghazi. (Photograph by author.)

name Zawaya. Abu al-Qasim al-Ghazi wanted to be alone, however, away from people, and so moved his zawiya twice. When he died, he was buried in a different location, about a kilometer to the east of the zawiya. His grandson, Sidi al-'Arabi, was also a 'Shaykh Hayy,' or Living Shaykh, who was able to further the teachings and writings of Abu al-Qasim al-Ghazi.[7] When he died, he was buried in his own separate *darih* (tomb) next to the zawiya.[8]

By the seventeenth century, the zawiya had become a major center for religious learning supporting a large mosque, a madrasa that housed up to sixty students, and a *khalwa* (a secluded place for contemplation) for *individual* study and prayer. It had also become an important place for religious scholars to study and to be buried. The khalwa and madrasa contain several tombs of religious scholars whose names are still known and are pointed out to visitors: Sidi Hanafi, al-Hajj 'Abd al-Karim, Sidi Ahmad bal-Hajj 'Abd al-Karim, and Ahmad (called) Zarruq.[9] In addition to these important figures whose names are remembered, there are forty-four walis buried in a special tomb next to the complex in what is the hospice's original graveyard,[10] as well ase one *waliya*, Lalla Toto Hamiya, whose tomb is separated from the men's by a short distance.

Zawiyat Sidi al-Ghazi was one of the richest in the Tafilalt, and in the mid-nineteenth century it rebuilt its main building in three individual sections: the *dar al-diyafa* (guest house) for visitors, recitations, and *dhikr* (ceremony to remember God); the *dar al-'abid* (the slave house), which housed up to forty slaves engaged in work for the zawiya (both domestic and agricultural labor); and the *dar al-kabira* (large or main house where the family lives), where the *muqaddam* (head of a zawiya) of the order lived (and still lives) with his family. The dar al-'abid has fallen into ruin, since there have been no slaves living in the zawiya since the 1950s; the other two sections are used for their original purposes to this day. The importance of the hospice was underlined in 1893 when Sultan Mawlay Hasan I made a point of visiting and bringing gifts to the hospice in person while in the area during a *mahalla* (royal procession around the country).[11]

Like many zawaya in Morocco, that of Sidi al-Ghazi also assisted in settling conflicts between local communities. The Adarasa were, and indeed still are, seen as more objective than the 'Alawi and their Filali allies in their decisions, since they engage primarily in religious scholarship and not in politics, unlike their cousins the 'Alawi and their Filali allies, who had established themselves firmly in the politics of the Tafilalt.[12] Zawaya in Morocco are frequently placed in areas between tribal territories, and their neutrality gives individuals from all neighboring tribes a place to both worship and settle major disputes. Zawiyat Sidi al-Ghazi is located between highly contentious and quarreling districts of the oasis, whose inhabitants frequently come to blows over water.[13] Ross Dunn notes that in 1894, for example, the Awlad Sidi al-Ghazi settled the dispute between the Awlad Abu 'Anan and Awlad Bil Giz of the al-Ghurfa district located to the east of the zawiya.[14]

Sources of income

Until the 1950s, Zawiyat Sidi al-Ghazi had a wide range of financial resources. A number of tribes from throughout Morocco gave annual gifts.[15] The zawiya used to hold a *mawsim* (*mawlid* or annual celebration of the founder's birth) once a year, from 10 to 11 Muharram, when each of the tribes presented both Zawiyat Sidi al-Ghazi and Zawiyat Sidi Muhammad bin Nasr with a female camel, a copper brazier and tea pot set[16], and a traditional knotted carpet.[17] Sidi al-Ghazi and Muhammad ibn Nasr were close friends and each gives the other credit for being the teacher of the other. Both zawiyas were founded at around the same time and the celebrations timed to more or less coincide. The *mawsim* has not been held since the early 1990s as a result of a severe drought that has created financial hardship for many of the pastoral tribes. Nonetheless, the close ties between the zawiya and the tribes have been maintained. It is still the practice of the zawiya to send the

Figure 3. Si Mustafa al-Ghazi, muqaddam-in-training of the zawiya of Sidi al-Ghazi.
(Photograph by author.)

son selected to be the next muqaddam to live with the nomadic tribes and come to know them and their languages (Berber and Arabic), learn tribal affairs and politics to be able to settle disputes, and to keep close contact with them. The current muqaddam-in- training, Si Mustafa al-Ghazi, spent many years of his youth in this way.

Among the hospice's most important sources of income are the agricultural lands it owns. Until the 1950s, the zawiya owned seven hundred hectares of agricultural land, most of which were scattered throughout the oasis—from Awfus in the northern district of al-Ratib to Tabubakrt in the extreme south.[18] Close to three hundred hectares have since been lost, mainly due to inheritance demands by members of the al-Ghazi family, although the hospice sold some of the property (in Awfus, for instance, the land on which the new mosque was built). The Ministry of Works appropriated one small plot—called al-Khaybata, located in Tizimi near the modern town of Arfud—in order to build an electrical power plant, without bothering to find out who owned the land. The zawiya lodged a legal suit in 2004 demanding compensation, since it would not be possible to have the land returned after the power station was built.

Today the zawiya owns two hundred hectares of agricultural land located mainly in Tizwint, a now-abandoned qasr (village or fortified village) along the Ghris River some fifteen kilometers south of Arfud. The land is farmed by sharecroppers mainly from the 'Arab al-Sabbah and Dhiwi Mni' tribes.[19] The zawiya takes three quarters of the production per year and the families retain the rest.[20] According to both the muqaddam of the zawiya and the sharecropper families, when the year is good the shares are based on thirds rather than quarters. Currently five families are working the land as sharecroppers, and their income is good enough to allow them to buy livestock as well as make improvements in the infrastructure: canals, well pumps, and the like.[21] In November 2003 Mawlay Ahmad, a wealthy member of the Ghazi brotherhood who lives in Casablanca, rented twenty hectares of land at Tizwint and employed several of the sharecroppers as workers. He has invested heavily in new equipment such as tractors, built a *sahrij*, or water storage tank, and dug new, deep wells for irrigation. He has replanted date palms and increased the amount of land under wheat, alfalfa, and bean cultivation. He is thus helping to revive the agricultural production of the zawiya's land as well as its financial wellbeing.

The zawiya sets aside part of its agricultural lands for use by people with no access to any form of support. Once a year landless poor people can ask the zawiya for five *feddans* to grow food for themselves.[22] The current muqaddam, Si 'Abd al-'Aziz bin Hanini al-Ghazi, sees this as an obligation of the zawiya and part of its traditional role in the community. Whoever is in need can thus come to the zawiya for help, and the hospice sets aside an area of its land for use by the poor. A number of families each year cultivate their feddans free of charge, and the families take all of the produce for their own subsistence.

The zawiya also has kept several small plots of land near the institution itself in Tabubakrt. These small plots are for the use of the muqaddam's family, where they grow a small amount of wheat, vegetables, and dates. The qasr's original water storage tank is still used, and when there is sufficient flow in the Ziz River it is filled to be used to irrigate the lands around the qasr.[23] One of the plots of land on the north side of the qasr has a line of date palms that were supposed to have been planted by Sidi al-'Arabi al-Ghazi himself, and special care is taken to keep them alive.

The last major source of income for the zawiya is the *hidiya* (sing. *hadiya*), or gifts from the adherents of the order *(muhibbin)*. Gifts can be in the form of money, food, livestock, books, and special objects brought from other countries.[24] The gifts of money are immediately reinvested in the food served to all guests who are present at meal times. The dar al-diyafa constantly serves rounds of highly sweetened mint tea, peanuts, almonds, and dates. Guests are expected to eat at the hopsice, and each meal is prepared with the assumption that between ten to fifteen people in addition to the large, extended family of the muqaddam will be present. The women of the muqaddam's family have now taken on the preparation of meals, since there are no more household slaves to do the task. Shopping is done by men in the Tafilalt, not by women, and the muqaddam and/or his sons must go to all three major market days per week to keep up with the supplies needed to feed large numbers of people.

Both Si 'Abd al-'Aziz and his son Si Mustafa have noted that the obligation to feed all who come to the zawiya is their largest single expense, averaging over 3,500 dirhams per month, other than the monthly electric bill which averages around 200 dirhams per month.[25] The zawiya is frequently obliged to ask for loans of money from wealthier members of the brotherhood in order to cover monthly expenses. These loans are not considered gifts and are expected to be repaid, but several of the wealthier members who help out this way prefer to not be repaid, at least not in full.[26]

Dispute with the Ministry of Habus

Most of Morocco's zawiyas have come under the control of the Habus (awqaf) in the past twenty years. The former minister, 'Abd al-Kabir 'Alawi Mdaghari,[27] made control of the zawiyas one of the cornerstones of his policy. Although most zawiyas have been brought under the general umbrella of the ministry, there remain notable exceptions—including some of the most influential zawaya in the country.[28] Once it took control of a hospice, the ministry would assume the responsibility of managing the finances and paying the bills, and made the muqaddams more or less government employees. The financial resources, including property, would be signed over to the ministry and it was argued that the pooled resources would improve conditions for all the zawaya. In addition, the ministry had the right to interfere with the rituals and practices of the muhibbin during *ziyara*s (visitations) and mawsims. Those practices seen by the ministry as un-Islamic would be severely curtailed or banned: Ribbon Trees usually associated with the semi-mythical spirit Lalla 'Aysha[29] and other practices engaged in mainly by women were particularly targeted.[30] The ministry also demanded that the zawiyas turn over all their manuscripts to ministry representatives, who collected them and took them to Rabat. The original justification was that the manuscripts would be cataloged and restored, and returned to the zawiyas; they have not, however, been returned and remain in Rabat.

When the offer to come under ministerial control was made to the muqaddam of Zawiyat Sidi al-Ghazi, he refused. He did not trust the persons sent with the offer and was highly suspicious of the need to sign over all of the hospice's property and manuscripts. He did not initially take issue with some of the other elements of ministerial oversight, but governmental restrictions, such as restricting or banning certain Ghaziya practices would have become problematic.[31] Discussions never got that far, however, as the muqaddam refused the offer almost immediately. He was disturbed not just by the requirement to turn over all of the zawiya's property, but, that being done, by the question of how the zawiya would be able to function as it had always done: how would it be able to provide all the services it traditionally gave to the community, and how could it be still seen as a neutral, impartial mediator in disputes between tribes and communities?

Since the muqaddam refused the ministry's offer, the zawiya has been left on its own to survive. It receives no governmental support of any kind. The government has instead given massive support to the expansion of the tomb complex of Mawlay 'Ali al-Sharif (d. 1657), who is the founder of the 'Alawi state. The tomb was not a zawiya or even a major shrine until Moroccan independence in 1956. In recent years the Moroccan government has expanded the tomb/mosque complex and built an Islamic school with a library next to it. A wide, well-paved road takes the visitor to a large open parking area in front of the tomb/mosque. While the government does not officially discourage visits to the local zawiyas, it definitely encourages Moroccan visitors to make a stop at Mawlay 'Ali al-Sharif: Visitors unfamiliar with the oasis could easily miss much of it because the 'main' road is so poorly marked—the only signs mark the way to the shrine of Mawlay 'Ali al-Sharif and the tourist destination of the Merzouga dunes some fifty kilometers southeast of the oasis. Indeed, the road to the shrine is twice the width of main road, which turns sharply at the shrine's entrance and is thus even harder to navigate. One would have to know where such places as Zawiyat Sidi al-Ghazi are in order to find them. The official support given by the Moroccan government to the shrine of Mawlay 'Ali al-Sharif has definitely hurt the older, traditional institutions in the oasis. Of the eleven zawiyas that once made up the Zawaya district, only Zawiyat Sidi al-Ghazi has been able to survive. Nothing remains of zawiyas such as those of Sidi al-Habib al-Mati and Sidi Sasi (in Qasr Bin Amar) apart from the 'saint's' tomb, which local people still visit for individual prayer or to make a wish and light a candle.

When asked why most of the older zawaya have lost much of their historical role, 'Abd al-Kabir 'Alawi Mdaghari suggested it was because there were too many of them located too close together, and that with the decline in income in the region, people decided to shift their support to one shrine—that of Mawlay 'Ali al-Sharif.[32] It is hard to believe that the distance between the zawaya and competition between them has much to do with the present situation. The zawaya existed for centuries and their recent collapse has less to do with their proximity than it does with the region's post-independence economics. As outlined above, however, official government support for Mawlay 'Ali al-Sharif has definitely played as big a role as the collapse of the local economy.[33] The fact that Zawiyat Sidi al-Ghazi has been able to survive is due to its past importance and to the strong characters of Si 'Abd al-'Aziz al-Ghazi and his son Si Mustafa al-Ghazi. They are determined that Zawiyat Sidi al-Ghazi will not suffer the fate of so many others—nor are they willing to bring themselves under control of the Ministry of Habus despite recent policy changes that are more favorable to Sufi brotherhoods.[34]

Conclusion

Zawiyat Sidi al-Ghazi has negotiated a path that secures its survival despite government favor to the shrine of the current dynasty's 'founder,' Mawlay 'Ali al-Sharif.[35] For instsance, the muqaddam and his son encouraged the creation of an association to gain access to other sources of funding[36] for the hospice. In 2006 the association published a small book of poems written by Sidi al-'Arabi al-Ghazi that it sold for 25 dirhams each. The book sold out within a year of publication and demand for it continues; they have not yet published a second edition. Book sales and agricultural profits give the hospice an assured and independent source of income. In addition, the zawiya is interested in developing cultural tourism as another source of revenue. They would like to host presentations on Islam and Sufism in the dar al-diyafa, a space traditionally open to anyone and intended to promote discussion. This plan has, however, been hampered by language barriers, since Arabic is the principle language at the zawiya, and few of the adherents know enough French or English to be able to explain things directly to tourists. In addition, their objection to the 'nakedness' of tourists at the nearby and popular Merzouga Dunes prevents them from developing contact with local tour operators.[37] Should cultural tourism be better developed in the region (and in Morocco), the hospice has potential for even higher earnings.[38] A secure financial base would obviate any need to ask for governmental support.

The zawiya did not enter into open conflict with the government when it refused sign over its property to the ministry, and it has tried to maintain its services to the community using its own sources of income. The change in the person of the minister of habus heralded a more positive attitude toward Sufism in Morocco in general, and although the hospice still receives no financial support from the Ministry of Habus, it has benefited from the more positive attitude. For example, the al-Ghazi *Sama'* group from Arfud has been included in recent festivals held in al-Rissani.[39] Zawiyat Sidi al-Ghazi remains a functioning traditional Islamic institution, and with the guidance of the current muqaddam and his son, it has been able to survive independent of government control. Its ability to diversify its sources of income demonstrates that to be traditional does not mean to lack imagination or the ability to adapt to current conditions.

Notes

1   All of these with the exception of Sidi Bu Ziyan are located in Morocco. The hospice of Sidi Bu Ziyan is in Algeria.

2   al-Ghazi and al-Ghazi, *Muqamah*, 4.

3   Dunn, *Resistance*, 43. The others included the current ruling dynasty of Morocco—the 'Alawis—as well as those of Sidi al-Habib al-Mati, which claim direct descent from Abu Bakr al-Sadiq. The main qasr (fortified village) of Zawiyat Sidi al-Ghazi is called Tabubakart, or the Place of Abu Bakr in Berber.

4   The claim to Sharifian descent by the Sa'dians was an important challenge to the legitimacy of the Bani Marin, who were Berbers from the plains near Oujda in eastern Morocco. Since the S'adian period, Morocco's rulers have established political legitimacy through direct descent from the Prophet Muhammad.

5   The Sa'dians themselves played such a role when they took over leadership of the resistance to the Portuguese in the Sus from the Shadhili leader al-Slamlali al-Jazuli.

6   Tamaghrut is 180 km from the Tafilalt and located along the Dra' River. Many of the same tribes who gave their support to the Nasiri zawiya also gave support to the Ghazi zawiya.

7   A 'Living Shaykh' is someone who has been able to establish a personal connection with God, whereas a muqaddam has and is able to pass on learning, but has not established this connection with God. Today in Morocco, Shaykh Hamza Qadiri Butshish, head of the Butshishi order, is considered to be a Living Shaykh.

8   al-Ghazi and al-Ghazi, *Muqamah*, 6.

9   Abu al-'Abbas Ahmad al-Burnusi (died 1494) was called Zarruq and founded the Zarruqi–Shadhdili order. He was more or less contemporary with the period of Sidi Abu al-Qasim, but the person buried at the zawiya is most likely not the same Ahmad Zarruq.

10   All forty-four were *wali al-salih*, or pious men whose learning gave them status during their lifetimes. The term *wali al-salih* is often translated into English as 'saint' but literally means 'sincere friend (of God).'

11   *Mahalla* refers to the expeditions of the Moroccan 'Alawi sultans to specific regions of the kingdom to collect taxes and/or extend the authority of the state over rebel leaders.

12   The 'Alawi contested the Sa'dian claim to the throne of Morocco and took control of the country in the 1660s from their base of tribal support in the Tafilalt. The Tafilalt remained a political training ground for young princes through the first part

of the nineteenth century. Many of the 'royal' palaces in the Tafilalt were built for prince–governors and their households of slaves and soldiers. Hasan al-Dakhil, founder of the 'Alawis, came to Morocco from Mecca in the thirteenth century at the request of the Filalis; his arrival broke a severe drought, proving the baraka (blessings of God) of the family. The Adarasa have been in Morocco since 788, when Idris I sought refuge with the Berbers of Volubilis. The Adarasa established their reputation as religious scholars and Sufi leaders after the fall of their state in the tenth century.

13   The prolonged drought that began in 1980 has caused qasrs to accuse each other of stealing water; in 2003–2004 several qasrs in Bani Muhammad and Wad Ifili were accused by the people of al-Ghurfa, Tazgizut, Zawaya, and al-Safalat of similar theft. Zawiyat Sidi al-Ghazi became a place for the matter to be discussed, and it was decided to call in government troops to patrol the canals.

14   See Dunn, *Resistance*, 86.

15   These tribes included the Ziyyan (Khanifra), Buhsusn (Mawlay Bu 'Aza), Zammur (Khamisat), Grushin (Khanifra), Ait BuHaddu (Mawlay Bu 'Aza), Qasba of Mawlay Sa'id (Bani Millal), Bani Sadn (Tawnat), Ait Khabbash (Tafilalt), Ait Murghad (Gulmima), Ait Atta (Tinjdad), Qasr Ait Bulman (Tinghir), Awlad al-Hajj (Zagura), Nisrat (Zagura), and Bani 'Ali (Zagura).

16   A *majmar* and *barrad*.

17   A *gtif*—a thick carpet usually red in color and with minimal design.

18   The zawiya owns land in the following places: Tizwint (Arfud), al-Khaybata (Arfud), al-Khaybata Awlad Bhar, Tizimi; the zawiya owns one feddan in each of the 32 qasrs, including Ma'adid, Qasr Fazna (al-Jurf), Zrigat (Awfus), Bahalil (near Sefrou), Sharratin (in Fas al-Bali), Hayy Zaytun (Meknes), Beni Sadn (Taounate), Oujda, Aknul (Rif), and Ouasil (Rif).

19   The 'Arab al-Sabbah were historically divided into two major sections: one had been settled in the oasis for several hundred years while the other remained pastoral nomads. The Dhiwi Mni' were primarily pastoral nomads (though some families owed palm groves in al-Ghurfa) until the severe drought that began in 1980 and the subsequent loss of most of their livestock forced the majority to settle. Being newcomers to the oasis, they had neither land nor water rights and were thus forced into sharecropper relationships with those who were already established. The 'Arab al-Sabbah were to a degree better off: members of the tribe had been settled in the qasrs, such as Qasr Awlad 'Ali, for generations, which enabled some of the recent migrants to gain access to land and water. The rural commune around Arfud is called 'Arab al-Sabbah and members of the tribe dominate commune politics.

20   The sharecropping relationship is referred to as *khums* (one fifth) because of the division of shares by fifths in most of Morocco. Even when other divisions are used, such as quarters or thirds, the relationship is still referred to as khums.

21   One of the more enterprising young men has enlisted in several income-generation projects offered by the Ministry of Agriculture and has become the foreman for the investor from Casablanca.

22   A *feddan* in local usage is not a set amount of land, but refers to an area marked out by a low, dirt wall. The other term used to denote landholdings is *jinan*, or garden, which usually refers to plots where fruit trees are growing.

23 The water storage tank was filled in 2004 and again in 2005 due to unusually heavy chance rainstorms. The older irrigation system was set up to preserve water when such things happened, and fortunately the original water tank at Tabubakrt is still functioning. Some of the other qasrs have not maintained theirs and are not able to take advantage of occasional stream flow or even floods by the Ziz and Ghris rivers.

24 These include incense from Saudi Arabia, the Arab Gulf, and Egypt; prayer beads in ivory, bone, and semi-precious stones from various countries, including Senegal, Saudi Arabia, and Egypt; calligraphy wall hangings mainly from Egypt; perfume from Europe or the Arab Gulf; collections of Sufi poetry from other orders in West and North Africa and the Arab East; and other such items thought to be of value or relevance for the order or the muqaddam.

25 It is difficult to get an idea of monthly incomes in most of rural Morocco as cash income is seasonally dictated unless there are family members abroad sending remittances. The usual monthly average in the country is between 800 dirhams and 1800 dirhams ($94 to $211), depending on the area. Incomes in the Tafilalt are in the lower range.

26 Mawlay Ahmad, the Casablancan renting the lands at Tziwint, is a good example of such a person. He decided to rent the land and pay the zawiya on a regular basis rather than continue to loan money. Both the muqaddam and Ahmad are happier with this arrangement.
Si Mustafa al-Ghazi estimates that the zawiya spends 600 dirhams per week on vegetables, meat, and fruit. In addition they buy wheat (the women of the family make their bread), sugar, tea, and cooking oil, which he estimates to cost around 950 dirhams a month. They often do not have ready cash and need to buy on credit. When the bills become too large, they ask wealthier members of the brotherhood for loans or those to whom they owe money to forgive the outstanding debt as a gift to the zawiya.

27 'Abd al-Kabir 'Alawi Mdaghari is originally from the Mdaghrah region of the Tafilalt. The Mdagharah tribe dominates the upper part of the oasis, starting at the new regional capital al-Rashidiya. While the tribe is of Berber origin, its elite are 'Alawi Sharifs who are close cousins to the ruling 'Alawi lineage.

28 The Wazzaniya order, based in the northern city of Wazzan, and the Butshishiya order, based in the northern city of Birkane (near the Algerian border), are among the most important and influential orders to refuse being brought under the ministry. Both of these have large numbers of adherents and a fairly large financial base. The Wazzaniya is headed by the Sharif al-Wazzan (a member of the Idrisi family), who was able to maintain autonomy from the central government until the 1950s.

29 Lalla 'Aysha is the name usually associated with Ribbon Trees. In popular Moroccan tales, Lalla 'Aysha is often described as a beautiful woman with cow's feet who can capture the souls of men and make them her devotees. The origin of the figure is thought to be a woman who lured Portuguese soldiers to their death during the troubled period at the end of Marinid rule. Another popular Lalla 'Ayshah figure relates to different walis who lived during the same time period. This Lalla 'Aysha is a beautiful woman who comes to marry the wali only to find him dead when she arrives and immediately dies to join him in paradise.

30 For example the Ribbon Tree at the shrine of Sidi Ahmad u-Musa in Illigh was cut down and *makhzani* police (auxiliary forces) are posted permanently at the shrine to

make sure women abide by a more 'Islamic' set of practices during their visits. Ex-minister Mdaghari, has recently been accused of encouraging 'Wahhabi' orthodoxy in Morocco.

31 The Ghaziya dhikr and *hadra* (literally 'presence'; refers to rituals where the inner soul or possessing spirit is called forth) include music, dance, and trance during which the muhibbin eat hot coals, drink boiling water, and perform other actions allowed by the muqaddam to demonstrate faith and submission to God. Men and women engage in this practice in separate but nearby spaces, where the women can hear the music and also go into trance. The music is accompanied by various types of drum, and the muqaddam controls the whole procedure through hand motions to the drummers, making sure that no one is injured and only those who are 'ready' are allowed to demonstrate their devotion. The more orthodox ministry frowns upon such populist practices.

32 Interview given by the former minister to Faiçal Medaghri, an Al Akhawayn student and close relative of the minister, March, 2004

33 The region has been greatly affected by the dam built in 1965 on the Ziz River above al-Rashidiya, which has changed the flow and amount of water available for irrigation. The whole Saharan region has also suffered from a prolonged and severe drought that began in 1980 and has been complicated by the interruption caused by the dam. The Tafilalt's trade had historically been as much south into the Sahara as it is north to Fez. The fact that the south has been closed off due to continued tensions between Morocco and Algeria has also caused economic hardship for the people. As a result of these factors, the Tafilalt has become one of the more isolated backwaters of Morocco when, a century ago, it was one of the country's most active financial centers. This, too, has affected the ability of local institutions like zawaya to remain viable.

34 In 2004 'Abd al-Kabir 'Alawi Mdaghari was replaced as minister after nearly twenty years by Ahmad Tawfiq, an intellectual and member of the Butshishiya order. Since he has become minister, there is a far softer approach to independent zawaya and to Sufism in general. It is far too early to see how this change will affect the survival of Zawiyat Sidi al-Ghazi.
In Morocco, the Minisry of Habus is the same as the Ministry of Religious Affairs. The term 'habus' is used instead of 'awqaf' but holds the same meaning: lands, other property, and the income from them, which is 'imprisoned.' In Morocco, the Ministry of Habus does not report to the prime minister but to the king and the appointed minister is a royal appointee answerable only to the king.

35 The actual founder is Hasan al-Dakhil, who came from Mecca to the Tafilalt in the thirteenth century. His tomb is located a short distance from that of Mawlay 'Ali al-Sharif, to the west of the town of al-Rissani, and is rarely visited. King Muham-mad V restored it shortly after independence, but little has been done to maintain or restore the tomb since then.

36 In the early 2000s Morocco created the Social Development Agency, which encour-aged people to organize into development and culture (or education) associations in order to access funding. Each association receives a small amount of money from the government, around 1700 dirhams, which is to be used as seed money to start up vari-ous projects. As a result of this initiative, every community in the oasis has at least one association, although most are no longer active. The zawiya formed the Association of Tabubakrt of Sidi al-Ghazi for the Development and Revival of Cultural Heritage.

37 The Merzouga Dunes are the usual destination for tourists. In the conservative view
    of local people, wearing shorts means they are naked.
38 Currently they depend on groups of students from Al Akhawayn University. The
    zawiya is included in most student visits to the oasis, which means between five and
    eight groups per year at around 2000 dirhams per visit.
39 *Sama'* refers to the sung form of religious poetry. Those performed by the Ghazi
    group were mainly written by Sidi al-'Arabi al-Ghazi and are in classical Arabic.
    The Sama' group performs many of the same songs that one can hear on any day at
    the zawiya.

Bibliography

Dunn, Ross. *Resistance in the Desert*. Madison: University of Wisconsin
    Press, 1977.

al-Ghazi, 'Abd al-Jalil, and Abd al-Majid al-Ghazi. *Muqamah fi dirasat
    mu'assasat al-shurfa' wa-l-tariqa wa-l-zawaya bi-l-Maghrib: al-
    mu'assasa al-gahziya namudhajan*. Maknas: Jami'at al-Shurfa' al-Ghaz-
    iyin Wilayat Maknas, 1993.

Lrediri, Saadia. "Zaouiat de Tafilalt: Sidi Al Ghazi." BA monograph, Meknes:
    Université Moulay Ismail, 1991.

Mezzine, Larbi. *Le Tafilalt: Contributions à l'histoire du Maroc aux XVIIe et
    XVIIIe siècles*. Casablanca: Najah al-Jadida, 1987.

6

Guild Waqf: Between Religious Law and Common Law

Nelly Hanna

The study of waqf is a field that has known intensive scholarly work, this institution having for many decades been explored by legal scholars and historians who have scrutinized waqf law and the provisions that regulated it. They have studied the application of this law on the ground in specific contexts, and they have explored the impact of waqf on societies and economies. The literature on this subject is consequently extensive and has allowed historians to understand waqf better than many other Islamic institutions. Studies on Mamluk waqf have been particularly developed, and as a result we now know a great deal about the role of waqf in running the city of Cairo, and specifically about the highly developed infrastructure it created, which facilitated commercial, religious, and charitable activities.[1]

Waqf in the context of the ruling class

By its nature, the creation of a waqf implied that an individual possessed wealth of some sort, which was endowed to a particular purpose. Waqf property was varied, but most waqf foundations—the great mosques, madrasas, and Sufi institutions—required huge sums not only to build but to maintain as functioning institutions. In short, these foundations were largely the domain of the ruling class. The literature in the field has, as a result, privileged the study of waqfs undertaken by members of ruling classes: sultans, amirs, Mamluks, and merchants. The analysis of waqf founders in the Mamluk period undertaken by Sylvie Denoix shows that waqf was overwhelmingly used by Mamluks and their families, including sultans and emirs, and to a lesser extent by religious and civilian elites. Her sample of 231 waqf founders included two artisans, who made up less than one percent of the total.[2] Regarding the Mamluk period, then, it is not entirely clear whether a) artisans and traders did not found waqfs; b) they did, but the documents regarding such waqfs have not survived; or c) the documents have survived but have not aroused the interest of historians. Regarding the subsequent period, our sources do provide us with numerous references to artisans and tradesmen who created waqfs. In contrast to the Mamluk period (1250–1517), merchants, artisans, and tradesmen have left numerous records of waqfs in Ottoman Egypt.

Waqfs of a more modest nature

The present study aims to consider waqfs established by some of those social groups that have not been incorporated in waqf studies for various reasons, and to broaden our understanding of the institution by considering a little-known type of waqf as it was used in the seventeenth and eighteenth centuries: namely, waqfs established by artisans within the framework of their guilds. In contrast with the Mamluk period, the period between the sixteenth and the eighteenth centuries has yielded rich sources in the form of court records, which show that ordinary tradesmen and artisans undertook to endow small properties that they owned: possibly a shop or a house or some other modest building or part of a building in their possession. These small waqfs, which were quite common in the Ottoman period, have not been the object of an academic study.

The subject of the present chapter, however, is not waqfs founded by tradesmen and artisans but more specifically guild waqfs, which served the guilds and were administered within the guild.[3] I base my conclusions on a dozen court cases of the late seventeenth and eighteenth centuries.

There are two kinds of court cases on guild waqfs: The first consists of deeds recording the appointment of a new shaykh to a guild. The deeds indicate the responsibilities of the new shaykh, among them ensuring that the guild waqf is properly administered. The second consists of deeds that focus on the guild member in charge of the waqf. At intervals, and especially when he passed his duties on to another guild member, this person presented the guild with the waqf's accounts. These deeds provide us with details of guild waqf property, the sources of revenue, and expenditures related to the waqf.

I will focus on the waqfs established and maintained by four guilds: the artisans who made linings *(batayniya)*; the tailors *(khayyatin)*; the weavers *(hayyakin)*; and the makers of cotton textile *(qattanin)*. Four guilds are not very many, but the number of people involved was relatively high since these guilds had many members. The weavers' guild was estimated to include about 4,600 persons at the end of the seventeenth century; that of the tailors about 3,000.[4] All these guilds were involved in some form of textile work, and the various stages of the textile manufacturing process employed more artisans than any other craft. Artisans working in textiles were also, according to the study of their estate inventories undertaken by André Raymond, the most prosperous artisans of Cairo.[5] The weight of these artisans in local industry gives their waqfs significance.

Another reason why it is important to study guild waqfs is that they appear to have existed in a number of Ottoman cities: notably, Damascus, Bursa, and Istanbul. Thus the guild waqfs of Cairo were not isolated phenomenon. The studies undertaken so far by Suraiya Faroqhi, Jeong Yi, and Brigitte Marino show certain features in common among guild waqfs in Cairo and guild waqfs in these cities.[6] For example, in all these cases, the property of guild waqfs consisted solely of copperware. Thus, even though not many guilds had a waqf, guild waqfs were spread over a wide region. It could therefore be important to try to examine what factors led to this broad trend.

Running a guild waqf

The real interest of these guild waqfs, at any rate, is not in the number of guilds or artisans. Rather, it is in the way that guildsmen used these waqfs, the way they were run, and the objectives of these foundations. Studying guild waqfs is also a way of exploring how traditional structures were being remolded and restructured to confront new conditions at a time of social and economic flux, when a Mamluk ruling class was emerging into political prominence on the local level and an intensification of commercialization was taking place on the regional level. Hence, guild waqfs can be situated in the context of broad transformations taking place in the region.

In many ways, these waqfs followed standard practice, sharing a number of features of mainstream waqf. For example, guild waqf included revenue-generating property. Some of the revenue was spent, as in many other waqfs, on charitable works. Like most mainstream waqfs, guild waqfs provided certain benefits for members of the guild, some of the money going toward helping the poor. The way the guild waqf was administered also bore resemblances to other waqfs. A person was designated to take the responsibility for administering the waqf—somewhat like the waqf supervisor—with specific duties related to the everyday running of the endowment, such as collecting rents and disbursing the necessary expenses. In guild foundations, as in other waqfs, keeping a careful record of expenses and revenue was an important part of the daily administration of the foundation.

In some important aspects, however, guild waqf deviated from standard practice, as will be explained further below. These differences may be related to the fact that artisans had much more modest means than ruling-class waqf founders, and this had a bearing on the size, composition, and functioning of guild waqfs. More importantly, some differences involved the core of the waqf institution itself. On some issues, the practices of guild waqfs directly contravened the provisions of waqf law. We could call guild waqf a variant of mainstream waqf, undertaken during a period when even mainstream waqfs were undergoing change.

Guild waqf versus mainstream waqf

There are some differences of variable importance between guild waqfs and foundations that followed established practice. These differences can be attributed to various factors—some of a general nature, affecting society and the economy during the late seventeenth and eighteenth centuries, and others more specifically related to the conditions of artisans and guilds and the modesty of their waqfs in comparison to the better-known ones. One could ask why, at this particular moment in time, these guild waqfs emerged in the way that they did. The answer cannot be simple and would require further exploration in order to fully understand the conditions behind this trend. Nevertheless, I will propose at least a partial explanation.

The fact that guild waqfs made use of unorthodox practices that did not conform to legal provisions can be attributed in part to the general history of waqf as an institution during the late Ottoman period: namely, that waqfs in general underwent changes and that these were manifested both on the ground, in the way that waqf was practiced, and at the scholarly level, since jurists were now coming to condone numerous practices that had been deemed unacceptable in the past. The period between the mid-seventeenth and the mid-eighteenth centuries was one of economic and political flux and a relatively high level of commercialization. This affected the institution of waqf in general, as it did other institutions like that of the tax-farming system. The implementation of unusual practices in guild waqf can be understood in the context of various new practices occurring in other waqfs as well. Waqfs in general were undergoing certain changes. With regard to the large princely or emiral foundations, the clearest manifestation is the alienation of waqf property. These allowed individuals with financial means to take possession of property that was in principle, and according to waqf provisions, inalienable and founded in perpetuity. Anyone working on the court records of late seventeenth and eighteenth century Cairo will have seen the innumerable cases of waqf alienation that were taking place.[7] These cases took many forms. Waqf property, which was supposed to be rented out for a short period (one to three years), was being rented out at fixed rates for ninety years. Such transactions were detrimental to the foundations, since as a result they were unable to benefit from market-driven rent increases.[8]

The perusal of court records from the late seventeenth and early eighteenth centuries shows numerous and—more significantly—very varied waqf transactions in the registers. New types of transactions in waqf property kept emerging. Long-term rent, for instance, long considered detrimental to the waqf and illegal except in exceptional cases, became commonplace. Hundreds of cases of rent of waqf property for thirty, sixty, or ninety years fill these registers. Even more amazing were the waqfs on long-term rent. In such foundations, rather than an actual property being made waqf, a long-term contract was itself made into an independent foundation. In other words, the use of property, rather than the property itself, was endowed. These deeds contradict basic waqf precepts, since long-term contracts did not have the quality of perpetuity required in waqf law. In fact, the very idea of what constituted property was also being adapted. We may see this as evidence that the process of commercialization affecting society and the economy at large was also penetrating the institution of waqf.

During the same period, the practice of *khuluw* became very widespread. It allowed a person to purchase not the waqf property but the usage of the waqf property, again with the same result: the waqf was deprived of anything but a small, stable, unchanging rent. The long-term rent contract and the *khuluw* contract were often themselves turned into waqfs. This too was against standard waqf practice because what was endowed was not property but use rights. Taken together, these and other practices along the same lines were part of the commercialization that affected waqf in the eighteenth century.

Where do guild waqfs stand in the framework of these changes? Guilds did not own real estate, nor did they attempt to acquire it. The similarity between the general and the specific cases lies in the fact that in times of change, new institutional forms may emerge and innovative practices crop up. In the specific case of guild waqfs, the form these practices took was heavily influenced by guild practices and by the general trend toward commercialization. It is also true, however, that in times of social flux, the consequences of change affected different groups in different ways. The emerging ruling class of Mamluks had encroached on the finances of the Ottoman treasury by appropriating large portions of the land tax; the alienation of waqfs was partly a reflection of their attempts to seize important urban property. Major properties in the cities had been integrated into waqfs over the decades. Through numerous transactions, these properties partially entered the real-estate market. Thus by the eighteenth century the ruling class commercialized certain aspects of waqf, and waqf properties were increasingly subject to market transactions.

We can therefore attribute the unorthodox nature of certain guild practices to the fact that the eighteenth century witnessed a number of innovations in waqf practice in general. For the most part, jurists had come to accept these innovations, and the unorthodox practices undertaken in guild waqf do not seem to have become a subject of debate among jurists. The innovative aspect of guild waqf was thus part of the general trend that touched waqf property. The specific practices that will be discussed below, however, were peculiar to guilds. On a broader level, the impact of commercialization could be felt in guilds too, and specifically on guild waqf. Guilds, as we shall see in the following pages, implemented commercial mechanisms in their administration of their waqfs.

Guild waqf: A form of common law

At some levels, the differences between guild waqfs and mainstream waqfs were not radical. Guild waqfs, less known and less studied, could be considered a variant of the better-known foundations. Features of mainstream waqfs were used in guild waqf, but not in exactly the same way. As these features filtered down to a modest category of people, they were adapted or molded to the conditions of a modest class who did not possess the means to construct or endow monumental foundations. One might compare this process of adaptation with the idea of 'appropriation' in the sense that as artisans and guilds made use of the waqf institution, they adapted it in order to fit their own conditions. Some of the objectives of waqf were adapted; the institution's rules and provisions were reformulated. In the process, some features traditionally associated with waqfs were either changed or discarded while other features were added to create a remade, reworked form of waqf. The guild waqfs thus shared features with other waqfs, but because they bore resemblances and parallels to the guild structure and guild practice, they diverged from standard practice in significant ways.

Some of these divergences bore little relation to accepted practice in waqf matters. Certain practices relating to guild waqfs can only have been innovated within the guild, since they had no parallel either in the legal provisions elaborated by jurists or in court practice. These could be perceived as unofficial or informal aspects of these waqfs, or as a kind of 'common-law' (*'urfi*) waqf, as opposed to legal or *shar'i* waqfs. Significantly, the term *waqf shar'i*, which we find in the legal deeds for mainstream waqfs, is not used in the deeds for guild waqfs.

In contrast, guild waqfs show significant similarities to guild structure and guild law. In fact there is some overlap between the guild structure, which had no status in religious law, and waqf, which did. Possibly, this overlap was behind some of the dissonance to be found in guild waqfs. We could also consider these aspects of guild waqf not so much a variant of ordinary waqf, but a parallel, a 'homemade' form, 'invented' by guild members who may not have had a perfect knowledge of the legal waqf provisions followed in court, but knew enough about the institution, in a general way, to realize that some of its features could be useful. Their waqf would be a combination of guild practice, some general knowledge of the waqf institution, and guild interests, which aimed to fulfill certain objectives.

Guild waqfs could therefore also possibly be seen as having been born from practice, rather than from a formal act. This matter requires further exploration, but if my hypothesis is accurate, it would reinforce the argument that guild waqf was a common-law institution *(waqf 'urfi)* rather than one which followed religious law *(waqf shar'i)*—bottom-up rather than a top-down, one might say—and an institution reflecting the specific conditions of artisans and guilds while showing less concern for strict adherence to legal waqf provisions.

An empirical examination of some guild waqfs will explore ways in which the institution was adapted to the context of artisans, their material conditions, and the specific nature and structure of guilds.

Unlike the better known waqfs established by the propertied Mamluk ruling class, guild waqf was created by a social stratum with limited financial resources. The waqfs in question were set up by weavers, tailors, makers of lining, and cotton producers—in other words, persons belonging to the artisan class rather than to the ruling class or the merchant class.

Consequently, property endowed as waqf was proportionately modest. Rather than real estate (buildings or land), the property in guild waqf consisted solely of copperware, such as bowls, plates, irons, cauldrons, and the like. Its value was estimated by its weight. The endowment of movable property rather than real estate had long been an accepted practice among most jurists. It meant that if, for instance, agricultural land was endowed, movable goods such as plows or other equipment could also be endowed. Hence at the level of jurisprudence this was not a novel practice. The noteworthy fact is the consistency with which copper was made waqf: none of the guild waqfs in question included any other form of property. Likewise, the property of the guild waqfs of Damascus and Istanbul also often consisted of copperware.[9]

It would appear that in these wares, the guilds had found the kind of property that was both appropriate for them and readily available in the market. Copper was infinitely more modest than the large foundations made up of monumental buildings of various kinds. Although expensive, it had the advantage of costing less than colleges, houses, commercial warehouses, baths, or most other urban property. Moreover, it was easily disposable, since it had its value in its weight; a waqf could be created even with a limited amount of capital—a few copper bowls or plates—and could be increased gradually by the addition of small or large pieces of copperware. Waqf in copper had another advantage: it served to create an income for the waqf, since generating revenue was an essential aspect of any waqf. In fact, numerous industries made use of copper utensils. For instance, sugar producers cooked sugarcane juice in large copper cauldrons in order to obtain molasses; copper utensils were also used in the process of dyeing cloth. The copper belonging to the guild waqf could consequently be rented out against the payment of a fee to those artisans needing such utensils for their work. This rent constituted an important source of income for the waqf. Presumably, the copperware, given the variety of shapes and sizes that are mentioned in the deeds, might also be rented out to people when elaborate food preparations were necessary or for the various feasts associated with public or private occasions throughout the year.

Influence of guild practice

The really distinctive feature of these waqfs is that guild interests and guild practice influenced them heavily, so that one can clearly see an overlap between the waqf framework and the guild framework. In fact, guild waqfs had certain features that were also evident in guild conduct, and consequently were characterized by an intermingling of guild rules with waqf rules. In some cases, guild rules conformed to legal waqf provisions and practice. For instance, the fact that a certain portion of the waqf revenues was set aside to help poor guild members conforms to both structures. The guild traditionally undertook to see to the welfare of its members; likewise, one of the very frequent objectives of making a waqf was charity of some kind.

In other cases, certain guild rules contravened waqf practice. One could consequently argue that the guild members used the waqf framework but changed or adapted some of its provisions in order to fit certain needs or requirements, and applied it in a way peculiar to them, largely inspired by guild practice. The result of this overlap led to waqf practices that we do not find in mainstream waqf, and that straddled the border separating legality from illegality.

The way the deeds present these waqf cases follows the pattern used for guild affairs. Acts within the guild were always undertaken in the presence of the guild shaykh and of the guild members. The names of guild members who attended and bore witness were mentioned in long lists. The deeds specify that a particular decision was taken after all the guild members, in the presence of the guild shaykh, had agreed to it. This is in keeping with guild practice. Moreover, the guild hierarchy was fully respected. As an example, in 1727 the guild of batayniya, or artisans who made linings, collectively agreed to a number of matters in the presence of their shaykh. Some of these matters were purely guild issues, like the fact that a member could only become a master craftsman *(mu'allim)* after his colleagues attested that he had mastered the craft. The same people, however, also collectively agreed to matters concerning the guild waqf: for instance, that a master craftsman should make a contribution to the waqf fund.[10] In a case dated 1726 regarding the waqf of cotton makers, the guild members in attendance are mentioned by name as collectively declaring that the person in charge of their guild waqf was no longer responsible *(bara'at zimma)* for the copper he had previously supervised, or for the waqf accounts.[11] In other words, the same procedures were followed whether the guild was considering a guild issue like the appointment of a guild shaykh or a waqf matter. The acts that guildsmen were used to undertaking for guild affairs they simply transferred to waqf affairs.

When we turn to the way that guild waqf was administered, we see the influence of guild practice again. As in guild practice, the guild shaykh had among his responsibilities to see that the waqf functioned properly. The actual running of the waqf in terms of its daily affairs was given to a guild member, with the title *amin al-nahhas* (keeper of the copper). This person, appointed from within the guild, was in charge of renting out the copperware, keeping accounts of the income, and paying the waqf expenses: namely, rent on a storeroom for the copper, payment for transporting it on a mule or donkey, and regular cleaning. In the court cases concerning guild waqfs, the *amin al-nahhas* presented the guild with the annual waqf accounts including income and expenses. These waqf matters were treated collectively within the guild, much in the same way as were other guild matters.

Guild interests

Waqfs had multiple purposes, and people who undertook to found a waqf probably had many reasons for doing so. Most waqfs had a charitable objective *(waqf khayri)* and allotted certain sums for the poor or for some other charitable or religious aim, such as feeding the poor; numerous, too, were the waqf foundations for important institutions such as colleges, elementary schools, mosques, or hospitals.[12] Many others allotted revenues for family members, sons and daughters, or slaves and freedmen *(waqf ahli)*. The majority combined these two objectives.

Guild waqfs, too, had more than one objective. The income was partly spent on charitable purposes. The guild of tailors, for instance, spent some waqf revenue on the poor guild members.[13] The guild of makers of cotton textiles likewise directed some of its waqf income to the poor, although it did not specify that the poor had to be guild members.[14] The guilds of weavers and of tailors both had provisions to use waqf income to pay for the shrouds and burial of poor guild members.[15] Other objectives were more directly related to guild issues. Some of the income of the waqf went directly to pay for guild expenses, specifically for the taxes that guild members owed.[16] A *multazim*, or tax farmer, collected the taxes imposed on crafts through the guild. This was one of the responsibilities of the guild shaykh, who collected it from the members. The allocation of waqf revenues to this purpose meant a degree of tax relief for these artisans. This feature must have acquired a certain importance at times when guild members were anxious about increases in the tax burden.

A closer scrutiny of some of the deeds related to guild waqf, however, allows us to see another dimension. The detailed accounts of the incomes and expenditures show us that the bulk of waqf revenues went neither to the poor nor toward the payment of guild taxes. The real reason for the creation of guild waqfs must thus be found elsewhere. In my view, they were established with the primary objective of consolidating the guild; the other objectives were secondary by comparison. From the amounts spent on one item or another, we can discern the priorities that the guilds had set for themselves and the emphasis they placed on certain objectives.

A deed regarding the guild waqf of cotton textile-makers, for example, shows that the expenses for the poor and for taxation represented a small portion of the actual income that came from renting the copperware. The deed specifies that the income of the guild waqf was 4,000 *nisfs*, without specifying any particular period; it is consequently not clear if this income covered a year or more. It also indicates the various expenses that were paid using this income. Certain administrative expenses had to be paid for, such as the rent of the storeroom where the copperware was kept (300 nisfs) and the cleaning of the copper (14 nisfs). Other payments went to guild members directly or indirectly, to acquit tax responsibilities or help poor members: these two items together totaled 380 nisfs. Hence, administrative expenses, payments for taxation, and payments for the poor together constituted less than a fifth of the waqf income. The bulk was spent on the purchase of more copperware, namely 25 plates and other copper items for 3,014 nisfs.[17] In this particular case, the expenses for the poor amounted to about a tenth of the money that was spent to purchase more copper for the waqf.

On the basis of these guild waqf accounts, one can make conjectures about the objectives of the foundation. Clearly, charity played a part; protection of individual guild members also played a part. But the bulk of the income was directed toward expanding the waqf and, by extension, consolidating the guild. In other words, the collective body, rather than any individual in the guild, was the main beneficiary.

This was not an isolated case. A similar pattern can be discerned with the waqf of the tailors' guild, although the information that the deed provides is less detailed. The accounts for the year 1742 indicate that between 1741 and 1742, sixty-two copper plates had been added to the guild waqf. Compared to this significant addition of copper, the expenses for charity that the waqf paid seem modest: 30 nisfs per year for each poor tailor, in addition to shrouds for the dead and fees paid to the scribes who recorded waqf accounts.[18] When Suraiya Faroqhi studied the guild waqfs of Bursa, she found that their objective was to help the artisans pay their taxes to the state, presumably at a time when taxes were increasing and weighing more heavily on the budgets of these artisans.[19] The case in Cairo was somewhat different. Judging from the accounts of these foundations, the expenses for tax payments disbursed by waqf funds were relatively modest. The bulk of the incomes went toward accumulation and expansion of the guild waqf itself. Consequently, it is not easy to classify such waqfs as within the oft-used categories of *waqf ahli* or *waqf khayri*. They do not fall neatly into either although they have elements of both—that is, if we consider the guild members as being the equivalent of family members.

Why was there a need to consolidate guilds at this particular moment? This is an important question which can shed light on the way guilds functioned, and to which different answers may be proposed. The emergence of the Mamluk ruling class was creating new conditions in Egypt. This class, as mentioned above, was expanding its financial resources by seizing tax farms and diverting the tax revenues to its own benefit. The Mamluk rulers' desire for wealth and ostentation led them to increase their consumption levels. This may well have had an impact on textile artisans, whose commodities were in high demand; consequently, it may have meant expansion in the textile market and textile production. Moreover, as André Raymond's work has shown, there was a growing market for Egyptian textiles, which may also have been a factor. France became a major importer of Egyptian textiles in the course of the eighteenth century. In what way could this encourage artisans to consolidate guild waqfs? There are various possible answers, and one can only conjecture, but the rationalization of guild finances could mean that a wealthier guild, one with funds, had some leeway in obtaining raw materials, or had enough influence to command a preferential price for them. Likewise, a strong guild was in a better position to negotiate prices when the goods its members produced were sold to merchants. Another possible reason why artisans might have wanted to consolidate their guilds involved their relations with the power structure. As the Mamluks rose to political prominence, they also tried to penetrate the economy, with various degrees of success. They had a strong presence in trading circles, and, no doubt, also tried to achieve the same preponderance in those areas of the economy that were linked to production. Members of the ruling class often tried to place their followers in guilds or even as guild heads, even when they did not have the right skills. Because local textiles were an important export product, this interference often occurred among textile producing guilds. Evidently, a stronger guild could resist such interference better than a weaker guild.[20] Any of these reasons could be behind a perceived need to consolidate guilds and could help explain why at this particular moment in time, artisans undertook to create guild waqfs.

The method by which expansion of its waqf funds helped consolidate the guild also requires some comment. In fact, the way in which waqf funds were increased is easily comparable to a business venture, as was the way the foundations were run. Over the years, some of these waqfs were clearly able to accumulate funds through the commercial activities in which they engaged. This implied a rationalization of guild practices. Specifically, the way these waqfs were administered aimed at expanding profits by channeling the incomes in a certain direction. For some guilds, this led to significant growth in their capital. Thus guilds too were influenced by the trend toward commercialization, and its repercussions—evident in other aspects of life—were also evident among artisans and their guilds.

Contradictions between guild practice and waqf

The commercialization of guild practice created certain anomalies in the way guildsmen implemented the waqf. As a result of the overlap between guild practice and waqf, indeed, guild waqfs were in a nebulous zone between legal and illegal spheres, or between formal waqfs that followed the legal provisions formulated by classical Islamic law and waqfs that, for whatever reason, did not follow or fully conform to these laws. This was because the waqf institution was subordinated to guild rules and used to forward guild interests.

The voluntary nature of waqf

Islamic waqf law requires a person who establishes a waqf to be in full possession of the property endowed, and to endow it (that is, to transfer it from the realm of private property to waqf) of his own free will. This means that for a waqf to be valid, a founder must have given up property willingly so that its revenues could be used for a charitable purpose or other beneficiaries. Creating a waqf is an individual decision ratified by the court. In many instances, however, the deeds of guild waqf showed that contributions to the waqf were not voluntary, but formed part of the rules of the guild: promotion through the ranks could be made conditional on such contributions, for example. The makers of textile for lining outlined the conditions of the guild when choosing a shaykh in 1727: any member who wanted to be promoted to master of the craft had to give the guild waqf five copper plates weighing a total of 10 *ratl*s.[21] Likewise the guild of cotton makers set similar rules in 1730: to become master craftsman, a member had to contribute 1,000 nisfs to the guild waqf.[22]

These payments replenished guild waqfs continually. They were also in keeping with another guild practice that had become common in the eighteenth century: that a guild member was required to pay a fine to the guild if he had violated a guild law. Prior to this period, violations of guild law could mean that a member was expelled from the guild. As time went by, however, the practice of paying fines seems to become increasingly widespread. These fines could be paid to the head of the guild, to a charity linked to a guild, and so on. Therefore obligatory payments to guild waqfs had a parallel in other guild practices. Such payments, even when they were relatively small, suggest that money, of which there were shortages in the seventeenth century, was available fairly easily in the eighteenth.

The fact remains that obligatory payments to the waqf violated a basic precept of waqf law, yet, despite this and other contradictions between guild waqf practices and the classical regulations pertaining to waqf, the deeds in question were made out in the presence of a *qadi* (judge) and registered in court. But why would a qadi place his seal of approval on a deed that did not follow the basic rules of waqf law? Two explanations can be offered. The simple one is that these deeds should not be considered waqf transactions. The more complex one is that, in the eyes of the law, the qadi could consider that he had notarized a deed without legalizing its contents. Such notarization of acts in court was a fairly commonplace procedure. It did not amount to a legalizing of the contents of the deed. We will return to this point below.

Waqf administration

There is another dissonance between guild waqf and waqf as it was formulated in law books and applied in courts, specifically related to the administration of waqf property. Pious foundations dealt with money, frequently large sums. The person who made the waqf also made provisions on how revenues were to be used. Since these provisions had to be carried out in perpetuity, the qadi had the duty to supervise the appointment of an overseer for the waqf after the founder's death. In the court registers, there are hundreds of such appointments *(qarar nazar)*, made when a supervisor had died and the qadi had to appoint a successor. This did not happen in guild waqf. Instead, appointments of supervisors for these waqfs were made internally. It appears from the wording of the various deeds that the head of the guild was responsible for running the waqf—that is, the waqf was administered according to guild law. We can therefore say that guilds were making use of the waqf institution as a framework without really bothering about all the provisions that Islamic law saw as necessary conditions to make a waqf legal. Thus there seems to be a contradiction between guild law, which was usually formulated by the guilds themselves, and waqf law, formulated by experts in jurisprudence.

Guild waqfs and the qadi

Why, then, were matters related to guild waqfs, which did not conform to the provisions of waqf law, considered by the qadi and notarized in the court registers? Two sets of reasons are plausible. In the first place, guild waqf could have the same standing as guild practice. When a guild chose a shaykh or took a decision, this was registered in court in the presence of the shaykh and guild members. Guild decisions, in other words, did not have any legal standing but are regularly found in court registers.

On a more general level, in a study on the approaches one could use in the study of court records, Magdi Guirguis noted that it was necessary to make a distinction between those cases where the qadi's stamp was a confirmation of the legality of the case and an indication that he had judged it on the basis of religious law; and those cases in which the qadi acknowledged that certain facts had taken place, either in his presence or according to the testimony of witnesses, regardless of the legality of the contents. Thus, not everything that was recorded in the court registers was by necessity a legal action. In support of his argument, he refers to some of the sixteenth-century manuals that were used by qadis to advise them on how to carry out their duties in court. One of these, written by Abul Su'ud al-'Imadi (d. 1574), made a distinction between what took place in the qadi's presence and what was a legal act based on the shari'a, upon which he based a sentence or judgment. This argument is also in line with the ideas expressed by another legal scholar, Darwish ibn Muhammad ibn Iflatun, who confirmed that, in his time (the 1570s), many of the acts that a qadi passed were in fact not legal or shar'i acts. He provided the qadi with advice on the way he should affix his seal to such cases.[23]

This could be another explanation for why the guild waqfs were registered before the qadi even though the provisions and the acts undertaken were not in conformity with waqf law. Applying Magdi Guirguis's argument, perhaps the qadi simply acknowledged that certain acts or decisions related to a guild had taken place in his presence without reference to whether or not they were legal acts.

In some ways, the conditions described above are reminiscent of the cash waqfs in sixteenth-century Anatolia that Jon Mandaville studied. It had become a common practice in this region for people to make a waqf from cash that would be lent at interest, with the revenue from the interest serving a charitable purpose. Even though lending at interest went against the teachings of Islamic law, this practice had not only become commonplace but was undertaken in the qadi's court. Only after long debates did some jurists deem it to be acceptable.[24] Mandaville's study shows how the cash waqf of Anatolia had its origin in practice rather than in theory or academic discourse. Only when cash waqfs became widespread among the population of this region was the matter taken up by the ulama and its provisions discussed and given a legal framework. This is a good example of how *'urf* became integrated into legal practice.

One cannot say the same about guild waqfs in terms of the process of legalization. Guild waqfs do not appear to have raised a discussion among religious scholars, possibly because they were never quite as widespread. The comparison between these two kinds of waqf is nevertheless interesting on two levels. First, it shows how certain practices that did not fully conform to provisions of jurisprudence were nevertheless carried out in the court; secondly, and most importantly, such a comparison reveals grassroots practices in both cases, initiated by ordinary people rather than by those in power or by the religious establishment, which fulfilled their needs but bordered on the illegal.

Summary and conclusion

We may draw a number of conclusions from the study of the guild waqfs established in the late Ottoman period. One of these has to do with the relationship between religious law and common law, the exact nature of which is open to debate. In a society where waqf played a major role, and most institutions—hospitals, colleges, and elementary schools, to name but a few—were run by waqfs, everyone knew what waqf was and probably had some direct experience of it in their daily lives. We can imagine that these artisans made use of an institution that fulfilled certain needs at a particular moment. They knew it could have many uses, but did not fully understand its more formal aspects and were not knowledgeable about its legal provisions. Waqf was part of their lived experience, since they drank from waqf public fountains, prayed in waqf mosques, and received their elementary education in schools funded by waqfs. Hence their experience of waqf was visible, concrete, and situated in the realm of the practical. It is possible that artisans had a heightened sense of pragmatism with regard to the usefulness of the waqf institution to their guilds, and this pragmatism shaped the way they used it. The way they administered it thus corresponded to *their* understanding of what waqf was, but not necessarily to what was in the books. Possibly, too, the word waqf had a different meaning for them than it did for others who were more closely involved with educated or scholarly circles. One noteworthy point that emerges from these explanations is that we can get an inkling of what waqf could mean not only to those who were scholars or qadis, but also to those whose concerns lay elsewhere, in more practical domains.

It seems that these persons of relatively modest social and economic status made use of a 'traditional' mechanism—that of waqf, a religious institution with old roots in Islamic society and a very pervasive presence in Cairo between the fourteenth and the eighteenth centuries—by adapting it to the framework of what they were familiar with: the guild. By doing so, they were better able to confront changing economic conditions. The guild waqfs can thus be placed in the framework of 'history from below' as the initiatives of persons outside the establishment and removed from the power structure who sought ways to protect themselves and innovated in the process.

The study of guild waqfs is also a way of understanding the breadth and variety of form that the waqf institution could have. Guild waqfs, an offshoot or a variant of mainstream waqf, can be considered as the outcome of particular circumstances. On a broad level, this was a period of social flux. The Mamluk households were emerging as a powerful force in society. They tried to control the financial resources and to penetrate various parts of the economy. At the same time, a growing commercialization was affecting many sectors of the urban society. As a result of these conditions, a number of important institutions were also undergoing change. Some artisans and guilds were more affected than others by these changing conditions. The anxieties created by these transformations led to many reactions from ordinary people. Some artisans closed their shops, some demonstrated in the streets, and some found their solace in Sufi circles. The change in guilds was consequently one of several channels by which artisans could confront conditions that were not always in their favor.

Notes

1   Amin, *al-Awqaf.*
2   Denoix, "Exploitation," 34–35.
3   Guild waqfs are discussed in some detail in Hanna, *Artisan Entrepreneurs.*
4   Raymond, *Artisans*, 229.
5   Raymond, *Artisans*, 229–30.
6   Faroqhi, "Ottoman Guilds"; Marino, "Copper Plates"; Yi, *Guild Dynamics.*
7   Hanna, *Habiter au Caire*, 31–35.
8   Crecelius, "Waqf."
9   Yi, *Guild Dynamics*, 62–62 and 85–87; Marino, "Copper Plates."
10 Zahid, reg. 690, p. 319, doc. 589.
11 Zahid, reg. 690, p. 271, doc. 490, 1726.
12 Sabra, *Poverty.*
13 Dasht, reg. 208, p. 340, 1690.
14 Zahid, reg. 688, p. 326, doc. 644, 1718, and Zahid, reg. 690, p. 271–72, doc. 490, 1726.
15 Zahid, reg. 692, p. 311, doc. 612, 1733.
16 Zahid, reg. 688, p. 326, doc. 644, 1718.
17 Zahid, reg. 688, p. 326, doc. 644, 1718.
18 a-Salih, reg. 351, p. 561, doc. 973, 1742.
19 Faroqhi, "Ottoman Guilds," 102–106.

20   Some aspects of this matter are discussed in more detail in Hanna, *Artisan Entrepreneurs*.
21   Zahid, reg. 690, p. 319, doc. 589, 1727.
22   Zahid, reg. 691, p. 164–65, doc. 297, 1730.
23   Guirguis, "Manahij al-dirasa."
24   Mandaville, "Usurious Piety."

Bibliography

Archival Sources
Ottoman Court Records
Dasht, reg. 208.
al-Salih, reg. 351.
Zahid, reg. 688, 690, 691, and 692.

Publications and Other Sources
Amin, Muhammad Muhammad. *al-Awqaf wa-l-hayah al-ijtima'iya fi Misr, 648–923 H, 1250–1517 M: dirasa tarikiya watha'iqiya*. Cairo: Dar al-Nahda al-'Arabiya, 1980.

Crecelius, Daniel. "The Waqf of Muhammad Bey Abu Al-Dhahab in Historical Perpsective." *International Journal of Middle East Studies*, no. 23 (1991): 57–81.

Denoix, Sylvie. "Pour une exploitation d'ensemble d'un corpus: Les waqfs mamelouks du Caire," in Randi Deguilhem, ed., *Le waqf dans l'espace islamique: Outil de pouvoir socio-politique*, 29–44. Damacus: Institut français de Damas, 1995.

Faroqhi, Suraiya. "Ottoman Guilds in the Late Eighteenth Century: The Bursa Case." in S. Faroqhi, *Making a Living in the Ottoman Lands 1480 to 1820*, 93–112. Istanbul: Isis Press, 1995.

Guirguis, Magdi. "Manahij al-dirasa al-watha'iqiya wa waqi' al bahth fi Misr." *al-Ruznama* 2 (2004): 273–74.

Hanna, Nelly. *Artisan Entrepreneurs*. Syracuse: Syracuse University Press, forthcoming.

———. *Habiter au Caire: La maison moyenne et ses habitants aux XVIIe et XVIIIe siècles*. Cairo: Institut français d'archéologie orientale, 1991.

Mandaville, Jon. "Usurious Piety: The Cash Waqf Controversy in the Ottoman Empire." *International Journal of Middle East Studies* 10, no. 3 (1979): 289–308.

Marino, Brigitte. "The Copper Plates of Ipshir Mustafa Pasha: Waqf al-Manqulat in Mamluk and Early Ottoman Damascus." Paper presented to the Seventh International Conference on the History of Bilad al-Sham, Damascus, 2006.

Raymond, André. *Artisans et commerçants au Caire au XVIIIe siècle*. Damascus: Institut français d'études orientales, 1974

Sabra, Adam. *Poverty and Charity in Medieval Islam: Mamluk Egypt, 1250–1517*. Cambridge: Cambridge University Press, 2000

Yi, Eunjeong. *Guild Dynamics in Seventeenth-Century Istanbul, Fluidity and Leverage*. Leiden: Brill, 2004.

7

Waqfs of Cyrenaica and Italian Colonialism in Libya (1911–41)[1]

Anna Maria Medici

In Cyrenaica, as elsewhere in the Muslim Mediterranean, waqf constituted a major resource and so was an important part of the Italian colonial authorities' efforts to sustain the initiative of occupation. The importance of waqf in the economic, strategic, and cultural fields, especially in Cyrenaica, and its relevance to the religious and cultural identity of the colonized people, meant that waqf policy was a crucial component of colonial projects. In this sense, it was repeatedly at stake in the struggle pursued by the colonial authorities to impose competing definitions of legitimacy and community.

Italy first occupied the Ottoman territories of Tripolitania and Cyrenaica in 1911; by the outbreak of the First World War, however, the implications of Italian control in Lybia were scarcely to be seen and were confined to the coastal towns. On the whole, while in Tripolitania the conquest began before fascists seized power in Italy (in 1922), in Cyrenaica Italian colonialism necessarily adopted a different policy. Political and geographical conditions in Cyrenaica dictated a different attitude for the colonial conquest of the region:[2] from 1922, the so-called reconquest of these territories heralded significant suffering, disruption, and oppression for the Libyan peoples as the interior was gradually 'pacified' by colonial forces.

The Italian attempt to conquer Cyrenaica met its main opposition in the Sanusiya brotherhood, a Sufi order established in Cyrenaica in the 1840s by a Maghrebi scholar, Muhammad bin 'Ali al-Sanusi (1787–1859). Italian rule was finally extended from the Libyan coast into the desert in the 1930s.[3]

A closer examination of the interplay between laws, customs, and colonial 'reform' of waqf—as well as the discourse on waqf produced by Libyan Muslims and Italians—tells the story of a ceaseless competition for resources between local communities and colonial authorities. It is also a story of the modification of Cyrenaica's physical and cultural landcape, and attempts to exercise control over social hierarchies.[4] There is evidence of how waqf structured the landscape in Muslim areas, and also of its great dynamism and resilience.[5] The institution in Cyrenaica was an instrument used by both Muslims and colonialists, though with opposite aims. Muslims (particularly notables, appointed and co-opted by the Italians to work on waqf administration boards) sought to turn the institution's complexity to their advantage. At first, they attributed the legitimacy of waqf to Qur'anic stipulations, hoping in this way to buttress the security of waqf assets and set up a barrier to colonial economic penetration. As for the Italians, they tried to interpret complex regulations pertaining to waqf in such a way as to take full advantage of resources 'from within.' At the same time, they were keen to show nominal respect for colonial policy, which stipulated the preservation of indigenous Muslim institutions. To reconcile their contra-dictory aims, they turned to two eminent Italian scholars of Islamic law: David Santillana and Carlo Alfonso Nallino.[6]

Cyrenaica's colonial conquest

In Libya, a first phase of colonial initiative was carried out on the part of the lib-eral state and was followed by the so-called fascist recovery.[7] These two phases together lasted only three decades, but had a lasting impact on waqf patrimony.

The colony was divided into two territories, officially joined in a single colony in 1934: Tripolitania (also including Fezzan), with a governor in Tripoli, and Cyrenaica, with a governor in Benghazi. These regions did not form a historical unit. Tripolitania was part of the Maghreb; Fezzan and the Kufra oasis were part of the Sahara desert, while Cyrenaica was linked to Egypt. After the colonial conquest, Italian governors had wide powers, including the command of armed forces, and they could select native 'advi-sors' (who received official nomination from the minister). A decree issued on 11 March 1917 established a 'Native Advisory Committees for Libya.' The system was inspired by French experience in Algeria and the *bureaux arabes*.

Italian colonian administration followed a distinction between 'pacified' areas on the one hand, which were under direct civil rule (these corresponded roughly to the towns and coastal areas), and, on the other, zones of indirect military rule (the hinterland). But borders between these two zones fluctuated, and were defined in accordance with the outcome of military operations.

This is also why colonial policy wavered between two administrative models until 1919: centralization and collaboration (or even joint management) with a hand-picked native hierarchy. Such hesitation, in the long term, generated ambiguous relations with local community representatives,[8] an ambiguity that greatly affected pious foundations.

There is a remarkable difference, in this regard, between Tripolitania and Cyrenaica. In Tripolitania, at the time of colonial conquest, waqfs were under the control of the Ottoman sultan's representative. Only in 1915 was the Ottoman Empire completely excluded from the management of charitable foundations, which were assimilated into the colonial system, even while waqf regulations and the rights of beneficiaries were being reaffirmed. In Cyrenaica, in contrast, most of waqf patrimony was under the control of Sanusi *zawaya* (plural of *zawiya*, or hospice). While in Tripolitania waqf assets were diversified, in Cyrenaica waqf patrimony was made up mainly of land.

In a bid for popular support of colonial rule, Italy was attempting to present itself as a defender of Islam. From the beginning of colonial rule, respect for Islamic institutions and local traditions was continually reiterated—not only in colonial propaganda but also in political records—and even presented as a pillar of Italian colonial policy. A 1911 decree specified that waqf properties would be managed as they had been before, "with absolutely no interference on the part of the Italian authorities."[9] The Italians, indeed, long considered it necessary to preserve the waqf system, at least in formal terms; reform was the only modification they were willing to contemplate.

The paucity of arable land available for settlement, however, as well as the vast extent and value of waqf patrimony, brought the colonizers face to face with an irresolvable contradiction: on the one hand, they had pledged to defend Islamic institutions; on the other, Italian colonialism was demographically oriented, and required a system that could 'associate' Italian settlers with the indigenous population in exploiting arable land. In other words, Italy had to adopt a policy that not only developed resources (as colonialist propaganda asserted), but also allowed for the settlement of Italian nationals on colonial territory, while enabling the acquisition of land and agricultural exploitation. In 1913, the Italian government therefore issued a decree initiating a process of property certification. In Cyrenaica, territorial Land Registry Offices were established for this purpose at Derna and Benghazi. Land surveys in the early years of colonial occupation show that Tripolitania and Cyrenaica did not have much empty land for Italian settlers to take over. A commission set up by the Africa ministry to survey Tripoli and its hinterland debunked the myth of Libya as Promised Land[10] as early as February 1912.[11] This evaluation was confirmed by a commission meeting in June 1913.[12] Extant title deeds obtained by the Italians show that land was divided into *mulk* (private), *miri* (state property), and waqf (charitable trusts).

By 1916, the question of waqfs was being explicitly defined in official records as the main obstacle to colonization: "The most serious issue that a colonialist state must face when it operates in a Muslim country endowed with ample lands that could assure the formation and development of a colony is, certainly, that of the availability of the land itself, which is for the most part set aside for constitution as *habus* [waqf] patrimony, and then immobilized. Hence the need to find a solution meeting these substantial requirements: first, avoiding any offense to Islamic basic principles; second, simultaneously allowing colonization of land constituted as *habus*. Above all, the solution must prevent land from being constituted as *habus* once more, which removes it [sic] from circulation, while allowing the colonization of the assets already constituted as *habus*."[13]

Italy therefore began a campaign of colonialist manipulation targeting waqfs.[14] A phase of closer examination was launched, with the creation of investigative commissions whose reports were scrutinized by Italian scholars of Islamic law.

First enquiries

The first measure taken by the colonial authorities was to establish a mixed commission, made up of Italians and indigenous Muslims, who were responsible for examining waqf assets and suggesting reforms. Libyans were appointed to this advisory body in accordance with the principle of the *associazione* of indigenous Muslims and the Italians' proclaimed respect for Islam. They were selected from among pro-Italian notables (Farhat Bey, Hassuna Basha, and Dawud Afandi, to cite a few names).

The deliberations of the commission began on 6 November 1915 and produced a tome of minutes and reports showing how unprepared the Italians were for this task. These records maintained that colonial development could be ensured while "respecting the principles of Islamic law" in two ways: either by exchanging waqf assets (as was attempted in Tunisia), or through long-term or perpetual tenancy (in Tunisia: *inzal*, in Egypt: *khuluw*).[15] Exchange appeared more feasible, but was not considered the best means of reform, because, although it moved individual properties back onto the market, it did not reduce the size of the patrimony alienated through waqf. In consequence, it did not enable the Italians to increase the overall amount of assets available to colonization.

It was then suggested that the inzal contract be considered as an option. The colonial administrators favored this legal instrument, especially because the French had used it in Tunisia to great benefit for the colonizers. According to the commission's final recommendation, "this form of contract [is] in accordance with both Islamic principles and colonial interests . . . . It could be the basis of a possible agreement with the Sanusiya."[16] The solution to be implemented, however, was subject to approval on the part of the waqf administrators.

A report authored by the scholar Carlo Alfonso Nallino painstakingly highlights the mistakes and naiveté in the commission's deliberations. Nallino noted a "fixation with imitating the French,"[17] and indeed a "true obsession" with inzal. As a scholar of Islam, he found this single-mindedness unreasonable, above all because such contracts were "utterly unknown in Libya"; instead, Tripolitanians used other forms of contract, "which are better."[18] Emphasizing the specificity of Libyan waqf practice, Nallino suggested that reforms be undertaken on the basis of local legal sources. As the judge appointed to the commission had already suggested, Nallino felt it would be best to use the *khuluw al-intifa* contract, entitling the lessor to rights of usufruct, for waqf property that had deteriorated. This made it possible to repair the waqf and was also customary in Egypt, where judges of the Maliki *madhhab* (school of religious law) recommended it. Other options suggested were the *hikr* contract (which Nallino interpreted as pinning rent to increases in the value of waqf assets) for agricultural land; and the *mugharasa*, or land lease—all instruments, he writes, that "are already customary" in Libya.[19]

The jurist, furthermore, astutely pointed out that these agreements had no foundation in religious law, but were rooted exclusively in local customs (*'urf*). Nallino argued strongly that the 1915 commission's gravest mistake was to believe that waqf was a Qur'anic institution: "The bias toward the 'religious nature' of waqf caused the Italian members [of the commission] to fall into the trap skilfully set by natives,"[20] he maintained. For this reason, Nallino was astounded by the fact that the Italians had not bothered to examine waqf documents before undertaking to propose appropriate reforms.

As for the commission's Muslim members, they repeatedly sought to take advantage of the Italians' incompetence and impede their territorial control. Nallino countered their attempts to reassert control over waqf assets in several instances. When, for example, the Muslim members suggested that waqf revenues earmarked for education should be set aside for the establishment of a 'Scientific Islamic University' in Tripoli (similar to Zaytuna in Tunis or al-Azhar in Cairo), Nallino, who considered such a proposal to be contrary to Italian interests, suggested that the money available for education should be set aside not to fund a university, but rather for an Islamic cultural institution to be established by the Italians (in keeping with the dual education system, Italian and native, set up by the colonial administrators).[21] Nallino thus sought to avoid precisely what the Libyans had hoped to achieve: including the university within a waqf, as one of the foundation's assets. Nallino wanted to obtain funding for the school from the waqf's revenue-generating assets, while preventing Muslims from exerting any influence over management or personnel selection.[22]

The Italian administration, therefore, did not attempt to dismantle the institution of waqf as such, principally because the colonial officials saw waqfs as permanent charitable foundations that appeared to be endowed with sanctity.[23] On the other hand, they did try to persuade local political and religious elites to join reform efforts that would ultimately allow the Italians to seize land assets belonging to waqfs. Although rural colonization was at the heart of Italian propaganda and expectations that drove the conquest itself, in Libya it developed slowly. In Tripolitania, between 1914 and 1922, just 3,612 hectares of land were given in concession to Italian settlers.[24] They had belonged to the Ottoman administration and had been seized by the colonial state after occupation. Starting in 1922, the Italians took concerted measures to increase the expanse of land under their control, decreeing that all uncultivated land would be considered state property. In consequence, settlement increased, and between 1922 and 1926 the colonial administration seized 58,000 hectares, most of which (31,000 hectares) were granted to Italian nationals.[25]

Only in 1926, however, after the start of fascist rule, did Italian settlement policy in Libya take a more definitive shape. In 1928, the governor of Libya, De Bono, enacted new legislation concerning state-subsidized colonization, and by 1931 the colonial state owned a remarkable 220,000 hectares, of which half was ceded for cultivation to a very restricted number of settlers (around 7,500).[26] In Cyrenaica, the situation was very different: for various reasons, the state had not implemented a similar policy of agrarian settlement, and therefore did not control such vast tracts of land.

In Cyrenaica

In Cyrenaica, the waqfs were closely connected with the existence of the Sanusiya brotherhood. The institution's evolution during colonial times followed the rhythm of relations between Italian authorities and the brotherhood.

Thus, the obstacle to colonial penetration represented by the Sanusiya, with their network of awqaf assets, was decisive in the first phase of conquest. Cyrenaica was a theater of Italian military operations until 1931, but the network of Sanusi hospices and the landed property they controlled enabled the brotherhood to check colonial designs on eastern Libya. Indeed, the Sanusiya seem to have prevented the Italians even from carrying out land surveys: in 1913 and 1914, the Italian government ordered the political and military administration of Cyrenaica to conduct a census of *zawiya* estates, but this initiative had no significant outcomes.[27]

A first attempt to seize the brotherhood's land assets was made through the governor's circular letters of February 1914, which decreed sequestration with judgments of confiscation by war tribunals.[28] These decrees merely enshrined the status quo reached by that point: The First World War had not yet unsettled military plans in this area, and the advancing Italians had asserted their control over Sanusi territories in western and central Cyrenaica.[29]

After the First World War, it was imperative for Italy to come to an agreement with the Sanusiya, and on 17 April 1917 the two parties came to a modus vivendi at Acroma (thirty kilometers south of Tobruk). The agreement was rife with ambiguities. Neither the Italians nor the Sanusi representatives were willing to relinquish their claim of sovereignty over the area. However, in light of difficult military conditions on the ground, the agreement gave Italians an advantage by closing one of the battlefronts. Meanwhile, Muhammad Idris al-Sanusi, the leader of the brotherhood, continued to wield sovereign power over almost all Cyrenaica.[30]

Two years later, in 1919, the Italians signed a further agreement with Muhammad Idris, in which Italy pledged to return all zawaya and attached assets that its forces had seized during the conquest. Applying Article 15 of the Acroma modus vivendi, the government of Cyrenaica also appointed a mixed commission that was responsible for conducting a census of all Sanusiya assets in that region.[31] Unlike its predecessor in 1913–14, this commission succeeded—albeit only partially—in giving the Italians an important basis for the verification of title to land, which would be used for confiscation after 1930. The two Italian executives heading the land offices of Benghazi and Derna, Massimo Colucci and Fernando Valenzi,[32] joined the commission, along with Sidi Idris al-Sanusi's representative, named in the document as Shaykh Muhammad Bu-Negima al-Fahasi. Colucci and Valenzi presented their report on 24 August 1919 (*"Relazione della Commissione per l'accertamento dei beni delle Zavie Senussite della Cirenaica"*). They had surveyed and registered the estates of only fourteen zawaya out of a total exceeding forty, which the above-mentioned agreement designated as land under de facto Italian occupation at that time. The 'Senusso' himself indicated the zawaya to the Italian government and appointed members of the brotherhood *(ikhwan)* to guide the members of the commission.[33] The commission would reach a zawiya, mark out the plots shown by the ikhwan, hold inquiries by cross-examining the interested parties to determine where individual plots ended, and subdivide the plots. It wrote up the procedures carried out for each property, but took no decisions, this prerogative being reserved to another political body that was supposed to take over when the commission had completed its survey.

This process does not correspond to stereotypical ideas of a colonial land grab. It seems clear that, in territory that was already subject to Italian military occupation, Sidi Idris al-Sanusi pointed out the zawaya to be inspected—a clear example of collaboration with the authorities. This interaction originated in the framework of the political agreement implicit in the modus vivendi of Acroma and turned out to be valuable for the Italians. Thanks to the cooperation of Sanusi leaders, the colonial authorities could overcome the hindrances resulting from Libyan reticence, especially when surveying vast coastal waqf lands. The reports produced by the mixed commission showed the careful outline of a remarkable part of the landed waqf property that was at brotherhood's disposal in 1919. The fourteen zawaya registered by the commission controlled an astonishing 45,033 hectares (ca. 450 square kilometres) along the Mediterranean coast. This survey, however, could not include the numerous other zawaya that resisted the Italians' survey efforts. Those of Jabal, the 'Abaydat, Marmarica, and a large part of the area south of Benghazi, as well as all the zawaya in territory controlled by the Sanusiya, yielded absolutely no information that the Italians could use in adducing proof of economic value.[34]

Italy's policy of association with the Sanusiya was legally defined in an agreement signed on 25 October 1920 at al-Rijma (not far from Benghazi). The agreement granted direct sovereignty over the Libyan coast and highlands to Italy, while entrusting the "self-governing administration" of the rest of Cyrenaica, including the inland oases, to Muhammad Idris al-Sanusi, named 'the Senusso' by the Italians. Article 15 of an agreement signed on 16 August 1921 further specified that the brotherhood could enjoy full control over its property. The association of Italian colonial rule with Sanusi self-administration was sealed by the Sanusi amir's solemn official visit to Italy, where he was welcomed by King Victor Emmanuel III. Italians who opposed this evolution in colonial policy complained that it was tantamount to acknowledging the existence of two distinct governments.

This was not accurate. Italy, which had proved unable to get rid of the Senusso, had attempted to reduce him to a mere religious leader: according to the agreements, he was obliged to refrain from collecting tolls, rates, tithes, and other taxes, and could only collect the *zakat* (Islamic tax). This attempt to circumscribe his authority, however, did not remove obstacles to agrarian settlement, as the Italians had hoped. On the contrary, the brotherhood was able to consolidate its hold on its waqf property. The example of Cyrenaica shows how waqf—in the case of uneven relations such as those between colonial rulers and native notables—could be used as both an offensive and a defensive weapon.

Common spaces, divided memories

Ten years after the conquest, the Italians had reached an impasse with regard to the waqf lands of Cyrenaica, due as much to the resistance put up by the Sanusiya as to the imperatives of colonial 'Islamic' policy. Although Italy took the French approach to the colonial reform of waqf (and particularly the example of Tunisia) as its model, Italy failed to effect legal reforms as France had done. The Senusso was therefore able to prevent the Italians from taking over waqf assets, on the grounds that these assets were bound by their religious vocation. Even as a mere religious leader, the Senusso could claim control over the landed property of zawaya—indeed, the brotherhood's leadership did so on the basis of the agreements concluded with the Italians.

Having failed in its bid to seize waqf assets through reform, Italy chose instead to address what it saw as blunders in colonial policy by force alone. It undertook a violent repression of the Sanusi resistance in the late 1920s before passing a confiscation decree in 1930. With the rise of Fascism, settling colonists on agricultural land arose as an urgent aim of colonial policy. The situation in Cyrenaica was further transformed by the outcome of the battle between Italian troops and brotherhood members.

From the outset, the logic of Italian intervention and colonial policy, whether liberal or fascist, was designed to populate Cyrenaica with Italians, who were to replace the area's original inhabitants. Inspiration could be found elsewhere, in the results other colonial powers had achieved in earlier decades. Times had changed, however, since the beginning of the colonial era,[35] particularly as far as waqf was concerned. On the one hand, the policy of 'respect' for local institutions—asserted by Italy—followed the trend set by the more 'advanced' manifestations of colonialism (exemplified by France's approach to waqf, which it modified over time). On the other, Italian attempts to effect 'colonial reform' of the institution, and the brutal assault the Italians ended up launching, occurred during a phase of reexamination within many Muslim societies—the outcome of a process already begun at the time of the nineteenth-century reforms. Although they were operating at cross-purposes, both these historical processes contributed to the dismantling of the waqf system. They overlapped and combined with particular force when the Italians carried out their assault on waqf lands in Cyrenaica, with unavoidable ambiguities. In this manner, the Italians exploited internal Muslim critiques of the waqf system during the late colonial period.

In practice, the Italian occupation devastated Libya's Bedouin communities and the Sanusiya brotherhood in particular. The Italians carried out a campaign of assassinations, incarceration in concentration camps, and the wholesale massacre of cattle.[36] The brotherhood's zawaya were bombarded, torn down, left to decay, or turned into Italian military posts.[37] Even Zawiyat al-Bayda—the oldest zawiya in Cyrenaica, established in 1840 by the brotherhood's founder, Shaykh Muhammad bin Ali al-Sanusi, and the center of the brotherhood until the establishment of the zawiya of Jarabub in 1855—was taken over to house government offices and a post for the Carabinieri.[38] In early 1931, the occupation of the holy city of al-Kufra (Cufra), and the bloody battle that took place there, made a great impression in Cyrenaica: Deputy-Governor General Graziani himself feared that, because of the mystical qualities associated with such oases, the occupation had perhaps "rekindled rather than deadened the religious spirit that inflames the combatants of the Gebel."[39]

Even during this decisive, violent phase of the occupation, the transfer of landed property from Sanusi to Italian ownership took place in three different steps: military seizures ordered by Graziani, which continued for many months; legal investigations, which were intended to legitimize the final transfer of the property to the colonial authorities; and finally, confiscation by royal decree.

On 29 May 1930, Graziani ordered all the zawaya in Cyrenaica to close and cease their activities; he had all the leaders arrested and confined in a single place, and all the assets seized ("measure for full confiscation to be submitted to Ministry")—with the exception of the assets that zawaya leaders had bequeathed to their families.[40]

Even when the authorities opted for the use of force, they avoided examining the institution of waqf from the legal and political points of view, and the Italian government sought to strike a difficult balance by refusing to abandon its 'Islamic' policy in relation to foundation assets. The ministry wanted to justify confiscation as a special measure, taken against rebels, and thus to dispel suspicions that it was carrying out an assault on the institution as such, which could have been interpreted as an anti-religious act. For this reason, the ministry insisted that confiscation should concern Cyrenaica alone, rather than extending to Libyan territory as a whole. Notwithstanding such scruples, in August 1930, Badoglio, the governor of Tripolitania, declared that he was willing "to issue a special decree [in Tripolitania] concurrently with the Royal one that will concern Cyrenaica's assets."[41] Minister De Bono emphasized, on the contrary, that the "radical difference in the political situation of the two Libyan colonies would not justify in any way the confiscation of the assets belonging to Sanussiyya in [Tripolitania]."[42] The minister added that, indeed, "the freedom allowed the Sanusiyya to continue their usual religious activities in Tripolitania plainly proves . . . that the measures taken against the brotherhood in Cyrenaica have no anti-religious nature." He specified: "It seems to me that such argument has a remarkable moral value and it is not advisable for us to refrain from using it."[43] For the same reason, the zawiya of Giarabub was excluded from any restrictive measure because many Muslims considered it a holy site (and also because it was bound by previous Italian agreements with Egypt).[44] Assets more closely related to religious functions were also spared confiscation. As the decree noted: "real properties consecrated for the purposes of mosque and burial retain their waqf nature, and join the public awqaf of the Colony."[45] In this way, Italy redefined the symbolic space reserved to religious institutions in Cyrenaica.

Still, as late as June 1930, the ministry did not consider the confiscation measure to be totally irrevocable. Italy's international status had been damaged by the long campaign to crush the Libyan resistance, but it could not relinquish its target of 'pacification.'[46] The plan to confiscate waqf property, however, had been on the back burner for years (having replaced the failed attempts at 'reform'), and, in the summer of 1930, De Bono could refer to the instructions already issued on the subject in 1928 by minister of colonies Luigi Federzoni.[47]

In preparation for the implementation of the confiscation program, a judge, Adolfo Fantoni, was requested to draw up a report on the legal nature of Sanusi assets in Cyrenaica with the purpose of finding legal arguments in favor of the colonial authorities' actions. The result was a legal opinion that, of course, 'advised' the authorities on how to proceed with the confiscation of remaining Sanusi assets. This was ultimately achieved with decree 22 of December 1930, n. 1944.[48] Legal arguments were clearly instrumental in this regard, since they supported the plan of colonial divestment. Soon after, Fernando Valenzi, another Italian expert already involved in evaluating waqf in Cyrenaica,[49] affirmed that the confiscation decree "brings to an end a series of measures previously issued with the same purpose—that of taking away the Sanusiyya's property."[50] The act, he added in his comment, "further preempts any theoretical issue."[51] The property confiscated was huge, encompassing hundreds of buildings and almost seventy thousand hectares of the best land in Cyrenaica.[52]

The arguments adduced by judge Fantoni, even if they were the work of "specious jurists,"[53] show some noteworthy features. The ministry's very choice to turn once more to jurists, after having used force to prevail over the Sanusiya, was not simply a reflection of political decisions—although these were of great importance.[54] It was also a last bid to maintain the illusion of an 'Islamic' policy. Referring to the Ottoman Land Code of 1858, Fantoni questioned whether most of the brotherhood's property was indeed waqf. In particular, he cited the Code and the fiscal policy of the *wali* Ali Kamal Pasha to argue that the founders of waqf had legal title only to land tenure, and only the state was entitled to full ownership of the land. In this way, Fantoni sought to invalidate the Sanusi foundations by arguing that they did not fulfill the essential condition of a waqf—to wit, that the founder be in full, legal owner of the assets he intended to endow.[55] The result was quite different from the Tunisian example the Italians had looked to for inspiration. Italy had not involved the ulama, not least because the colony could not boast a group of eminent scholars comparable to those linked to Zaytuna in Tunis. Italy therefore had to do without the skills of Muslim jurists, although these scholars would have proved invaluable in redefining the waqf system, even after the end of colonialism.

The Italian colonial initiative in Libya came so late, in comparison with other European endeavors, that it coincided with the outcome of a deep crisis in waqf as an institution in the Arab world (and above all in neighboring Tunis and Cairo), where debates highlighted the 'uneconomic' and 'reactionary' nature of the institution, as well as the undisputed need for its radical reform.

While the Arab world was preparing to rethink waqf—in line with a process begun by nineteenth-century reformists and aimed at consolidating new state-building projects in a later phase—Italian colonial officials in Libya were looking for ways to overcome the limits of their own 'Islamic' policy, and to legitimize late colonial bids to seize waqf property in Cyrenaica. In his report, Fantoni referred not only to Ottoman policies, but also to the advice of experts in Islamic law, from nineteenth-century reformers to twentieth-century jurists. Fantoni hoped he could turn the debates about waqf that were being conducted among Muslims to the advantage of Italy and its colonial policies. With regard to inzal contracts, for instance (whereby usufruct could be ceded to a third party), the criticisms of the renowned *'alim* (plural, ulama) Ibrihim al-Rihahi of Tunis and the Maliki mufti of Tunisia, al-Shadhili bin Salah, were cited in support of the argument that contracts of this kind took different names in Algeria, Tunisia, and Egypt—with the purpose of fragmenting "the great evil of mortmain in the East."[56] By that point, the Italians had long abandoned an idea, popular in early colonial times, of applying the Tunisian inzal model in Libya for colonial purposes (an idea sharply criticized by Carlo Alfonso Nallino).

In other Arab countries, colonial policies on waqf had been shaped by the crisis besetting the institution. In 1928, the minister of colonies, Federzoni, recalled that the mood had already changed at the turn of the century: "It is necessary to take into account that, during [the] European War [First World War], in Egypt, a Muslim country, the assets of Sayyid Sanusi in Siwa, Farafra, Bahariya, Dakhla, and Kharga were confiscated; and the French, when fighting against the Sanusiyya, had no qualms about destroying *zawaya*. As for Muslim public opinion, everybody knows that France let pass, with hardly any protest, the suppression and divestment of Brotherhoods in Turkey."[57]

With regard to the validity of Sanusi waqfs, an Italian report cited a professor of Islamic law at Cairo University as affirming that such foundations were not religious institutions and were therefore to be abolished.[58] There is, unsurprisingly, no reference to views on the issue expressed by Libyan ulama[59] Fantoni concluded his report in August 1930, writing that "the abolition of the Sanusi *zawaya* does not conflict with religious law. Rather, it is in keeping with the advice of the most authoritative scholars of Islamic law."[60]

Conclusion

In Cyrenaica, therefore, waqfs were dismantled mostly through the confiscation and expropriation of their landed assets. The methods adopted by the Italians had needlessly tragic consequences for local communities and resulted mainly from the lacunae and contradictions inherent in Italian colonial policy. At the core of such contradictions with regard to waqf was the Italians' religious policy, exalted in the 1930s by Fascism, which promoted itself as the "sword of Islam."[61] Islam was a concern of colonial policy, and it was also at the core of waqf lands that the Sanusiya controlled. The contradiction was settled in a pragmatic way through military force. In theoretical terms, Italian officials sought to dissolve waqf as an Islamic institution into the local society's customs—indeed, into the Libyan landscape. Paradoxically, after some initial naiveté and the formation of the first commissions of inquiry (which turned to the Qur'an to find a basis for waqf as practiced by the Sanusiya), Italy's colonial policy, in both its liberal and its fascist manifestations, seems to have sought to outdo even Islamic scholars on the topic of waqf.[62] Referring to plans for modernization and development launched by the Ottoman reforms, or *Tanzimat*, the Italians ended up by acknowledging unambiguously 'religious' assets—mosques, cemeteries, the oasis of Jarabub—as the only ones bound by waqf. The confiscation of 1930 was of course devised to allow the colonial appropriation of lands, but the legal report that paved the way for this measure referred explicitly to a redefinition of the country's resources and their allocation and, obliquely, to a redefinition of the local landscape as well as the role reserved for religious codes.

Italian references to the possibility of exploiting resources that had been 'locked up' in waqf[63] actually revived the concept of *maslaha*, or public interest—a concept that had been used by Muslim jurists elsewhere to help redefine the commonweal in the envisaged aftermath of waqf. The state of waqfs in Cyrenaica also contributed to the failure of the institution in Libya: the legal deeds established by the founders did not allow the Italians to define waqf in a consistent manner, or to document the foundations' assets easily. To the contrary, beneficiaries' claims appeared weak in light of such elastic definitions. Compounding the confusion in Cyrenaica was the absence of a reformed waqf administration, integrated within the state apparatus, comparable to those established early on in both Tunis and Cairo.

Confiscation was not merely the transfer of vast resources from the ownership of the inhabitants to that of the colonial power. Such resources shaped the local cultural environment (and the symbols of the ruling class), due to the specific nature of the assets (agricultural land) and to the quality of the waqf relationship that bound most of Cyrenaica's oases and gardens to the history of Sanusiya. For over a century—and therefore in the direct experience of many Libyan Muslims and their forefathers—Cyrenaica's landscape had been associated with the Sanusiya and their zawaya. Shared spaces (from madrasas to date groves) were marked by the enactment of rituals, the names of saints, and the complex customs that regulated 'mixed' waqf property (whose management was reserved to the ikhwan).

The brotherhood thus called upon the very same landscape as a witness to its authority and modeled itself on that landscape. Long after the Ottoman conquest, this relation between the Sanusiya and the assets they controlled gave Cyrenaica's inhabitants a specific sense of belonging and a connection with the region. The Italians severed this special connection through their confiscation campaign. They saw in waqf an ideal instrument that enabled them to manipulate the complex relations between political groups and people (through territory), both to thwart the power of the brotherhood and to favour the penetration of settlers. Control of waqf property gave even the colonial authorities the opportunity to 'take shape'—to acquire, and assert, a territorial form.

Ironically, the Italians tended to set aside a symbolic part of the resources obtained through confiscation to emphasize the Islamic aspects of their policies—another intended aim being to marginalize, or at best to eliminate, Sanusi management. Federzoni, for instance, suggested that part of the proceeds of the confiscated assets should be earmarked for the creation and administration of "a middle or high school for Islamic studies, which could replace the Sanusi one in Jarabub." It was seen as advisable, however, to avoid choosing the same location for the Italian school: by placing it in Jarabub, the Italians feared, they might give the impression that it was the heir to the brotherhood's cultural traditions. Rather, Federzoni suggested that the school be built in Sidi Rafaa, outside Cyrenaica, where a *marabut* (holy man) and a retreat had existed long before the rise of the Sanusi mission and the brotherhood's establishment.[64] Waqf was an eminently versatile instrument for intervening in the landscape and the symbolic systems related to it. Areas closer to large urban centers, in contrast, were earmarked as reservoirs for urban growth, which encouraged a process of haphazard expansion.[65]

With regard to the lands taken away from the Sanusi waqfs, in 1932 Italy established an organism for the colonization of Cyrenaica (*Ente di colonizzazione della Cirenaica*, ECC), which was responsible for managing these assets.[66] The Fascist National Institute for Welfare Services (*Istituto nazionale fascista di previdenza sociale*, INFPS) also played a role; in fact, as Federico Cresti writes: "from 1935 onwards, in the agrarian colonization launched by the state, it played a role more important than historiography has acknowledged until today."[67] The ECC, later renamed the organism for the colonization of Libya (*Ente di colonizzazione della Libia*, ECL), still focused most of its efforts on Cyrenaica, but these endeavors rapidly came to an end in 1942.[68]

Between 1940 and 1943, war buffeted Libya, and particularly Cyrenaica, more and more harshly.[69] After the Italian occupation, the political and diplomatic events connected with the territory's destiny displaced the issue of waqf from the heart of the debate. Already under British military administration, and even more so when the war ended, the Libyans expected that waqf lands would be restored to them. This expectation might have reopened the case of Italian waqf policy as an aspect of decolonization. But UN General Assembly Resolution 388(V) of 1950 determined that agrarian questions should be settled through a direct agreement between Italy and Libya and stipulated that Italian settlers' properties should be preserved. The ECL had the final say on the property confiscated from the Sanusiya: the Italian government made the organism responsible for the final phase of agrarian development, which followed the Italian–Libyan agreements of 1956.[70]

Thus despite its ambitious 'Islamic' policy, when Italy made its exit as a colonial power it left behind the legacy of its confiscation campaign and the consequences thereof for Sanusi assets in Cyrenaica. Its failure to conceive of a consistent plan for the dismantling of waqfs and the efficient administration of their assets is among the reasons why Italy's impact on the landscape of the postcolonial state endured even after independence.

Notes

1   The present essay is part of an ongoing research project on Cyrenaica's waqfs under Italian occupation. It is based on archives kept at the Historical Archives of the Italian Africa Ministry (Archivio Storico del Ministero dell'Africa Italiana [ASMAI]) in Rome.
2   Atkinson, "Geographical Knowledge"; Atkinson, "Nomadic Strategies"; Fowler, "Italian Colonization."
3   Del Boca, Gli italiani, vol. 1; Del Boca, Gli italiani, vol. 2.
4   Vikør, "Sufism."
5   Deguilhem, Le waqf.
6   Baldinetti, David Santillana; Baldinetti, ed., Carte private di Carlo Alfonso.
7   Santarelli, "L'ideologia della "riconquista" libica (1922–1931)," in Santarelli et al., Omar al-Mukhtar, 9–51.
8   "Indeed, an administration being unable to avoid the ambiguity between direct administration (the assimilation of French provenance) or indirect administration (the indirect rule dear to Great Britain)." Novati, "Amministrazione," 367.
9   Decree Borea–Ricci of 7 October 1911. Novati, "Amministrazione," 387. See also Marongiu Buonaiuti, Politica e religioni, 32 ff. (It is reasserted there what Fascism meant by 'respect'—and indeed 'absolute respect'—for local religion: "Not the mere toleration, but rather a proper safeguard of native religious institutions" (Marongiu Buonaiuti, Politica e religioni, 32–33).

10 The report was signed by Franchi, Tucci, De Cillis, and Trotter (Del Boca, *Gli italiani*, vol. 1, 254).

11 Del Boca, *Gli italiani*, vol. 1.

12 Commission for the agrarian study of Tripolitania, set up by Bertolini (Del Boca, *Gli italiani*, vol. 1, 256).

13 ASMAI, b. 113/1, Sistemazione.

14 Califano, *Il regime*; Colucci, *Il diritto*; Castaldo, *Le fondazioni pie*; Colucci, *Il regime*, vol. 1.

15 ASMAI, b. 113/1, Sistemazione.

16 ASMAI, b. 113/1, Sistemazione.

17 ASMAI, b. 113/1, Libya, f. (1911–19), report of Carlo Alfonso Nallino, "Progetto di ordinamento dell'amministrazione dei Beni Auqaf," 27 July 1916.

18 ASMAI, b. 113/1, Libya, f. (1911–19), report of Carlo Alfonso Nallino.

19 ASMAI, b. 113/1, Libya, f. (1911–19), report of Carlo Alfonso Nallino.

20 ASMAI, b. 113/1, Libya, f. (1911–19), report of Carlo Alfonso Nallino.

21 Cresti, "Per uno studio."

22 ASMAI, Libia (1911–19), b. 113/1, report of C. A. Nallino, 27 July 1916.

23 Franzoni, *Colonizzazione*, 91.

24 This was land allocated on the basis of a government decree defining rent procedures for state-owned lands: Cresti, *Oasi*, xxi and xxxii.

25 Cresti, *Oasi*, xxii–xxiii.

26 Cresti, *Oasi*, xxiv.

27 In fact, with a few exceptions (for instance, the *zawaya* of Tilumim and Gsur, or those of Driana and Tocra), all offices reported that the zawaya within their jurisdiction owned nothing; or, as in the case of the zawaya that were under the authority of the commander of Derna, they communicated only their overall land revenues with no reference to individual assets. ASMAI, Libya, b. 150/7, Valenzi report (*"Relazione sull'accertamento del patrimonio delle zavie senussite in Cirenaica"*), 14 April 1931.

28 The measure applied to the zawaya of Cyrene, al-Bayda, al-Faydiya, al-Tart, al-Asqafa, Umm Hufayn, Umm al-Rizam, al-Maraziq, Khashm Rzaiq, Umm al-Shakhnab, al-Qusur, and Dariyana.

29 In August 1915, the Italians occupied the coastal strip of Cyrenaica and created a line of five fortified positions on the territory (Bengasi, al-Merg, Cirene, Derna, and Tobruk). Del Boca, *Gli italiani*, vol. 1, 335.

30 Del Boca, *Gli italiani*, vol. 1, 334–41.

31 ASMAI, b. 150/7, (1919–34), "Commissione per l'accertamento."

32 The offices of Derna and Benghazi were set up in 1914 for the verification of land rights.

33 They were the following: Benghazi, Driana, Tilimum, Tocra, Merg, Tolmetta, Cirene, Beda, Faidia, Hania, Hamama, Tert, Derna, Habbun. From Valenzi's report (he had already written an earlier report with Colucci, 24 August 1919), ASMAI, b. 150/7, 1931.

34 Because the case was being conducted for the commission about waqf, the report of the lawyer Valenzi required an examination by a distinguished Italian Islamologist. David Santillana, who esteemed the work of Valenzi, conducted the examination; but as it was a data-gathering work, it was only useful, Santillana writes, "to

a certain extent" (ASMAI, b. 134/20, February 1920, "Parere prof. Santillana").
See also: Baldinetti, *David Santillana*, 65–74.

35 In the first decades of the twentieth century, the victims of colonialism were not the
only voices challenging European pretensions to usurp land from its native population.

36 Under Italian colonization, the Bedouin population was reduced by half or even two
thirds due to death and emigration. On the death toll, as well as the acts of violence,
deportations, and decimation of livestock carried out by the Italians in Libya, see
Rochat, "La repressione"; Evans-Pritchard, *Sanusi*; Segre, *L'Italia*; Del Boca,
Italiani, brava gente?.

37 In 1931, there were forty-nine zawaya of Cyrenaica registered in Italian documents:
"Bengasi (Bengasi, Oriana, Tocra); El Abiar (Omm Sheganeb, Asgafa); Soluk
(Msus, Tilimum); Barce (Barce, Gasfein, Graberbi, En-Neian, El-Haueizi, Mirad
Messaud, El-Gsur, Tolmetta); Agedabia (El Gtafia, Marada, Augila, Gikerra, El
Ergh, El Lebba); Cirene (Cirene, Argub, Gfonta, Hania, Hanana, Beda, Faidia);
Derna (Derna, Tert, Marazigh, Ez Zeiat, Ain Mara, Martuba, Bscira, Umm-Er-Rzen,
Umm-Hfein, Mechili, Kascem-El-Rzeik); Tobruk (Umm-Rukba, Gianzur o Defna,
Mrassas, Habbun o Gerfan); Giarabub (Giarabub); Cufra (al-Giof, al-Tag, El Hauari,
El Rebiana, Tazerbo)."

38 Guida d'Italia del Touring Club Italiano, *Possedimenti*.

39 Del Boca, *Gli italiani*, vol. 2.

40 ASMAI, Libya, b. 150/7, telegram 29 May 1930/VIII no. 03803. Graziani (deputy
governor of Cyrenaica, at Benghazi) wrote the general direction for Northern Africa.

41 ASMAI, Libya (1925–30), b. 150/7, 19 August 1930, from the governor of Tripolitania Pietro Badoglio to the minister of colonies, Emilio De Bono.

42 ASMAI, Libya, b. 150/7, 8 August 1930, from the minister, Emilio De Bono, to the
governor of Tripolitania and Cyrenaica Pietro Badoglio.

43 ASMAI, Libya, b. 150/7, 8 August 1930, from the minister, Emilio De Bono, to the
governor of Tripolitania and Cyrenaica Pietro Badoglio.

44 The oasis of Jarabub, which housed the tomb of the Sanussiyas' founder, had been
the object of diplomatic agreements with Egypt in 1925, and the Italians occupied
it in February 1926. Through the Milner–Scialoja agreement of April 1920, Great
Britain had already granted it to Italy (Pace, *Libia*). In the agreement with the
Egyptians, which granted the oasis to Italy in 1925, the Italians pledged themselves
to issue a decree "declaring the inviolability of Islamic Sacred Sites, unrestricted
access to them, as well as freedom of worship at Giarabub" (Marongiu Buonaiuti,
Politica, 253–55).

45 Under clause 8, last paragraph of R.D. 3 July 1921 no. 1207.

46 A ministry note quotes: "The sole fact being able to change our mind, it would be
an unconditional subjection of Idris and his followers; which is the goal we want
to achieve." An extreme measure like confiscation appeared not to be workable in
a short time, and—although not fostering excessive expectations in a subjection of
the Senusso—the intents of confiscation were immediately conveyed to the Italian
legation at Cairo, so that Idris al-Sanusi could be indirectly informed on. ASMAI,
Libya, b. 150/7, coded telegram from the Ministry of Colonies to the governor in
Tripoli, June 1930, no. 5336.

47 The minister of colonies at the time considered that the "fear of upsetting religious
awareness of our people and moving Muslim public opinion," which had hampered

for a long time Italian initiative was "definitely exaggerated." "*Beni delle zavie senussite*." "The Zavie, in Cirenaica, do not currently fulfill any of the functions that justified their existence from the Islamic point of view . . . . All natives know that land revenues . . . . are neither given to charity nor worship . . . . Therefore, a measure against such assets would not be interpreted as an attempt against religion" (ASMAI, Libya, 150/7, no. 5179, 15 June 1928).

48 ASMAI, Libya, 150/7, Fantoni report, 11 August 1930.

49 ASMAI, Libya, i. 150/7, 1931.

50 ASMAI, Libya, i. 150/7, 1931.

51 ASMAI, Libya, i. 150/7, 1931.

52 ASMAI, Libya, 150/7, Fantoni report, 11 August 1930.

53 Evans-Pritchard, *Sanusi*.

54 The importance of the measure of confiscation was far greater than any hypothesis of action according to the police regulations in force at the time, and for this reason Minister De Bono reminded the governor of the "need that it should be taken in the form of royal decree." ASMAI, Libya, b. 150/7, n. 65681 of 8 August 1930.

55 ASMAI, Libya, 150/7, Fantoni report, 11 August 1930.

56 ASMAI, Libya, 150/7, Fantoni report, 11 August 1930, 25.

57 ASMAI, Libya, 150/7, no. 5179, 15 June 1928, "Beni delle zavie senussite." Federzoni was complaining that the assets had not yet been removed from the brotherhood's control; according to him, the reasons were: "from one side, the fear of upsetting religious awareness of our people and moving Muslim public opinion, from the other side, the survival of a mentality that did not dismiss possible agreements with the Brotherhood."

58 ASMAI, Libya, 150/7. For an inquiry on Italian policy in Egypt in connection with Libyan conquest, see Baldinetti, *Orientalismo*.

59 Graziani, asked pro-Italian Libyans to make statements in favor of closing the zawaya; these statements were widely broadcast. Mohammed al-Rida al-Sanusi had given in to Italian pressure, and in the document he disavowed the actions of his brothers, the rebels Muhammad Idris and Ahmad al-Sharif, inviting the rebels to submit. The editor of a Benghazi magazine also sided with the confiscation (ASMAI, Libya, 150/7).

60 ASMAI, Libya, 150/7, Fantoni report, 11 August 1930, 22.

61 Galoppini, *Il fascismo*.

62 As written by the minister De Bono, introducing the report of Fantoni, the inquiry should bear out how "the Senussia was able to establish to its benefit in Cyrenaica a series of economic privileges that have no serious foundation even in Islamic law" (ASMAI, Libya, b. 150/7, 17 October 1930, from minister De Bono to the Governor of Cyrenaica).

63 ASMAI, Libia, b. 150/7, Valenzi report ("Relazione sull'accertamento del patrimonio delle zavie senussite in Cirenaica"), 14 April 1931.

64 ASMAI, Libya, 150/7, n. 5179, 15 June 1928 ("Beni delle zavie senussite").

65 Cresti, *Edilizia*; Cresti, *Projet social*; Cresti, *City and Territory*; von Henneberg, *Construction*.

66 Cresti, *Oasi*, xxv.

67 "For INFPS it was not easy to conciliate its routine activities with such an extraordinary chapter of its story." There was also rivalry between INFPS and ECC, which

were in competition to obtain from the colony's government the richest lands among those few available (Cresti, *Oasi*, 253).

68   Cresti, *Oasi*, 257.
69   Rochat, *Le guerre italiane*.
70   Cresti, *Oasi*, 254. In the following years, and from the Italian point of view, Federico Cresti writes that "Italian policy about the Libyan issue, and particularly about agrarian colonization, shows a substantial continuity between the fascist period, the postwar period, and the birth of the Republic: it was a point still argued in the early fifties, that Italy should stay in the country 'at any cost'" (Cresti, *Oasi*, 260).

Bibliography

Archival Sources
Archivio Storico del Ministero dell'Africa Italiana (ASMAI), Rome
Inventario: Ministero dell'Africa Italiana, vol. 2 (1859–1945)
Buste Descrizione

113/1 (1911–19) Assetto Servizi civili
1) Primo assetto Servizi pubblici
2) Sistemazione dei Beni Auqaf (1911–16)
3) Bandi emanati (1911–13)

133/1 (1911–26)
11) Interpellanza Somaini pel migliore assetto politico-economico della Colonia: I Beni Auqaf: Relazione Lavison (1914)

134/20 Libia (1920) Convegno dei Capi della Cirenaica e Tripolitania. Beni senussiti (gennaio–febbraio 1920)
142) Situazione politico-militare. Relazioni e notiziari, Convegno di Capi della Cirenaica e Tripolitania, Beni senussiti (gennaio–febbraio 1920)

143/6 (1918–22)
Rapporti con gli Anglo-Egiziani circa i confini e la Senussia
53) Zavie e beni senussiti in Egitto 55-A
54) Beni senussiti in Egitto (1920) 55-A
56) Beni senussiti in Egitto (1920) 55-A

147/1 (1911–19) Senussia e suoi Capi
Fasc. 4) Zavie senussite in Cirenaica e in Egitto (1912–19)

150/7 (1919–34)

15) Commissione per l'accertamento dei beni delle zavie senussite in Cirenaica (Relazione Colucci e Valenzi)

Natura dei beni delle zavie senussite (Relazione Fantoni)

16) Decreti confisca beni ribelli (1925)

Confisca beni della Senussia (R.D. 22/12/1930 N. 1944) (1925–30)

17) Chiusura zavie senussite (1930)

18) Beni zavie senussite (Gruppo Di Agedabia) 1931

19) Beni zavie senussite (Gruppo Di Bengasi) 1931

20) Beni zavie senussite (Gruppo Di Derna) 1931

21) Beni zavie senussite (Gruppo Di Barce) 1931

22) Beni zavie senussite (Gruppo Di Cirene) 1931

150/8 (1914–38)

25) Arabi confinati a Ustica Confino Capi zavie senussite (1926–38)

Publications and Other Sources

Atkinson, David. "Geographical Knowledge and Scientific Survey in the Construction of Italian Libya." *Modern Italy* 8, no. 1 (2003): 9–29.

———. "Nomadic Strategies and Colonial Governance: Domination and Resistance in Cyrenaica 1923–1932," in Joanne P. Sharp, Paul Routledge, Chris Philo, and Ronan Paddison, eds., *Entanglements of Power: Geographies of Domination/Resistance*, 93–121. New York: Routledge, 2000.

Baldinetti, Anna. *Carte private di Carlo Alfonso e Maria Nallino: Inventario.* Roma: Istituto per l'Oriente C. A. Nallino, 1995.

———. *Modern and Contemporary Libya: Sources and Historiographies.* Rome; Istituto per l'Oriente C. A. Nallino, 2003.

———. *Orientalismo e colonialismo: La ricerca di consenso in Egitto per l'impresa di Libia.* Rome: Istituto per l'Oriente C.A. Nallino, 1997.

Baldinetti, Anna, and David Santillana. *David Santillana, l'uomo e il giurista (1855–1931): Scritti inediti, 1878–1920.* Rome: Istituto per l'Oriente C.A. Nallino, 1995.

Ben Achour, Mohamed-El Aziz. "Le Habous ou waqf: L'institution juridique et la pratique tunisoise," in S. Ferchiou, ed., *Hasab wa Nasab: Parenté, alliance et patrimoine en Tunisie*, 51–78. Paris: Centre national de la recherche scientifique, 1992.

Calchi Novati, Gianpaolo. "Amministrazione e politica indigena in Libia nella prima fase del colonialismo italiano (1911–19). *Studi urbinati*, new series, a. 57–58, no. 41–42 (1988–90): 361–99.

Califano, Giuseppe. *Il regime dei beni auqaf nella storia e nel diritto dell'Islam, seguito da note ed appunti sugli auqaf della Tripolitania e da uno schema di progetto per la riorganizzazione della amministrazione degli auqaf el giauama in Libia.* Tripoli: Tip. Internazionale, 1913.

Castaldo, Augusto. 1940. *Le fondazioni pie mussulmane: Manomorta islamica (waquf–auqaf–hubus).* Rome: Tip. Ferraiolo.

Colucci, Massimo. *Il diritto consuetudinario della Cirenaica.* Rome: Lit. Ferri, 1931.

———. *Il regime della proprieta fondiaria nell'Africa italiana.* Vol. 1, *Libia: A cura del Ministero dell'Africa italiana: Ufficio studi.* Bologna: Cappelli, 1942.

Cresti, Federico. "City and Territory in Libya during the Colonial Period: Sources and Research Documents," in Anna Baldinetti, ed., *Modern and Contemporary Libya: Sources and Historiographies,* 141–68. Rome: IPO, 2003.

———. "Dalla repressione alla politica araba nella colonizzazione agraria della Libia." *Africana* (1999): 79–95.

———. "Edilizia ed urbanistica nella colonizzazione agraria della Libia (1922–1940)." *Storia urbana* a. 11, no. 40 (1987): 189–231.

———. *Oasi d'italianità: La Libia della colonizzazione agraria tra fascismo, guerra e indipendenza (1935–1956).* Turin: SEI, 1996.

———. "Per uno studio delle 'élites' politiche nella Libia indipendente: La formazione scolastica (1912–1942)." *Studi storici* 1 (2000): 121–58.

———. "Projet social et aménagement du territoire dans la colonisation démographique de la Libye." *Correspondances* (Institut de Recherche sur le Maghreb contemporain) 58 (October–December 1999): 11–15.

Deguilhem, Randi, ed. *Le waqf dans l'espace islamique: Outil de pouvoir socio-politique.* Damascus: Institut français de Damas, 1995.

Del Boca, Angelo. *Gli italiani in Libia.* Vol. 1, *Tripoli bel suol d'amore 1860–1922,* 2nd ed. Milan: Mondadori, 1993.

———. *Gli italiani in Libia.* Vol. 2, *Dal facismo a Gheddafi.* Rome: Laterza, 1988.

———. *Italiani, brava gente? Un mito duro a morire.* Vicenza: Neri Pozza Editore, 2005.

Evans-Pritchard, Edward E. *The Sanusi of Cyrenaica.* Oxford: Oxford University Press, 1973.

Fowler, Gary L. "Italian Colonization of Tripolitania." *Annals of the Association of American Geographers* 62, no. 4 (1972): 627–40.

Franzoni, Ausonio. *Colonizzazione e proprietà fondiaria in Libia: Con speciale riguardo alla religione, al diritto ed alle consuetudini locali.* Ròme: Athenaeum, 1912.

Galoppini, Enrico. *Il fascismo e l'Islam.* Parma: All'insegna del Veltro, 2001.

Graziani, Rodolfo. *Cirenaica pacificata.* Milan: Mondadori, 1932.

Guida d'Italia del Touring Club Italiano. *Possedimenti e Colonie.* Milan: Touring Club Italiano, 1929.

Henneberg, Krystyna Claran von. *The Construction of Fascist Libya: Modern Colonial Architecture.* New York and London: Palgrave, 2002.

Marongiu Buonaiuti, Cesare. *Politica e religioni nel colonialismo italiano (1882–1941).* Milan: Giuffrè, 1982.

Ministero delle Colonie. *Norme per la trascrizione italiana e la grafia araba dei nomi propri geografici della Tripolitania e della Cirenaica.* Ministerial decree of 1 February 1915, Rome, 1915.

Pace, Biagio. *La Libia nella politica fascista (1922–1935): La riconquista, la definizione dei confini, l'ordinamento.* Milan: Messina, 1935.

Raincro, Romain H. *La politica araba di Mussolini nella seconda guerra mondiale.* Padova: Cedam, 2004.

Rochat, Giorgio. *Le guerre italiane 1935–1943: Dall'Impero d'Etiopia alla disfatta.* Turin: Einaudi, 2005.

———."La repressione della resistenza araba in Cirenaica nel 1930–31 nei documenti dell'archivio Graziani." *Il movimento di Liberazione in Italia* 110 (1973): 3–39.

Salerno, Eric. *Genocidio in Libia: Le atrocità nascoste dell'avventura coloniale italiana (1911–1931).* Rome: Manifestolibri, 2005.

Santarelli, E., G. Rochat, R. Rainero, and L. Goglia. *Omar al-Mukhtar e la riconquista fascista della Libia.* Milan: Marzorati, 1981.

Segre, Claudio. *L'Italia in Libia: Dall'eta giolittiana a Gheddafi.* Milan: Feltrinelli, 1978.

Teruzzi, Attilio. *Cirenaica verde.* Milan: Mondadori, 1931.

Triaud, Jean-Louis. *La légende noire de la Sanusiyya: Une confrérie musulmane saharienne sous le regard français (1840–1930).* 2 vols. Paris: Maison des sciences de l'homme, 1995.

Vikør, Knut. "Sufism and Social Welfare in the Sahara," in H. Weiss, ed., *Social Welfare in Muslim Societies in Africa*, 80–97. Stockholm: Nordic Africa Institute, 2002.

Zarcone, Tierry. "Waqfs et confréries religieuses à l'époque moderne: L'influence de la réforme des waqfs sur la sociabilité et la doctrine mystique," in

F. Bilici, ed., *Le waqf dans le monde musulman contemporain (XIXe–XXe siècles): Fonctions sociales, économiques et politiques*. Proceedings of the Round Table, Istanbul, 13–14 November 1992, 237–48. Istanbul: Institut français d'études anatoliennes, 1994.

8

The Waqf System: Maintenance, Repair, and Upkeep

Dina Ishak Bakhoum

It is essential that the principles guiding the preservation and restoration of ancient buildings should be agreed and be laid down on an international basis, with each country being responsible for applying the plan within the framework of its own culture and traditions."

—The Venice Charter

Successive Islamic regimes in Egypt constructed a variety of magnificent buildings such as mosques, *sabil*s (water dispensaries), *sabil-kuttab*s (water dispensaries with Qur'anic schoolrooms above), *wikala*s (warehouses with an inn), madrasas (Islamic theological colleges), *bimaristan*s (hospitals), houses, and *khanqah*s (monastic residences for Sufis).[1] Although many of these buildings no longer exist, some are still in relatively good condition and functioning; they have survived earthquakes, man-made alterations, interventions, and destruction. Their existence for hundreds of years was possible not only because of the advanced structural engineering and construction techniques used to build them, but also due to the fact that a system for their upkeep, maintenance, and repair existed through waqf. Jukka Jokilehto, who has researched the history of architectural conservation in great depth, wrote that "Islamic society also had a traditional system of maintenance and repair of community properties; this was organized within a type of endowment called the *waqf*."[2] The waqf system was acknowledged and institutionalized further as an entity responsible for maintenance and restoration activities through the founding of the *Comité de Conservation de Monuments de l'Art Arab* (AD 1881–1961) (hereafter *Comité*), established by Khedive Tawfiq under the Wazarat al-Awqaf (Ministry of Endowments), for the conservation and restoration of Islamic and later also Coptic monuments. Although the *Comité* was under the administrative aegis of the Ministry of Endowments, it did not necessarily follow the concepts and systems of maintenance that the waqf system had put in place, especially since, as some argue, its foundation came about as a result of pressure from Europeans interested in Arab art.[3] The relationship between the Ministry of Endowments and the *Comité* (and later the Supreme Council of Antiquities, or SCA) is a dynamic one and might seem to be—or is—conflicting in some cases.

This article will introduce the waqf system and its relation to maintenance and repair activities from a historical perspective, using specific examples from the Mamluk period (1250–1517). Nevertheless, in order to place this historical research in its current context, I will allude briefly to the conflict between the Ministry of Endowments and the Supreme Council of Antiquities (SCA) with regard to waqf properties, especially those buildings that are registered as historic monuments. The current disagreement and the lack of any clear system for management and administration of waqf monuments must be tackled and conflicting issues settled for the sake of the built heritage and its living traditions.

Accordingly, this chapter will emphasize the benefits to be gained by scholars and restoration-conservation specialists from the study of waqf documents and guiding principles. More specifically, it will highlight the beneficial and valuable ideas that inhere in the traditional system and which can be useful for the protection of the built heritage. I will attempt to demonstrate that the fundamental principles of the waqf system with regard to maintenance and protection of property are in line with many of the current conservation protection laws of the built heritage.

Brief description of the waqf system

The literal meaning of the word 'waqf' is 'to stop' or 'the act of stopping.' The waqf (plural *awqaf*) is the system of endowment that existed and still exists in numerous Muslim countries. Another word that is also used describing the same system is *habs*.[4]

One definition states that waqf is the prohibition of *tasarruf* (selling, giving away, buying, mortgaging, making inheritable, bequeathing, and donating) relating to a person's property. Revenue generated from that property, once it has been made into waqf, is to be used solely for a charitable cause.[5] Accordingly, the formula consecrating a property as waqf asserts the characteristics of this property, which has been alienated from its owner and placed in the service of God. In waqf documents, the endower states that he endowed *(waqafa, habasa)*, set aside for God's sake *(sabbala)*, perpetuated *(abbada)*, prohibited, that is, from being subjected to transactions *(harama)*, and gave as charity *(tasaddaqa)* the property described in the endowment deed.

Three important entities were involved in the act of endowment, and understanding their characteristics helps us understand how waqf operated as a system. The first was the person who endows, the *waqif*, who had to be a free adult, in good heath and mental condition, cognizant of his or her actions, and owning the endowed property. The second was the endowed property, the *mawquf* (plural *mawqufat*). The endowed property had to confer a benefit *(manfa'a)*: it could be a revenue-generating property or an institution that provided services. The third was the beneficiary (*mawquf 'alayhi* or *mustahiqq*). All the stipulations the founder saw fit to make were written in the *waqfiya*, the legal endowment deed. As Crecelius noted: "A *waqf* document is like a cut gemstone. It has many facets and can be admired, even enjoyed, from different angles. *Waqf* documentation contains a wealth of material that scholars of many disciplines can exploit."[6]

Waqif, mawquf, and mawquf 'alayhi in relation to maintenance and repair

There were slightly different types of endowments, two of which will be examined here with a view to understanding how they contributed to the maintenance and repair of the architectural heritage.[7]

In the first type, when a founder endowed property (for example, a shop, agricultural land, a public bath, mill, sugar refinery, oil press, commercial warehouse, or coffee shop that generated revenue),[8] the income from these properties could be spent on pious and charitable causes. Money could be given to the poor, provide treatment for the ill, give people an opportunity to perform the pilgrimage in Mecca, care for orphans, or allow family members to bury deceased relatives. It could also be stipulated that revenues be used to purchase lamps, oil, carpets, the *kiswa* (cover) for the Holy Sanctuaries and other mosques, or for the upkeep and maintenance of religious buildings. The second and more common type was when the founder endowed a hospital, sabil, mosque, madrasa, or khanqah for the public to use and benefit from. Income from commercial properties included in the waqf[9] was spent on the upkeep and running of the public or charitable institutions. The institution as well as the revenue-generating properties were considered part of the waqf and could not be subject to any transaction (sale, gift, pawning or mortgaging, and so on) once the foundation had been established.

Although most schools of Sunni jurisprudence considered waqf to be lawful only when it is endowed in perpetuity, followers of the Maliki school believed that perpetuity is not a necessary condition for validity; hence, even a temporary waqf could be legally valid and binding.[10] Nevertheless, most waqf deeds stated the founder's intention that the waqf remain beneficial in perpetuity. To ensure the continuity of the waqf and its benefits, the most important stipulation as stated in many waqf documents was that the waqf supervisor *(nazir)* had to spend revenue on the *'imara*[11] (actions that keep the building operational) of endowed buildings or institutions.

For example, in the waqf deed drawn up by Sultan Qalawun (r. 1279–90) for his hospital, the supervisor was bound by the following orders:

"He should start with the *'imara* of what requires *'imara*, in terms of repair, restoration, or construction of a collapsed section, in a way that does not harm or cause injustice or damage."[12]

Similarly, the waqf deed of Sultan al-Ghuri (r. 1501–16) stipulates:[13]

> The supervisor of this *waqf* should use it in a lawful *(shar'i)* manner; he must begin by spending the revenue on its *'imara* and *maramma* (minor restoration work) and on that which preserves revenue and perpetuates benefit. He must replace any blue ceramic tiles that have fallen from the dome right away; these are to be replaced *in situ* on the same day they fall. This should be done when the *waqif* is alive and also after his death, always and forever. As for the plots of land, [the supervisor] must provide for their upkeep, digging canals and excavating the banks of the river so that they continue to produce. Only then should he spend on the beneficiaries and workers.

In the endowment deed of Sultan Barsbay (r. 1422–38), the section discussing the stipulations binding this waqf and its beneficiaries mentions that *istibdal*[14] (exchange, for example, an exchange of dilapidated waqf property for private property in good condition, whereby the private property was alienated as waqf) was not allowed, even if this endowment's revenue-generating properties fell into ruin. It would appear that some supervisors saw this as an expedient means of preserving the perpetuity of an endowment, while avoiding the costs and time that regular maintenance work required. An endower like Sultan Barsbay could therefore anticipate potential laxity on his supervisor's part by forbidding specific transactions related to the waqf and insisting upon the need for proper upkeep. Indeed, immediately after prohibiting istibdal, Barsbay's endowment deed mentions the importance of 'imara, thus implying that maintenance should be carried out in order to prevent the endowed property from falling into disrepair. The deed stipulated that any revenue from income-generating properties endowed as part of the waqf was to be spent first on 'imara, restoration *(tarmim)*, repair *(islah)*, and "that which allowed the endowed property to remain" *(wa ma fih baqa' 'aynahu)*, while ensuring the perpetuation of the property's income-generating capability *(dawam manfa'atuh)*, even if most of the revenue was spent on these requirements.

According to al-Khassaf,[15] regardless of whether an endowed property's 'imara is specifically mentioned in the endowment deed, maintenance should still be carried out using the revenue generated by the waqf.[16] When people claimed that restoration was not a stipulation of waqfs, the *qadi* 'Abd al-Rahman ibn 'Abd Allah al-'Amri (early ninth century) replied: "Without restoration, *ahbas* would not remain for the people."[17] This clearly indicates the strong link between maintenance (or restoration) and the function and benefit of the building, emphasizing that the essence of all maintenance and restoration activities is to preserve the building's use value and its benefit to the community.

To maintain important and large-scale institutions such as the monumental mosques, hospitals, and schools endowed in the Mamluk period, an organized system existed. Numerous people took part in this system and played different roles in the upkeep, maintenance, and repair of these institutions.

The judge

Judges played an important role in the maintenance and supervision of endowed buildings. Some judges paid special attention to waqfs. Abu Tahir 'Abd al-Malik ibn Muhammad al-Hazami, for example (late eighth century), personally visited endowed properties on three designated days every month and gave orders to restore, repair, and sweep them.[18] The abovementioned judge 'Abd al-Rahman ibn 'Abdallah al-'Amri was very strict in matters concerning the 'imara of endowed properties, and used to watch over restoration work himself and supervise the builders for days on end.[19]

According to the Mamluk chronicler al-Maqrizi, quoting al-Sharif ibn As'ad al-Juwani, during the Fatimid period, three days before the month of Ramadan, judges visited the mosques and the shrines in Cairo to survey them, check their mats, lamps, and upkeep, and rectify anything that had fallen into disrepair.[20]

The supervisor (nazir)

The waqf supervisor was responsible for all the operations affecting the endowed property. The founder could occupy this position himself or assign it to someone else. He had to make sure that everything was running according to the waqf's stipulations and that the revenues were being collected and spent in the correct manner. He also had to ensure that maintenance and restoration operations were carried out whenever needed.

The shahid al-'imara

The endowment deed of Sultan Mu'ayyad Shaykh (r. 1412–21) stipulates that two good and honest men should be hired as shahid al-'imara to regulate construction and repair work.[21] According to 'Abd al-Latif Ibrahim, the shahid al-'imara was responsible for spending on the renovation, repair, and restoration of the buildings, endowed lands, and properties, and providing accounts of work and expenses to the supervisor of the waqf.[22]

The shadd and the shadd al-'ama'ir[23]

Another of the many functions associated with the upkeep and maintenance of waqf foundations was that of the shadd al-'ama'ir al-mawqufa. He was "a Mamluk amir responsible for the royal buildings and for the supervision of the architects and craftsmen involved in royal construction."[24] An individual occupying this position had to be knowledgeable in matters of engineering and construction and able to supervise a variety of tasks related to maintenance and restoration. In a document pertaining to the endowment established by Sultan al-Ghuri, two men were paid to collect revenue from the income-generating properties and ensure that activities related to upkeep were being carried out as well as possible.[25]

In a document pertaining to the endowment of Gamal al-Din Ustadar, it is written that the shadd must assist the endowment collector in gathering revenue and help the supervisors in activities related to 'imara. He also had to make sure that waqf employees working on the waterwheel and in other service positions were fulfilling their responsibilities.[26]

In sum, the shadd had to deal with the collection of money while the shadd al-'ama'ir had to supervise and control the maintenance and restoration work.

The engineer and the *(mi'mar)*[27]

In the waqf of al-Ghuri the supervisor chose two skilled engineers, experienced in building and repairs, for the job of the *mi'mariya* (tasks related to the supervision of construction, restoration, and repair); these tasks were assigned to an engineer or a mi'mar or, in some cases, to a chief artisan *(mu'allim)*. They had to visit the endowed buildings and survey the materials, builders, and other requirements related to the 'imara. They controlled the scaffolding, demolition, and construction activities.[28]

The waqf deed of Qaytbay (r. 1468–96) mentions that the mi'mar responsible for this waqf had to be present when the 'imara (construction or maintenance and repair) took place, in order to supervise the workers and prevent them from neglecting their work.[29]

In the waqf of Gamal al-Din Ustadar, the mi'mar assigned, being well trained and experienced, had to carry out activities related to the mi'mariya; he had to constantly visit the endowed buildings, monitor and inspect their condition as well as emphasize the importance of maintenance and repair ('imara and *islah*).[r·]

The *murakhkhim* (marble mason)

The marble mason was responsible for installing marble during construction and for maintaining and repairing it whenever needed. In the waqf of Qaytbay, a marble mason was assigned the responsibility of inspecting and restoring the marble on a monthly basis, using an allocated sum of money for this task.[31]

In the waqf of al-Ghuri two marble masons had to regularly inspect the marble paving and skirting of the madrasa and the dome; they had to fix and return to their original places the pieces that had become detached or were about to fall, immediately and with mastery.[32] This shows that Mamluk waqf founders prioritized regular monitoring and preventive maintenance, which are currently among the most important conservation principles.

The plumber

In the waqf of Qaytbay a plumber had to restore the pipes and drains of the endowed buildings.[33] In the waqf of al-Ghuri the supervisor had to select an experienced plumber to do the necessary plumbing work and maintain the pipes and the drainage, fastening and fixing them when the water stopped.[34]

From this one deduces that an extensive network of water pipes and drainage existed during that time and it was important to keep it running. The maintenance of these networks was necessary, as water was crucial for ablutions and other purposes related to the performance of religious duties.

The *farrashin* (cleaners)

Among the work required in many waqf deeds was the regular cleaning of the endowed properties. Many of the deeds assigned to numerous cleaners the responsibility of sweeping, washing, and cleaning the different areas on a daily basis. In the waqf of Qaytbay four cleaners were assigned to the complex: one in the mausoleum, two in the mosque, its courtyard and its surroundings, and one in the ablution area.[35]

The waqf of al-Ghuri describes in great detail the tasks to be done by six different cleaners, who were required to be knowledgeable in the art of cleaning *(fann al-firasha)*.[36] Four were assigned by the supervisor to sweep, wipe, and otherwise clean of all parts of the madrasa. They had to clean the mats every Friday, wash the marble, and spread all the carpets for the Friday prayers; after the worshipers had finished praying and left, the carpets had to be removed and folded. Another cleaner was responsible for the large ablution area. He had to clean[37] all its toilets and wash the water fountains. The last was responsible for the second ablution area and assisted the four cleaners responsible for the madrasa.

The *waqqadin* (lamp lighters)

The lamplighters were responsible for the oil lamps; they had to light and clean them as well as check their oil. In the waqf of Qaytbay, two lamp lighters were assigned the responsibility for all the oil lamps in the mosque, the madrasa, and the ablution area. They had to light them, extinguish them when they were not in use, and keep them in good condition.[38]

The *muzzamalati* and money for the cistern

When a sabil and a cistern were part of the endowed building, a *muzzamalati* was responsible for them. He had to be trustworthy and loyal, good looking, cleanly dressed, healthy, strong, and smart. His job was to bring water from the cistern to the water tank that filled the basins. He then distributed water to the people from sunrise until sunset, and then for a while at nighttime. He also had to hang curtains on the sabil windows when the sun shone into the cistern during the summertime; every afternoon when the sun was about to set he had to remove, clean, and fold them for the next day. He was also responsible for cleaning the marble, sweeping and washing it continuously. There was money allocated specially for the cistern as well, to fill it with water from the Nile and to clean, wash, and perfume it with incense.[39]

Of course, there were numerous other positions that existed for the maintenance and cleaning of specific places and elements of the building. For example, when the endowed building comprised a waterwheel *(saqiya)*, a man had to be responsible for it. Also, a carpenter would be requested to carry out maintenance and repair work.

Waqf deeds always specified a sum of money for each service provider and allocated set amounts for the purchase of materials and equipment required for operation and maintenance.

Architectural description in the waqf deed

Waqf deeds (*waqfiya*s) contained elaborate sections that described the architecture of the endowed institution and its revenue-generating properties. Such detailed descriptions were an important part of the deed because the *waqfiya* was the legally binding document of the waqf, and accordingly the architectural description served legal purposes. It also confirmed the value of the building through the description of its spaces, materials, and decorative elements. Of course, for historians of art and architecture, these descriptions are invaluable documents.

"As legal documents, the *waqfiya*s had to be drawn up according to certain prototypes provided in law books."¹ This is also true as regards their descriptions of architecture. There were common rules and methods by which the architecture of various edifices was described and followed by the scribes who wrote up the waqf deeds.

Architectural descriptions were presented as though one were walking inside the building and moving from one space to the next, determining the social and functional aspects of the different areas.

The façade was briefly described, then the function of the building was specified and the different spaces were identified. These spaces were described, with mention of their shape and size but giving no specific dimensions. Also, the construction technique and decorative materials of all walls, floors, and ceilings were listed. For example, a waqf deed could specify that the grilles of an endowed building were made of bronze, or the ceiling painted in gold and lapis lazuli; such details clearly demonstrate that the goal of the endowment deed was not only to document and identify a building precisely, but also to establish the value, quality, and richness of the endowment. In contrast, decoration patterns were rarely mentioned.

The study of the architectural descriptions contained in waqf deeds provides information concerning the terminology of architectural and decorative elements. Valuable research carried out by Laila Ibrahim and Muhammad Amin in their book *Architectural Terms in Mamluk Documents* lists all the architectural elements, spaces, materials, and decorative descriptions mentioned in the waqfiyas and other archival documents, and provides a detailed explanation of these terms.[41] In cases where buildings no longer exist, the waqf deeds provide valuable information that can be used to reconstruct their layout.

Prior to the execution of any restoration and conservation project, primary and secondary sources have to be consulted to provide a clear understanding of a building and its architectural history. Information on the building's initial condition can be obtained from the waqf deeds, while its architectural history can be gleaned from the writings of Mamluk chroniclers such as al-Maqrizi and government officials like the nineteenth-century secretary of public works 'Ali Mubarak, as well as court reports available for the Ottoman period, the *Corpus Inscriptionum Arabicarum*, travelers' accounts and drawings, and *Comité* reports. A waqf deed can be very beneficial for archaeological excavation of an endowed building, since in some cases a well, cistern, or waterwheel was mentioned in the deed; excavations and interventions should therefore try to find these elements.

The living built heritage of Historic Cairo

In order to contextualize the idea that waqf principles can be beneficial for current restoration and maintenance practice, I will briefly describe the current situation for the different types of built heritage and waqf properties in Historic Cairo.[42]

There is a difference between the condition of registered monuments that are placed under the auspices of the SCA and those under the joint responsibility of the SCA and the Ministry of Endowments. In the Egyptian Law on the Protection of Antiquities (law no. 117 of 1983, amended in 2010),[43] there are only two clauses regarding waqf properties. The first, clause 6, states that waqf authorities (represented by the Ministry of Endowments) are the owners of waqf properties; the second, clause 30, states that the SCA is responsible for carrying out conservation, maintenance, and restoration work while the Ministry of Endowments must bear the cost (which is currently not the case). Clause 30 also states that the SCA may authorize other organizations and missions to carry out interventions. There are no further clear written guidelines, regulations, or procedures regarding the protection, conservation, and maintenance of waqf properties.

Each type of waqf property has special conditions. Religious structures such as historic mosques, under the auspices of both the SCA and the Ministry of Endowments, are those structures where most of the conflicts over use and restoration occur. The mosques are a living heritage, constantly used by congregations of worshipers. The Ministry of Endowments therefore assigns them a guard and a shaykh. Continuous use ensures that these structures are regularly maintained and not left to decay and deteriorate. In many cases, however, they are considered only for their function and not for their historical and artistic value; accordingly, many actions take place that cause harm to the buildings, even though the intention may be to benefit them. For example, the application of black cement mortar on the walls of mosques, carried out by users to enhance their appearance, negatively affects the limestone and causes it to deteriorate due to the presence of large amounts of salts in the cement. This is one of many examples. For users and the Ministry of Endowments, the important thing is to have a functioning building that is of benefit to the community. For historians and conservationists, in contrast, the value of the mosque lies in the historical and artistic significance of the building. If we return to the waqf stipulations, however, founders always evinced keen interest in the physical and aesthetic aspect of the buildings they endowed. Nor do historians and conservation specialists disregard the significance of mosques as a living religious heritage.

A number of conservation and restoration projects of historic mosques are being carried out in collaboration with the SCA; these of course pay attention to the historic and artistic fabric as well as the requirements of the mosque users. The problem remains, however, of how a mosque will be maintained after the project is completed and handed over to the SCA and the Ministry of Endowments to start regular prayers there, and of how to ensure that users will appreciate the mosque not only for its function but also for its heritage value.

As mentioned above, original waqf deeds stipulate that the benefit, and hence the function, of the endowment must be in perpetuity. This does not mean that the artistic value of endowment properties must be neglected, however. Waqf founders took great pains to build magnificent and lavishly decorated structures, drafting careful stipulations for their maintenance and upkeep. It can be argued that demolishing or disregarding the artistic and architectural value of these structures runs contrary to the founders' stipulations.

Other buildings that do not have a religious function can be divided into two groups. The first includes structures that no longer fulfill their original function, such as sabils, palaces, or caravansaries. The second includes buildings that are still being used, such as houses and other residential units. Often, the units are not registered as historic buildings, leading to many of them being destroyed and lost, with newer units being built in the place of the historic, endowed structures. Advocates of function over form will argue that the purpose of the endowment (to provide residential units) was respected; as mentioned above, however, waqf stipulations placed a premium on maintenance of the original structure. The demolition of residential units that are part of waqf destroys not only the historic buildings in which these units were located, but also the whole urban landscape and fabric of many parts of Historic Cairo.

The buildings belonging to the first group are registered and are thus protected, at least from being demolished. Yet, they suffer from overall neglect, as many of them are closed and not being used. Some of these buildings are currently being restored by various organizations in coordination with the SCA. After the completion of conservation and restoration projects, it is important to consider appropriate continuous reuse of these structures along with a maintenance plan, as the lack of either will lead inevitably to the deterioration of these structures once again.

Waqf and conservation principles

A number of significant ideas related to maintenance and upkeep can be drawn from careful reading of the waqf stipulations. Certainly, these were not always respected, but it is not my purpose here to explain why the system did not continue. Rather, I wish to demonstrate how these principles established a number of interesting and important ideas in regard to maintenance and repair and how these are actually strongly in line with many current conservation principles.

Sources of funding to be used primarily for maintenance and repair activities

The waqf system provided the sources of funding that were used primarily for the maintenance and repair operations. If no sources of funding were available, the waqf deed provided suggestions such as renting the waqf property to expedite the necessary repairs and restorations.

The economics of investing in cultural heritage is currently a major concern. Despite the availability of donors and funds for the preservation and conservation of the cultural heritage, sustainability issues and problems need to be addressed. To give an example: even if sources of funding are available for a restoration project, if further funding is not available for maintenance, deterioration is inevitable and hence investment in the initial restoration project is not really worthwhile. Therefore, following the very basic idea of the waqf system, it is important that those institutions responsible for the cultural heritage provide possible sources of funding and constant revenue for extant monuments. This money should be used, as in the past, primarily for the maintenance and repair of the monuments.

Supervision and regular maintenance and repair

Under the waqf system, supervision, maintenance, and repair were priorities. The waqf supervisor and a team of engineers, architects, plumbers, marble masons, and other artisans had to regularly inspect waqf institutions, making sure that things were functioning properly and undertaking any action needed if something had to be fixed. The idea of regular maintenance and repair is very important, because it prevents buildings from decaying. If done properly, there would not be a need for huge restoration projects requiring the outlay of enormous funds. It is therefore important to consider establishing an institution or hiring a company that is specialized in regular maintenance and conservation to conduct regular and continuous visits to all monuments, both those recently restored and those in need of restoration, and carry out all necessary repairs in order to protect buildings from further decay.

Preservation of a building's function and benefits

When restoring a mosque it is easy to respect this stipulation, as the mosque will return to its original function after restoration. This is not true of many other buildings that have lost their function and use over time and due to modernization. It is not always possible to restore the function of many of these buildings: sabils, for example, are no longer in use due to the existence of a water supply system. Accordingly, these buildings are often closed and at risk of becoming 'dead heritage,' subject to continuous degradation and decay. It is important that these buildings be restored and revitalized; since their original function cannot be restored, however, new functions must be considered. Buildings must be useful and beneficial to the people. The same applies to houses, madrasas, palaces, khanqahs, and numerous other types of buildings that are no longer in use according to their original function. The adaptive reuse of monuments would ensure their maintenance and upkeep as well as their continued use and benefit. If a restored building remains closed, it is likely to deteriorate again and be of no benefit to anyone.

A clear and legally binding management system that regulates the above-mentioned issues should be drafted to ensure the protection of the cultural heritage. This would be a lengthy process and would require the willingness and sincere cooperation of all parties involved. It should thus be begun immediately, as the lack of such a system will likely result in further deterioration of waqf properties. In undertaking this exercise, the parties involved must learn to respect the different yet not necessarily conflicting values of the various stakeholders and beneficiaries, all of whom seek to preserve a vibrant living heritage.

The Venice Charter states in its preamble:

Imbued with a message from the past, the historic monuments of generations of people remain to the present day as living witnesses of their age-old transition. People are becoming more and more conscious of the unity of human values and regard ancient monuments as a common heritage. The common responsibility to safeguard them for future generations is recognized. It is our duty to hand them on in the full richness of their authenticity.

It is essential that the principles guiding the preservation and restoration of ancient buildings should be agreed and be laid down on an international basis, with each country being responsible for applying the plan within the framework of its own culture and traditions.

Notes

1 Parts of this article are based on the author's MA thesis. See Bakhoum, "The Waqf."
2 Jokilehto, *A History,* 12.
3 For further information on this subject, see Reid, "Cultural Imperialism and Nationalism." For more information on the Comité, see El-Habashi, *Athar.*
4 Also *hubus, hubs, ahbas.* These are often used in Morocco, Algiers, and Tunis, and "hence in French legal language: *habous*" (Heffening, "Waḳf," 1096).
5 Abu Zahra, *Muhadarat fi-l-waqf,* 7.
6 Crecelius, "Introduction," 251.
7 It is important to mention that there are numerous other forms of waqfs: in the early period of Islam, for example, weapons and horses used in battles to spread religion were endowed (Peters, "Wakf, I," 59).
8 The revenue had to come from a lawful and religiously accepted source, otherwise it would not be considered a lawful waqf.
9 These revenue-generating properties were sometimes, but not always, attached to or near the institution. For further information regarding waqf and urban development, see Denoix, "A Mamluk Institution," and Akar in this volume.
10 For a more detailed discussion on the perpetuity of waqf (also in twentieth and twenty-first century laws), see Abu Zahra, *Muhadarat fi-l-waqf,* 70–86.
11 The term *'imara* denotes any action that allows a building to remain operating and in good condition *('amir).* Nevertheless, in some cases it could also mean building and construction operations. The term, when taken from the Arabic text to be used in this research, will not be translated to English; instead the word *'imara* will be used because there is no one single word that could define it, and also because in each text it could have had a different meaning.

12   Amin, "Watha'iq waqf al-Sultan Qalawun," 361–62. It is clear here that the term *'imara* is related to maintenance and repair operations.

13   Waqf of al-Ghuri, Awqaf 883, 178.

14   *Istibdal* literally means exchange. It is a system of exchanging damaged or ruined waqf properties that were structurally dangerous to the people or not generating any (or enough) revenue and were not beneficial to the system for better ones. Although as an idea it was in favor of the beneficiaries and the system as a whole, it was often misused to obtain waqf properties for personal reasons, even if these properties were actually in a good condition. The istibdal and its misuse will not be discussed in detail in this paper, but will be mentioned whenever applicable. For further information regarding the istibdal of waqfs and urban development, see Fernandes, "Istibdal."

15   al-Khassaf was the imam al-Shaybani, Abu Bakr Ahmad ibn 'Umar, a judge *(qadi al-qudah)* in Baghdad in the ninth century. He wrote a work on waqf stipulations titled *Ahkam al-awqaf.*

16   al-Khassaf, *Ahkam al-awqaf,* 320.

17   al-Kindi, *Kitab al-wulah,* 394–95.

18   al-Kindi, *Kitab al-wulah,* 383.

19   al-Kindi, *Kitab al-wulah,* 395.

20   al-Maqrizi, *al-Khitat,* vol. 2, 295.

21   Waqf of al-Mu'ayyad Shaykh, Awqaf 938, 56.

22   Ibrahim, "Silsilat al-watha'iq," discussing "Wathiqat al-Amir Akhur," 250, referencing the Waqf of al-Ghuri, Awqaf 883, line 1592; *wathiqat* Badr al-Din Wafa'i, *mahkama* 221; Waqf al-Mu'ayyad Shaykh, Awqaf 938.

23   The shadd or mushidd was responsible for collecting the revenue of endowed properties. For more information about this position see Rabie, *Financial System,* 151–53.

24   Behrens-Abouseif, "*Muhandis,*" 295. Behrens-Abouseif mentions that the distinction between the *muhandis al-'ama'ir* and the *shadd al-'ama'ir* is not easy to make. But apparently *shadd al-'ama'ir* was responsible for financial matters, so "he could have dealt with the feasibility of the projects and the estimation of the costs involved."

25   Waqf of al-Ghuri, Awqaf 883, line 1571, studied by 'Abd al-Latif Ibrahim, quoted in Amin, *al-Awqaf,* 307.

26   Amin, *al-Awqaf,* 307, discussing the waqf deed of Jamal al-Din Ustadar.

27   A *mi'mar* was "a specialist for repair and restoration and should not be mistaken for an architect, for whom this term never applied in Mamluk terminology" (Behrens-Abouseif, "*Muhandis,*" 296).

28   Waqf al-Ghuri, *al-Awqaf,* 318, quoting Waqf of al-Ghuri, Awqaf 883, line 1603ff., studied by Dr. 'Abd al-Latif Ibrahim.

29   Mayer, *Buildings of Qaytbay,* 70–71.

30   Amin, *al-Awqaf,* 307, discussing the waqf deed of Jamal al-Din Ustadar.

31   Mayer, *Buildings of Qaytbay,* 71.

32   Amin, *al-Awqaf,* 319, quoting waqf of al-Ghuri, Awqaf 883, line 1608 ff., studied by Dr. 'Abd al-Latif Ibrahim.

33   Mayer, *Buildings of Qaytbay,* 71.

34   Waqf of Sabil al-Mu'minin, Waqf 884, 468; sabil restored by al-Ghuri.

35   Mayer, *Buildings of Qaytbay,* 72.

36   Waqf of al-Ghuri, Awqaf 883, 191.

37   The Arabic word used here is *tathir,* which literally means 'to purify.'

38   Mayer, *Buildings of Qaytbay*, 72–73.

39   Waqf of al-Ghuri, Awqaf 883, 203, 204, 219–20.

40   Fernandes, "Notes," 5–6.

41   The study was conducted not only by comparing waqfiyas with existing buildings, but also by using other sources pre- and post-dating the Mamluk period.

42   Looking into some questions, while outside the immediate scope of this article, would shed further light on the issues raised here: for example, the history of conservation of waqf properties, how the waqf authorities stopped being responsible for the maintenance of these structures, and how the Comité and later the Egyptian Antiquities Organization (currently the SCA) were formed. I am currently researching these issues and hope to explore them further within the context of a PhD dissertation.

43   The Egyptian Law on the Protection of Antiquities, Law no. 117 of 1983, was modified by Law no. 3 of 2010.

Bibliography

Archival Sources

Ministry of Endowments, Waqf of Barsbay, Awqaf 880.

Ministry of Endowments, Waqf of al-Ghuri, Awqaf 883.

Ministry of Endowments, Waqf of al-Mu'ayyad Shaykh, Awqaf 938.

Ministry of Endowments, Waqf of Sabil al-Mu'minin, Waqf 884.

Ministry of Endowments, Waqf of Sultan Hasan, Awqaf 881.

Ministry of Endowments, Waqf of Qaytbay, Awqaf 889.

Publications and Other Sources

Abu Zahra, Muhammad. *Muhadarat fi-l-waqf.* Cairo: Dar al-Fikr al-ʻArabi, 1972.

Amin, Muhammad Muhammad. "Un acte de fondation de waqf par une chrétienne (Xe siècle h., XVIe s. chr.)." *Journal of the Economic and Social History of the Orient* 18, no. 1: (1975): 43 52.

———. *al-Awqaf wa-l-hayah al-ijtimaʻiya fi Misr, 648–923 H, 1250–1517 M: dirasa tarikhiya watha'iqiya.* Cairo: Dar al-Nahda al-ʻArabiya, 1980.

———. "Watha'iq waqf al-Sultan Qalawun ʻala al-Bimaristan al-Mansuri." Published as appendix in Ibn Habib, *Tadhkirat al-nabih fi ayyam al-Mansur wa banih,* vol. 1, 295–396. Cairo: al-Hay'a al-Misriya al-ʻAmma li-li-Kitab, 1976–86.

Amin, Muhammad Muhammad, and Laila Ali Ibrahim. *al-Mustalahat al-miʻmariya fi-l-watha'iq al-mamlukiya, 648–923 H/1250–1517 M.* Cairo: American University in Cairo Press, 1990.

Bakhoum, Dina Ishak. "The Waqf in Relation to Maintenance and Repair: The Medieval Sources and Their Uses for Contemporary Practices." MA thesis, American University in Cairo, 2004.

Behrens-Abouseif, Doris. "*Muhandis, Shād, Mu'allim*—Note on the Building Craft in the Mamluk Period." *Der Islam* 72 (1995): 239–309.

———. "Waḳf, II. In the Arab Lands: 1. In Egypt." In *Encyclopedia of Islam*, 2nd ed., vol. 11, 63–69. Leiden: E.J. Brill, 1960, repr. 1986.

Behrens-Abouseif, Doris, ed. *The Cairo Heritage: Essays in Honor of Laila Ali Ibrahim*. Cairo: American University in Cairo Press, 2000.

Crecelius, Daniel. "Introduction." *Journal of the Economic and Social History of the Orient* 38, no. 3 (1995): 247–61.

Denoix, Sylvie. "A Mamluk Institution for Urbanization: The Waqf," in D. Behrens-Abouseif, ed. *The Cairo Heritage*, 191–202.

Fernandes, Leonor. "Istibdal: The Game of Exchange and its Impact on the Urbanization of Mamluk Cairo," in D. Behrens-Abouseif, ed. *The Cairo Heritage*, 203–22.

———. "Notes on a New Source for the Study of Religious Architecture during the Mamluk Period: The Waqfiya." *al-Abhath* no. 33 (1985): 3–12.

El-Habashi, Alaa El-Din. "Athar to Monuments: The Intervention of the Comité de Conservation des Monuments de l'Art Arabe." PhD diss., University of Pennsylvania, 2001.

Heffening, W. "Waḳf." In *E.J. Brill's First Encyclopedia of Islam, 1913–1936*, edited by M. Th. Houtsma, vol. 8: 1096–1103 (repr. 1987). Leiden: E.J. Brill, 1913–1936.

Ibrahim, 'Abd al-Latif. "Silsilat al-watha'iq al-tarikhiya al-qawmiya, majmu'at al-watha'iq al-mamlukiya." *Majallat kulliyyat al-adab* (Cairo University) 25, no. 2 (1963): 183–251.

Jokilehto, Jukka. *A History of Architectural Conservation*. Oxford: Butterworth-Heinemann, 1999.

al-Khassaf, Ahmad ibn Amr al-Shaybani. *Kitab ahkam al-awqaf*. Cairo: Maktabat al-Thaqafa al-Diniya, 1904.

Kindi, Abu 'Umar Muhammad ibn Yusuf. *Kitab al-wulah wa kitab al-qudah*. Beirut: Matba'at al-Aba' al-Yasu'iyin, 1908.

al-Maqrizi, Taqiyy al-Din Ahmad. *Kitab al-mawa'iz wa-l-i'tibar fi dhikr al-khitat wa-l-athar*, 2 vols. Cairo: Bulaq Press, AH 1270.

Mayer, L.A. *The Buildings of Qaytbay as Described in His Endowment Deeds*. London: Arthur Probsthain, 1938.

Mubarak, 'Ali. *al-Khitat al-tawfiqiya al-jadida li-Misr al-Qahira wa muduniha wa-biladiha al-qadima wa-l-shahira*. 20 vols. Cairo: General Egyptian Book Organization, AH 1306.

Peters, R. "Waḳf, I. In Classical Islamic Law." In *Encyclopedia of Islam*, 2nd ed., vol. 11, 59–63. Leiden: E.J. Brill, 1960, repr. 1986.

Rabie, Hassanein, *The Financial System of Egypt AH 564–741/AD 1169–1341*. London and New York: Oxford University Press, 1972.

Reid, Donald M. "Cultural Imperialism and Nationalism: The Struggle to Define and Control the Heritage of Arab Art in Egypt." *International Journal of Middle East Studies* 24 (1992): 57–76.

al-Tarabulsi, Ibrahim ibn Musa ibn Abi Bakr. *Kitab al-is'af fi ahkam al-awqaf.* Mecca: Maktabat al-Talib and al-Jami'i, AH 1406.

The Venice Charter, International Charter for the Conservation and Restoration of Monuments and Sites. Venice: International Council on Monuments and Sites, 1964.

9

The Role of Waqf in Shaping and Preserving Urban Areas: The Historical Commercial Center of Adana

Tuba Akar

In the Ottoman Empire, waqfs or pious endowments were the main force behind construction and public works. The Ottoman state, rather than discharging a modern state's duties of providing social welfare, left such tasks to institutions like the waqf. Social, cultural, economic, and educational services were provided and maintained by waqfs of different sizes and varying degrees of importance; so, as waqfs served public welfare, they also contributed to shaping space throughout the empire, especially in the urban areas. Mosques, madrasas, khans, baths, shops, and other facilities that existed thanks to waqf revenues offered social, cultural, and educational services to the public.

This study examines the impact of waqf on built urban areas in terms of formation, development, and preservation. I take as my case study the historical commercial center of the city of Adana in Turkey. Endowment deeds (*waqfiyas*), and the extant physical features of the historical commercial center are the basic data on which I have relied in this study.[1] In particular, I have focused on the waqfiyas[2] of Piri Mehmed Paşa, the founder of the Ramazanoğlu waqf, to which the historical commercial center belonged. These waqfiyas make mention

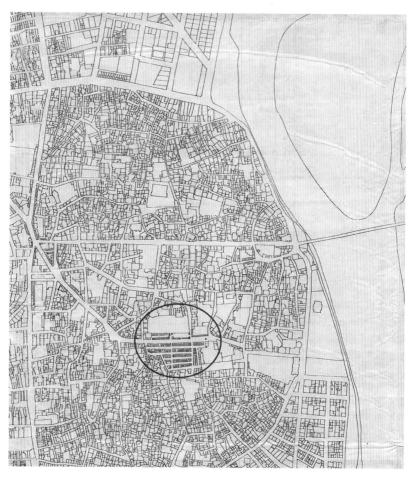

Figure 1. The historical settlement of the city of Adana (Oral 1996).

of endowed properties, employees of the waqf, their salaries, management of the waqf, the duties of the supervisor (*mutevelli*; Arabic *mutawalli*), and so on. As is customary in endowment deeds, the endowed properties are described and situated with reference to surrounding buildings or areas. Furthermore, the deeds specify conditions for preservation of the buildings, financing of repair activities, and the responsibilities of technical staff.

Using information from the waqfiyas and the extant conditions in Adana, I was able to trace the formation of the historical commercial center.

When attempting to determine the role waqfs played in shaping and preserving an urban area, it is useful to return to the definition of a waqf, perhaps best defined as the act of appropriating movable or immovable properties to a religious, charitable, and social cause for the purpose of gaining God's approval by providing permanent social and public services.[3] In this definition, two points are particularly important to our topic of waqf and its impact on urban space: the appropriation of immovable properties and the idea of permanence.

The immovable properties to which the definition refers usually consist of real estate: mosques, madrasas, khans, shops, and baths that anchor and structure urban space durably. Such durability, as mentioned, was intrinsic to the definition of the waqf, and was indeed the reason for which founders earmarked income and stipulated the terms for continuity of service.

Figure 2. The historical commercial center of Adana and immediate surroundings. After base map from the Municipality of Adana.

Clearly, then, when we examine the ways in which waqfs contributed to shaping built areas in the Ottoman Empire, it becomes apparent that these institutions were a central force, in addition to their social, cultural, and economic functions. Apart from housing, construction activities in the Empire tended to fall into one of two categories: the construction works carried out by the central government (generally military installations, defensive structures, and public works including towers, ramparts, roads, bridges, and so on); and the public buildings erected on the initiative of individuals seeking to contribute to religious, social, and cultural aspects of urban life, and brought into existence by means of the waqf.[4] Services we might expect today from the central government or local municipal authorities were provided by waqfs, which catered to the community's needs in the domains of religion, education, health care, transport, welfare, and infrastructure.

On a larger scale, waqfs played a significant role in shaping and developing urban centers. This came about through the creation of *kulliye*s or building complexes, which included such edifices as a madrasa, a khan, and a public bath, generally located around a mosque in a new district of

Figure 3. View along Ali Münif Yeğenağa Street toward the clock tower, 2001. (Photograph by author.)

the city. Thus were new neighborhoods brought into existence, with increasing numbers of inhabitants and activities coalescing around the nucleus formed by the kulliye. It may be said that kulliyes drew up urban development plans, since a city tended to develop in the direction they dictated.[5]

To ensure the continuity of waqfs, founders included revenue-generating properties as well as public welfare institutions in their establishments. Thus, a waqf would include a mosque, school, or hospital, as well as an orchard, a commercial warehouse, or rental apartments, with the revenues from the second group allowing for the maintenance in perpetuity of the first. Keen to perpetuate this relationship, waqf founders made sure to stipulate terms for the repair of their foundations, sometimes appointing personnel for this purpose. Thus, waqf deeds include not only detailed instructions for repair and maintenance, but also stipulations regarding the personnel to be employed and the salaries they were to receive.[6]

Historical commercial center of Adana

The city of Adana is located in southern Turkey, in the Çukurova plain (historical Cilicia). The city had an important place in history because of its location on the caravan route between Anatolia and the Arab regions of the Ottoman Empire. The goods produced in Adana also made the city a lively commercial

Figure 4. Shops on Ali Münif Yeğenağa Street, 2001. (Photographs by author.)

Figure 5. Shops arranged in *arasta* pattern, 2001. (Photograph by author.)

Figure 6. Different shop units, 2001. (Photograph by author.)

center in Ottoman times. The peak of its development, however, was reached in the time of the Ramazanoğlu Principality (late fourteenth to early seventeenth century), a frontier principality incorporated by the Ottomans in the early sixteenth century. There were twenty waqfs in Adana in the sixteenth century, and the most important and largest of all was the Ramazanoğlu waqf;[7] the others were small mosque waqfs. After the Ramazanoğlu Principality Ottoman rule prevailed, but did not play as important a role in urban life as the Ramazanoğlu Principality had. Adana continued to grow, but few large-scale monuments were built after the early seventeenth century.

Today, the historical commercial center of the city is located in the heart of the old residential areas, between two *külliye*s (Figure 1): Ulu Cami Külliyesi and Yağ Cami Külliyesi. These were built in the sixteenth century. A public bath located southwest of Ulucami was also built as part of the Ramazanoğlu waqf in the sixteenth century. A clock tower was built in 1882 (Figure 2). Other monumental buildings in the vicinity of the commercial area are the Hasır Pazarı Mosque (sixteenth century) and Inkılap School (nineteenth century).

The historical commercial center of Adana features buildings organized in an *arasta* pattern (shops aligned along a covered or uncovered street); a covered bazaar; a newly built area known as Vakıf Çarşısı; and a khan. Commercial activities have continued here since the area's inception—a remarkable example of functional continuity—with some spatial and architectural alterations, as well as a shift in the type of commercial activity practiced. The main functions seen in the historical commercial center today are the production and sale of shoes and candy (Figures 3–6).

In general architectural terms, space is organized to serve commerce in the area, with shops lining both sides of the streets. The plots are completely built up. The shops are built entirely of brick, to a rectangular plan of approximately three meters by four meters. The street façades of the shops are completely open. The superstructure is generally a brick barrel vault perpendicular to the street. Small domes may also be seen in the superstructure of a few of the shops. The plan dimensions of the shops fall into three main categories: unit, half unit, and large unit.

Although the shops have similar features, some differences can be seen in volume, plan, façade, construction material, or details. Most of the façades are brick with timber beams. There are variations in the height of the façades, the form of the arches, and the details of the cornices. Walls are raised above the vaults and finished with special details.

Today, nearly all the shops belong to private owners. Only the completely new area (Vakıf Çarşısı) is the property of the General Directorate of Pious Foundations as Ramazanoğlu waqf property.

Information from the waqfiyas

There are eight waqf deeds (AH 945–62/1538–55 CE) relating to endowments established by Piri Mehmed Paşa.[8] In this study I will take into account only the information related to the commercial center and commercial activity in Adana. This information can be found in the first three foundation deeds, which tell us that the Ramazanoğlu Waqf Bazaar was a big commercial area with different types of buildings: shops, khans, bazaar, and market areas, manufactories like sesame oil presses, and so on. It had unique features, such as the surrounding walls, which were pierced by seven gates. The bazaar was actually made up of two commercial areas, the bazaar and the market, with streets named according to the more specialized activities that were presumably located there (for example, Cobblers' Street, Saddlers' Street, Bazaar Street).[9]

Although the area belonged to the Ramazanoğlu waqf, not all the buildings were built by the waqf. The differences in the shop façades suggest this; the third endowment deed, moreover, mentions that the founder had constructed some of the buildings and bought other existing buildings or shops within the walls surrounding the commercial area.

Endowment deeds and physical evidence: A comparison

In planning the restitution of the area, the information taken from the waqfiyas, the buildings' architectural features, and site analysis results were mapped out to determine the layout of the area in the sixteenth century (Figure 7).

Where Inkılap School stands today, there may have been an *imaret* (soup kitchen erected as charitable foundation for the distribution of food to the staff of the waqf and the needy) in the sixteenth century.

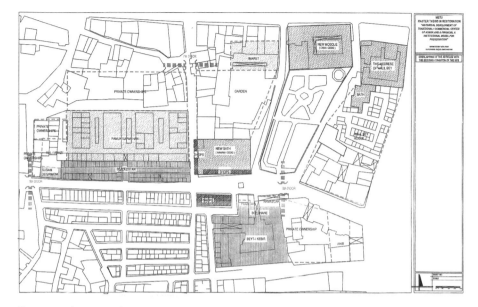

Figure 7. Information from the waqfiyas superimposed upon current conditions in the historical commercial center (by the author).

According to the waqfiyas, there were shops adjacent to the southern and western façades of the Çarşı Bath. Today there are still some shops located on the southern side of the bath.

In the place of Yeni Han, the waqfiyas mention a big building (Beyt-i Kebir) for flour merchants.

In the place of the covered bazaar, there was a clothing market (Bezestan).

The Pamuk Kapan Khan (Cotton Weighers' Khan) stood to the north of this area in the sixteenth century.

The eighth gate may have been on Ali Münif Yeğenağa Street at the east of the clock tower, whereas the fifth gate may have been on the same street to the west of the covered bazaar. However the seventh gate may have been on the street located to the west of Çarşı Bath.

The road the waqfiyas refer to as Bazaar Street could be present-day Ali Münif Yeğenağa Street.

A site analysis carried out with the help of the foundation deeds provides clues that are helpful in our effort to understand how the commercial area was formed. For example:

The northern wall of Inkılap School is different from the school's other walls, and originally might have been the wall of a different building.

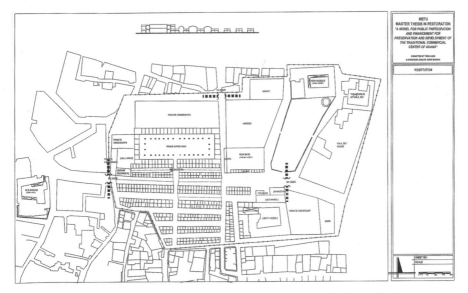

Figure 8. Restitution of the historical commercial center (by the author).

The waqfiyas mention that there were thirteen shops to the south of Çarşı Bath. The current cadastral map shows the same number to be extant today.

When the shops on 29th Street are examined, it becomes clear that the street had a similar superstructure (which has since collapsed) to that of the covered bazaar.

The entrance of Vakıflar Çarşı shows the architectural features of a khan entrance.

The junction of the walls of the covered bazaar and Vakıflar Çarşı shows no organic link between the stones. This suggests that the buildings were not constructed at the same time; Vakıf Çarşı may have been constructed before the covered bazaar.

The courtyard wall to the south of Vakıflar Çarşı could have been one of the walls of the Pamuk Kapanı Khan or the surrounding wall of the commercial area.

Yeni Khan might be the big building (Beyt-i Kebir) mentioned in the waqf deed. Although a date inscribed on Yeni Khan dates the building to the eighteenth century, this might be the date when the building was repaired.

On the 1938 cadastral map, Ali Münif Yeğenağa Street is shown as Bazaar Street, which is also mentioned in the waqfiyas.

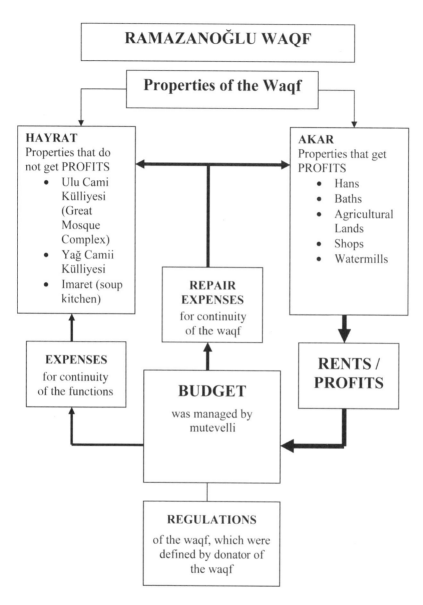

Figure 9. Ramazanoğlu waqf (by the author).

When Ali Münif Yeğenağa Street and 6th Street are examined, they show traces of a superstructure between building lots 93 and 94. Old photographs of the area prove this impression correct.

The heterogeneous architectural features and details of the shops indicate that the commercial area was not built all at once, but rather dates from different periods.

In light of this analysis, we may put forth some tentative conclusions regarding the layout of the site in the sixteenth century:

Pamuk Kapanı Khan was located where Vakıflar Çarşı is today.

The Bezestan was made up of two buildings: the covered bazaar and the section on 29th Street.

An imaret was located at the place of Inkılap School.

The boundaries of the commercial area cannot be determined with much precision. To the north, east, and west the plan (Figure 8) may be accurate; to the south, however, the commercial area must have extended much farther, since the waqf deeds mention an animal market, which seems to have been located to the south of the shops.

Organization scheme of the waqf

With information taken from the waqfiyas, we can deduce the organization of the Ramazanoğlu waqf (Figure 9). As in any waqf, rents and profits from real estate owned by the foundation were used to defray operation costs, provide welfare services, and pay for repairs. The founder made special stipulations to ensure that the waqf properties would be repaired in perpetuity.

Conclusion

The Ramazanoğlu waqf exerted a powerful influence over the historical commercial center of Adana, shaping the area over a long period of time. The waqf also played an important role in urbanization, acting as a commercial pole of attraction and providing social and religious services as well.

This influence was gradual and piecemeal, however. Even the arasta pattern of the Ramazanoğlu waqf bazaar was not put in place all at once, as can be seen in the architectural features. The waqf deeds tell us that the commercial area was planned, then the constructions were carried out over a period of time, as the foundation included not only shops but also empty plots—gaps to be filled in, as it were, by more shops. Thus, we may conjecture that the founder envisaged a fluid planning scheme: one that provided a structure but was sufficiently flexible to adapt to organic urban growth during the decades that followed the waqf's establishment.

Notes

1   This study is based on the writer's unpublished master thesis.
2   There are eight waqfiyas drawn up by Ramazanoğlu Piri Mehmed Paşa in the archives of the General Directorate of Pious Foundations, Turkey.
3   *Islam Ansiklopedisi*, vol. 13, p. 154, s.v. "vakıf."
4   Madran, "Organization," 25.
5   Barkan, "Osmanlı," 239–43.
6   Bakırer mentions that while there are more general repair terms in thirteenth- and fourteenth-century waqfiyas, the deeds written in the classical Ottoman period include detailed information on the repair of the buildings and the personnel to be employed in the repairs (Bakırer, "Vakfiyelerde," 121).
7   Kurt and Erdoğru, *Çukurova*, lx.
8   Waqfiyas of Piri Mehmed Paşa.
9   Bazaar Street, shown on the Cadastral Map of 1938, is named Ali Münif Yeğenağa Street today.

Bibliography

Archival Sources

Waqfiyas of Piri Mehmed Paşa, original notebook 646—translated notebook 1961, registration no. 367–93, translated by Refik Şallı in 1936. Archive of the General Directorate of Pious Foundations.

Publications and Other Sources

Akar, Tuba. "The Historical Formation of the Traditional/Commercial Center of Adana and a Financial and Institutional Model for Preservation." Master's thesis, Graduate School of Natural and Applied Sciences, Middle East Technical University, Restoration Program, Department of Architecture, Ankara, 2002.

Bakırer, Ömür. "Vakfiyelerde Binaların Tamiratı ile İlgili Şartlar ve Bunlara Uyulması." *Vakıflar Dergisi* 10 (1973): 113–26.

Barkan, Ömer Lütfi. "Osmanlı İmparatorluğunda İmaret Sitelerinin Kuruluş ve İşleyiş Tarzına Ait Araştırmalar." *İktisat Fakültesi Mecmuası* 23, no. 1–2 (1963): 239–96.

Cezar, Mustafa. *Typical Commercial Buildings of the Ottoman Classical Period and the Ottoman Construction System*. Istanbul: Türkiye İş Bankası Cultural Publications, 1988.

Kurt, Yılmaz. "16. yy Adana Tarihi." PhD diss., Hacettepe University, Ankara, 1992.

Kurt, Yılmaz, and Akif M. Erdoğru. *Çukurova Tarihinin Kaynakları IV*. Ankara: Türk Tarih Kurumu, 2000.

Madran, Emre. "The Organization of the Field of Restoration in the Ottoman Empire: 16th–18th Centuries." PhD dissertation, Middle East Technical University, Ankara, 1996.

Oral, F. Duygu. "16.yy'da Adana Kentinin Fiziksel Yapısı." Master's thesis, Çukurova University, Adana, 1996.

Yediyıldız, Bahaeddin. *XVIII. Yüzyılda Türkiye'de Vakıf Müessesesi.* Ankara: Türk Tarih Kurumu Publication, 2003.

———. "Sosyal Teşkilatlar Bütünlüğü Olarak Osmanlı Vakıf Külliyeleri." *Türk Kültürü* 219 (1981): 262–71.

———. "Vakıf." *İslam Ansiklopedisi,* vol. 13 (1986): 153–72.

Conclusion

Ottoman Waqfs as Acts of Citizenship[1]

Engin F. Isin

The waqf as an institution of beneficence is well known among Islamic scholars. The idea that waqfs provided many of the social and cultural services to 'citizens' of diverse Islamic polities ranging from the Mamluk and Ottoman empires to India, Indonesia, and Iran would not surprise many scholars. But to interpret the Islamic waqf as an 'act' of citizenship is at best unconventional. This argument requires changing our modern understanding of citizenship as contractual status. It requires considering the ways in which the concept of citizenship has evolved through history and how it enabled a division between modern and traditional and occidental and oriental.[2] Once we fulfill these requirements, new avenues of thought open up through which we can interpret Islamic waqfs as acts of citizenship. There are many historical and political advantages to interpreting waqfs as mechanisms for producing and managing citizenship; I suggest a few in the present chapter.

At first glance, interpreting waqf as an act of citizenship may surprise the reader. What is the relationship? Citizenship (its modern version that we are familiar with) was born of the state (seventeenth and eighteenth centuries) and then the nation-state (nineteenth and twentieth centuries), which allocated certain rights and obligations to individuals under its authority. Modern citizenship rights that draw from the nation-state typically include civil (free speech and movement, rule of law), political (voting, seeking electoral office), and social (welfare, unemployment insurance, and health care) rights. The precise combination and depth of such rights vary from one state to another, but universal citizenship rights and obligations are attributes expected in every modern state. By contrast, Islamic, and more specifically, Ottoman, waqfs are popularly known as pious foundations, mostly for avoiding state taxes and bequeathing family property.[3] The two institutions could not seem more dissimilar, yet a critical analysis reveals affinities between them and indeed suggests that rethinking waqf as an act of citizenship is not merely an academic exercise, but a political necessity. Critical reflections on both citizenship and waqf will help to illustrate the relationship I wish to establish, and ultimately why this relationship is important.

The recent history of the concept of citizenship, as indicated above, is in relation to the state and nation-state. But while a particular variant of citizenship as status may have been articulated in Europe in the late eighteenth and early nineteenth centuries, it is by no means the only possible variant, let alone the most politically acceptable form, especially in its collapsing of citizenship into nationality. Indeed the conflation of citizenship and nationality has contributed to racism, xenophobia, and discrimination. As long as citizenship has been understood as nationality, state authorities have not hesitated to commit atrocities and genocides in its name.

The institution of citizenship has, however, had a much longer history than the modern state. It is usually traced to ancient Greek politics and Roman law, both of which understood citizenship as a city-based identity, albeit with differences. Recent critical scholarship, however, has demonstrated the limits of the modern European or Western conception of citizenship—especially understood as nationality—and has thus opened up new practices and rituals as objects of study, extending its boundaries beyond Europe and North America.[4] Some scholars have identified a form of Mesopotamian 'citizenship' that existed centuries before the Greek polis or Roman law. Similarly, scholars have questioned the 'Westernization' of this institution and have begun studying citizenship in ancient China, ancient India, and ancient Judaic, Christian, and Islamic traditions. In all these studies, citizenship appears much less as state membership, let alone nation-state membership, and more as an institution symbolizing generalized routines, practices, and rituals that constituted humans as political beings, enabling them to deal with each other via political rather than violent means. In general terms, citizenship can be defined as the art of negotiating difference and claiming recognition through political means rather than using violence to annihilate difference. While this may appear as an idealist conception, it does not presuppose any results of negotiation and claim making. If citizenship cultivates human beings who perceive themselves as beings with rights and are able to recognize the rights of others, this merely constitutes the foundations of political coexistence, not its guarantee. Thus, citizenship can be thought of as the foundation of justice and injustice simultaneously. Nonetheless, cultivating such a political identity requires practices, rituals, and habits, and that is why citizenship is increasingly defined by those elements rather than by a status that may be a result, not a cause.

As critical studies began challenging the idea of citizenship as a uniquely Western and nation-state institution, scholars have also reexamined the notion that contemporary nation-state citizenship is a universal status.[5] The reasons behind this questioning are no doubt associated with broader transformations such as globalization, the emergence of new international regimes of government, new international migration, new rationalities of government such as neoliberalism, new regimes of accumulation, as well as new social movements and their struggles for recognition and redistribution. All these have forced upon scholars, practitioners, and activists alike an urgent need to rethink the meaning of citizenship under these transformations. Major social issues such as the status of immigrants, aboriginal peoples, refugees, diasporic groups, environmental injustices, and the status of national minorities have increasingly been expressed through the language of rights and obligations, and hence of citizenship. Moreover, not only are the rights and obligations of citizens being redefined, but what it means to be a citizen and which individuals and groups are enabled to possess such rights and obligations have also become issues of concern. The three fundamental axes of citizenship, *extent* (rules and norms of exclusion), *content* (rights and responsibilities), and *depth* (thickness or thinness), are always being redefined and reconfigured. The modern conception of citizenship as merely a status held under the authority of a state has been contested and broadened to include various political and social struggles for recognition and redistribution as instances of claim making, and hence, by extension, of citizenship. Various struggles based upon identity and difference (whether sexual, 'racial,' 'ethnic,' diasporic, ecological, technological, or cosmopolitan) have found new ways of articulating their claims as claims to citizenship, understood not simply as a legal status but as political and social recognition and economic redistribution. Many scholars now are exploring and addressing concepts of sexual, ecological, diasporic, differentiated, multicultural, cosmopolitan, or Aboriginal citizenship. These studies, taken together, focus much more on rituals, practices, and routines that cultivate different forms of citizenship than an ostensibly universal status.

Of course, if we understand citizenship in its narrow, Eurocentric meaning, there is absolutely no relationship between waqfs and citizenship. But if we understand citizenship in its broadened and deepened meaning as the foundations of both justice and injustice and consider the role of social, cultural, and religious institutions in the formation of citizens as beings capable of making claims and recognizing the claims of others, then the waqf institution presents itself as a significant object of study. After all, this Islamic institution of beneficence existed for centuries before the Ottoman Empire, and was then taken up by the Ottoman authorities, which institutionalized, codified, and systematized it. By the eighteenth century this institution provided almost all social, cultural, religious, and economic services.

Why was such an institution overlooked in interpretations of the Islamic city or even Islamic citizenship? To answer that question, it is crucial to discuss Weber's work on the city, which had an enormous influence on the interpretations of social and cultural difference between the Orient and the Occident.

Citizenship after Orientalism

As is well known among scholars of urban history, Weber defined the city in terms of five characteristics (fortification, market, autonomous law and administration, association, and autocephaly), and thus argued that what made the occidental city unique was that it arose from the establishment of a fraternity, a brotherhood in arms for mutual aid and protection, and the usurpation of political power.[6] In this regard, Weber always drew parallels between the medieval 'communes' and ancient 'synoecism.' For Weber: "The polis is always the product of such a confraternity or synoecism, not always an actual settlement in proximity but a definite oath of brotherhood which signified that a common ritualistic meal is established and a ritualistic union formed and that only those had a part in this ritualistic group who buried their dead on the acropolis and had their dwellings in the city."[7] As we shall see below, while Weber consistently emphasized that some of these characteristics emerged in China, Japan, the Near East, India, and Egypt, he insisted that it was only in the Occident that all were present and appeared regularly. Thus, he concluded: "Most importantly, the associational character of the city and the concept of a burgher (as contrasted to the man from the countryside) never developed [in the Orient] at all and existed only in rudiments."[8] Therefore, "a special status of the town dweller as a 'citizen,' in the ancient medieval sense, did not exist and a corporate character of the city was unknown."[9] He was convinced that "in strong contrast to the medieval and ancient Occident, we never find the phenomenon in the Orient that the autonomy and the participation of the inhabitants in the affairs of local administration would be more strongly developed in the city . . . than in the countryside. In fact, as a rule the very opposite would be true."[10] For him this difference was decisive: "All safely founded information about Asian and Oriental settlements which had the economic characteristics of 'cities' seems to indicate that normally only the clan associations, and sometimes also the occupational associations, were the vehicle of organized action, but never the collective of urban citizens as such."[11] Above all, for Weber, only "in the Occident is found the concept of *citizen* (*civis Romanus, citoyens, bourgeois*) because only in the Occident does the *city* exist in the specific sense of the word."[12]

As important as it is to question the differences Weber posits, it is still necessary to examine why he thought they existed in the first place. Broadly speaking, Weber provided two reasons why the city as confraternity arose only in the Occident. First, since the occidental city originally emerged as a war machine, the group that owned the means of warfare dominated the city. For Weber, whether a group owned the means of warfare or was furnished by an overlord was as fundamental as whether the means of production were the property of the worker or the capitalist.[13] Everywhere in the Orient the development of the city as a brotherhood in arms was prevented by the fact that the army of the prince or overlord dominated the city.[14] Therefore, a prince or king always dominated 'oriental cities,' because in their origins and development, in India, China, the Near East, Egypt, and Asia, the question of irrigation was crucial. "The water question conditioned the existence of the bureaucracy, the compulsory service of the dependent classes, and the dependence of subject classes upon the functioning of the bureaucracy of the king."[15] That the king exercised his power in the form of a military monopoly was the basis of the distinction between the Orient and the Occident: "The forms of religious brotherhood and self-equipment for war made possible the origin and existence of the city."[16] While elements of analogous development occurred in India, China, Mesopotamia, and Egypt, the necessity of water regulation, which led to the formation of kingly monopolies over the means of warfare, stifled these beginnings. So for Weber the decisive issue became the harsh climate of oriental cities and the development of bureaucracies equipped to handle it.

The second obstacle preventing the development of the city in the Orient, according to Weber, was the persistence of magic in oriental religions. These religions did not allow the formation of "rational" urban communities. Eventually, however, the magical barriers between clans, tribes, and peoples, which were still known in the ancient polis, were set aside and so the establishment of the occidental city was made possible.[17] What makes the occidental city unique is that it allowed the association or formation of groups based on bonds and ties as rational contracts rather than through lineage or kinship.

In various studies written between *The Agrarian Sociology of Ancient Civilizations*[18] and *The City*,[19] Weber's argument that the city as a locus of citizenship was the characteristic that made the Occident unique and his reliance on synoecism and orientalism appeared more consistently than his emphasis on rationalization— and with increasing urgency.[20] Let us take a closer look at both the premises and conclusions of his argument.

Weber accepted various similarities between the occidental city and its near- and far-eastern counterparts.[21] Like the occidental city, the oriental city was also a marketplace, a center of trade and commerce, and a fortified stronghold. Moreover, he noted that merchant and artisan guilds could be found in oriental as in occidental cities.[22] Even the creation of autonomous legal authority could be found in both cities, though to varying degrees. Moreover, all ancient and medieval occidental cities, like their oriental counterparts, contained some agricultural land belonging to the city. Throughout the ancient world, the law applicable in cities differed from that in rural areas. In the occidental medieval city, however, such difference was essential, while it was insignificant and irregular in the ancient oriental city. The ancient occidental city almost always arose from a confluence and settling together of strangers and outsiders. While Weber used this as evidence of why the city always manifested a social and cultural differentiation, he often underlined its unity over diversity.[23] While he recognized that the urban population consisted of very diverse social groups, what was revolutionary in the occidental city was the free status of this distinct population. The fact that the city was a center of trade and commerce led rulers to free bondsmen and slaves so as to pursue opportunities for earning money in return for tribute.[24] The occidental city arose as "a place where *the ascent from bondage to freedom* by means of monetary acquisition was possible."[25] The principle that "city air makes man free," which emerged in Central and Northern European cities, was an expression of the unique aspect of the occidental city: "The urban citizenry therefore usurped the right to dissolve the bonds of seigniorial domination; this was the great—in fact, the *revolutionary*—innovation which differentiated the medieval occidental cities from all others."[26] The common quality of the ancient polis and the medieval commune was therefore an association of citizens subject to a special law exclusively applicable to them. In ancient Asia, Africa, or America similar formations of polis or commune constitutions or corporate citizenship rights were not known.

Weber's essential emphasis was, therefore, on the collective character of the city, which provided its dwellers with a distinct status. As he suggested: "The fully developed ancient and medieval city was above all constituted, or at least interpreted, as a fraternal association, as a rule equipped with a corresponding religious symbol for the associational cult of the citizens: a city-god or city-saint to whom only the citizens had access."[27] A significant difference between the occidental city and the ancient oriental city was that in the former there was no trace of magical and animistic castes. It was the belief of ancient occidental citizens that their cities originated as free associations and confederations of groups.[28]

Thus Weber argued that in the ancient oriental city, kinship ties persisted regularly, while in Greek *poleis* and medieval cities they progressively dissolved and were replaced by spatial and occupational relationships. In Greek *poleis* this process becomes visible beginning with colonization, which required the settling together of strangers and outsiders to become citizens. In addition, the shift in the military organization of the *polis* from heroic to hoplitic warfare intensified the dissolution of clan ties. Although many Greek *poleis* maintained such ties for a long time, they became more ritualistic and less significant in the everyday life of politics. Similarly, the warrior associations of the wandering Germanic tribes in Europe after the fall of the Roman Empire were organized around leadership and military prowess rather than clan ties. The development of spatial units such as the 'hundreds' as a method of distributing obligations impeded clan development.

Weber thought that Christianity dissolved such clans and effectively removed the barriers to the development of citizenship as a common identity. He said:

> When Christianity became the religion of these peoples who had been so profoundly shaken in all their traditions, it finally destroyed whatever religious significance these clan ties retained; perhaps, indeed, it was precisely the weakness or absence of such magical and taboo barriers which made the conversion possible. The often very significant role played by the parish community in the administrative organization of medieval cities is only one of many symptoms pointing to this quality of the Christian religion which, in dissolving clan ties, importantly shaped the medieval city.[29]

By contrast, the oriental city never really dissolved the tribal and clan ties and failed to develop citizenship as a common identity.

One can make two major criticisms of Weber's argument. The first is that Weber severely overestimated the importance of synoecism. Other scholars have interpreted the formation of corporations in early modern Europe not as an expression of communal freedom, but as a sign of its end.[30] When Weber argued, for example, that the oriental city did not have an associational or communal character, he assumed that "the medieval city, by contrast, was a commune from the very beginning, even though the legal concept of the 'corporation' as such was only gradually formulated."[31] It is not possible to assume that, by the time the concept of corporation was formulated in European legal thought during the sixteenth and seventeenth centuries, the city maintained its communal or associational character.[32] The second concern is Weber's orientalism. Weber already assumed that oriental despotism hindered the development of active citizens without secondary affinities and loyalties. He was then most concerned with explaining how this situation had come about. Thus, his orientalism provided the premise for his conclusion of synoecism, and synoecism, in turn, was the premise for his conclusion of orientalism.

How do we approach citizenship without synoecism and orientalism? Approaching citizenship without orientalism will require overcoming fundamental assumptions about synoecism and an ontological difference between the Occident and Orient mobilized by presences and absences. Moreover, it will require abandoning teleological, historicist, and presentist ways of interpreting histories of citizenship. Appropriating various strands of thought that range from legal and sociological thought to psychoanalysis and social psychology, I have argued elsewhere that it is possible to rethink occidental citizenship by analyzing the formation of groups as a generalized question of otherness and of the ways of being political without appealing to an ontological difference between the occident and the orient. Such an analysis regards the formation of groups as a fundamental but dynamic process of self-articulation. Through *orientations*, *strategies*, and *technologies* as forms of being political, beings develop *solidaristic*, *agonistic*, and *alienating* relationships. I maintain that these *forms* and *modes* constitute ontological ways of being political in the sense that being thrown into them is not a matter of conscious choice or contract.[33] It is through these forms and modes that beings articulate themselves as *citizens*, *strangers*, *outsiders*, and *aliens* as possible ways of being rather than as identities or differences. It is therefore impossible to investigate 'citizenship,' as that name which citizens—as distinguished from strangers, outsiders, and aliens—have given themselves, without investigating the specific constellation or figuration of orientations, strategies, and technologies available for deployment in producing solidaristic, agonistic, and alienating multiplicities.

Each of these figurations is a moment that should be understood not merely as a temporal but also as a spatial way of being political. Each moment is constituted as a consequence of analysis and exists only through this analysis. Each moment crystallizes itself as that space that is called the city. The city should not be imagined as merely a material or physical place but as a force field that works as a difference machine. The city is a difference machine because groups are not formed outside the machine and encounter each other within the city; instead, the city assembles, generates, and distributes these differences, incorporates them within strategies and technologies, and elicits, adjures, and incites them:

> The city is a crucial condition of citizenship in the sense that being a citizen is inextricably associated with being *of* the city . . . . [Therefore,] the city is neither a background to these struggles *against which* groups wager, nor . . . a foreground *for which* groups struggle for hegemony. Rather, the city is the battleground *through which* groups define their identity, stake their claims, wage their battles, and articulate citizenship rights, obligations, and principles.[34]

This condensed summary aims to highlight two issues regarding relations between the city and citizenship. First, while many critics of Weber have emphasized lacunae in his interpretation of the oriental city, they have tended to assume that his account of the occidental city is fundamentally correct. I argue that the unification Weber attributes to the occidental city and its ostensible expression—citizenship—is questionable. I called this 'synoecism' and argued that we must begin interpreting the history of occidental citizenship itself differently and accept that that history itself was articulated as an invented tradition that needs to be interrupted. Second, the constitution of the occidental city has not been without reference to the ostensible features of the oriental city. That 'orientalism' is not merely a representation but a strategic orientation that has mobilized various practices as a result of which some cities have been constituted as the bedrock of citizenship and others with their lack of it should be an object of critical analysis. I doubt that remaining within the terms of a discourse that employed an orientalist—if not imperialist, racist, and colonialist—difference between cultures and nations to dominate for at least two centuries our sense of being political, will enable us to articulate new understandings of the ways in which humans become political beings.

Whether we like it or not, citizenship has institutionalized specific ways of being political in world history, and leaving its investigations to either occidentalist or orientalist forms of thought is not an attractive option.

Ottoman citizenship

Approaching citizenship without orientalism opens up new possibilities for investigating the ways in which, at various moments in world history, distinct groups have articulated themselves by mobilizing orientations, assembling strategies and technologies, and producing different forms of otherness through which different ways of being political are rendered possible. Approaching citizenship this way removes the burden of comparing and contrasting various cultures or civilizations with a view to establishing the superiority or inferiority of one over the other. Weber focused incessantly on Judea, China, India, and Islam to compare corporate organization, contractualism, and so forth with ostensibly occidental institutions.[35] The aim in approaching citizenship without orientalism is not to abandon difference among various world historical moments, but to refuse to reduce them to fundamental ontological differences along the axis of inferiority or superiority.[36] Nor is it simply about abandoning occidental ways of thought. Rather, it is about revealing multiple and critical traditions of both occidental and oriental thought and appropriating them for alternative and critical interpretations.

Without these caveats, the notion of 'Ottoman citizenship' would be an apparent oxymoron. If citizenship is taken to mean what was articulated during the eighteenth and nineteenth centuries in Europe, then the only moment of emergence of Ottoman citizenship would be during and after the reform period (1839–76) known as the *Tanzimat*. It can further be argued that, until the promulgation of the 1869 'citizenship' law, and 1876, when a new Ottoman constitution was drawn up, citizenship had not been institutionalized in the imperial governing order.[37] One may even argue that these were moments of proto-citizenship, and that properly modern citizenship did not emerge until the new Turkish republic was formed in the 1920s, clearly adopting and articulating citizenship laws.[38] I would reject these arguments. Whatever reasons one gives to limit analysis of Ottoman citizenship to its modern incarnations, one should not approach it with already defined and understood notions of citizenship and search for the traces, development, and emergence of this construct. Such an approach fosters orientalist or reverse orientalist modes of thought that agree to recognize the existence of citizenship only if it is found in a particular, Western form. Besides, when this approach is followed faithfully, one can argue—as recent European Union documents have done—that even Turkish citizenship has not yet arrived since it still does not conform to its European counterpart.

The constitution of the Turkish republican citizenship began much earlier than the 1920s and was indeed a European project. Turkish identity and citizenship, founded on a racialized and ethnicized Turkishness, became prevalent in the late Ottoman Empire and the early Turkish republic.[39] This must, however, be understood in the context of a broader movement toward Westernization that incorporated racist and nationalist discourse on the purity of Aryan races and their ostensible superiority.[40] European discourse on race began in the late eighteenth century and continued well into the 1940s, which was a crucial moment of transformation of the Ottoman Empire into the Republic of Turkey. The discourse was not only implicated in various European projects of imperialism, colonialism, and orientalism, but also provided direct justification for them. It is often argued that the Ottomans did not use race or nation as operative concepts with which to organize their practices of belonging, identity, and difference.[41] But when the Ottomans were faced with the question of identity as a response to the declining empire, they drew upon Western sources and theories of race, identity, and nation. Ottoman intellectuals drew upon Western anthropology, archaeology, philology, and psychology—ways of seeing and thinking that allowed them to perceive themselves as modernizing and Westernizing forces.[42] Just as many European intellectuals and intelligentsia constituted European nations as authentic, *sui generis* polities with racial and ethnic purity and homogeneity, so, too, did their Ottoman counterparts in their quest to define a nation emerging from the fragments of an empire. While the intellectuals of the early republic attempted to set themselves apart from the Ottoman legacy, they nonetheless inherited the fundamental assumptions of the late Ottoman search for Turkish origins and, in some ways, intensified and deepened it.[43] Thus, it would be a mistake to consider the birth of republican citizenship without reference to the broader context in which orientalism played a crucial role.

I have insisted that to take orientalist assumptions about citizenship as given and deploy them in analyses that interpret various ways in which citizenship was used in republican institutions leads to orientalism and reverse orientalism. An opposite danger is to find in Ottoman institutions conceptions of 'the art of living together' that avoided the racism of modern European citizenship and that are more progressive and developed than an honest analysis warrants. In recent years, there has been a development in this direction that interprets certain Ottoman institutions from the point of view of tolerance.[44] For instance, the well-known system by which the Ottomans allocated certain rights to minorities—the millet system—is increasingly interpreted as a sign of Ottoman tolerance and accommodation of difference.[45] The problem with these arguments is not their plausibility or implausibility; it may well be that Ottoman institutions that were overlooked by orientalist interpreters did indeed involve certain forms of tolerance and accommodation that were alien to the emerging nineteenth-century national-ist and racist forms of constituting modern otherness. Yet to discover forms of tolerance, pluralism, and accommodation in the Ottoman Empire in terms understood in the late twentieth and early twenty-first centuries generates more problems than it solves. First, it serves as still another form of oriental-ism wherein Ottoman institutions are once again justified using ostensibly European standards, albeit in contemporary rather than historical figurations. Second, and perhaps more importantly, it also serves as a form of occiden-talism wherein ostensibly progressive Ottoman institutions are shown and demonstrated to be superior to their European counterparts.[46]

I suggest, rather, that investigating Ottoman citizenship must avoid orientalist, reverse orientalist, and occidentalist approaches. Understanding citizenship as a generalized problem of otherness would generate more useful theses by which to investigate the institution and rethink its con-temporary figurations. These suggestions raise the question: What kinds of investigations can one undertake about Ottoman citizenship without succumbing to orientalism? There are a number of problems that suggest possible investigations. The first is, of course, the formation of Turkish citizenship during the long century between the 1830s and the 1920s.[47] The debate over the Westernization of the Ottoman Empire in that period and the role of military-intellectual cadres (the Young Ottomans and later the Young Turks) is extensive. But the debate over the formation of citizenship during this period is more limited and embodies various orientalist assump-tions. Often citizenship is taken to mean modern republican citizenship as defined in Europe. A second cluster of problems concerns the formation and treatment of minorities in the Ottoman Empire, especially during the period of its expansion in the sixteenth and seventieth centuries. The debate over the millet system has dominated the investigations of this question and, as far as I know, the question of minorities has not been interpreted from the perspective of Ottoman citizenship. The question of the status and practices of non-Muslim groups in the Ottoman Empire has so far extensively focused on quintessential occidental categories such as autonomy, tolerance, recog-nition, and accommodation.[48] Analyses of these practices that refrain from relying on such categories have yielded remarkably rich interpretations.[49] The following section draws upon investigations concerning the second cluster of problems and illustrates how negotiations of difference and identity and claims for recognition for the so-called minorities of the Ottoman Empire also revolved around rights and obligations concerning the founding and maintaining of waqfs.

Waqfs, beneficence, and citizenship

As the Ottoman Empire expanded into three continents during the fifteenth century, encounters with the Other became a generalized condition of governing the empire. From the moment of its conquest by the Ottomans—and the Ottoman realization that governing the city would involve dealing with already constituted religious sects—Constantinople always had to deal with negotiating differences among groups. After Constantinople was conquered in 1453, Mehmed II began to repopulate it with people transferred from other conquered areas, such as Salonika (modern Thessalonica) and the Greek islands. By about 1480 the population had risen to between sixty and seventy thousand.[50] While the Hagia Sophia and other Byzantine churches were transformed into mosques, the Greek patriarchate was retained and was moved to the Church of the Pammakaristos Virgin (Mosque of Fethiye), later to find a permanent home in the Phanar quarter. The capital of the Ottoman Empire was transferred to Constantinople from Adrianople (Edirne) in 1457. Within a century, *Konstantiniye* (as Ottomans called the city for a long time) was transformed into a 'cosmopolitan' imperial city, with inhabitants drawn from all corners of the empire. In the process of negotiating their differences, these inhabitants invented various legal, political, social, and cultural institutions.

Modern historians of the empire call these institutions for negotiating difference collectively the 'millet system.' Millet was a generic term used to describe Muslim or non-Muslim religious groups and their affiliations. Millet is often translated into English as 'nation,' though it would be anachronistic to define these as modern nations. What complicates this history is that these millets did indeed develop and fulfill national aspirations in the modern sense in the nineteenth century. I prefer to use the sociological concept of 'social group' or simply 'group' in referring to the millets, to avoid anachronism.

These groups had various governing rights and privileges within the framework of Ottoman imperial administration.[51] The four main non-Muslim groups were Armenian, Catholic, Jewish, and Orthodox; of these, the last was the largest and most influential. These groups enjoyed various collective rights and privileges. A religious authority governed each and was also responsible for its obedience to imperial administration. The head of the Orthodox millet, for example, was the ecumenical patriarch of Constantinople. The patriarch's position as leader of that millet also gave him substantial secular governing powers. Whether to call these rights and privileges 'autonomous' or even 'autocephalous' is controversial. But, not unlike the guilds and corporations of medieval European cities, these groups were able to negotiate considerable scope for rights and privileges that obviously prompted many historians to use such terms as 'autonomy' with relative ease.

Much has been written about Ottoman millets, the way their subjects governed themselves, and regulation of relations between these millets and the Ottoman imperial administration.[52] Ottoman waqfs as acts of beneficence have also been investigated quite extensively, although not to the same degree.[53] What interests me is the way in which waqfs were used by millets to govern relationships of authority within them, between themselves and other millets, and between imperial authorities. We know that through thousands of waqfs established throughout the empire, neighbourhoods and cities were built and governed. Especially in Istanbul, the waqf became a charitable act that provided a considerable number of what we would call social services, ranging from libraries to soup kitchens, baths, fountains, hospitals, and religious buildings. We also know that, while the principle of waqf was Islamic, waqfs were also founded by non-Muslim groups to provide various services and were recognized by Ottoman authorities as legitimate and indispensable mechanisms of group governance. An Islamic act of beneficence that had existed for centuries before the Ottoman Empire, therefore, was then taken up by the Ottoman authorities and institutionalized, codified, and systematized. By the eighteenth century, this institution provided almost all social, cultural, religious, and economic services.

Under Ottoman rule, the waqf became a systematic method of building cities by providing various services in well thought-out nuclei (*külliye* or *imaret*) through which a definitive shape was given to cities. Well-known külliyes that have given shape to Istanbul, for example, include Süleymaniye, Fatih, Şehzade, Eyüp Sultan, and Lâleli külliyes. Throughout the empire, thousands of madrasas, schools, libraries, mosques, caravanserais, commercial centers (*hans*), bazaars, fountains, bridges, hospitals, soup kitchens or almshouses, lodges, tombs, baths, and aqueducts were founded either as part of such külliyes or imarets or as stand-alone buildings. Waqfs could include immovable property, such as rural land, which yielded income, as well as movable property, such as cash, books, and other valuables. One waqf scholar, Nazif Öztürk (1995), estimates that throughout the Ottoman Empire more than thirty-five thousand waqfs were founded, each including many buildings. That means the vast majority of Ottoman cities were built, maintained, or managed by means of the waqf system. According to Öztürk, waqfs, by employing vast numbers of people and providing income, made up about 16 percent of the Ottoman economy in the seventeenth century, about 27 percent in the eighteenth, and about 16 percent in the nineteenth century. Another waqf scholar, Murat Çizakça,[54] estimates that by the end of the nineteenth century, waqfs were providing more than 8 percent of total employment in the Ottoman Empire.

Yet this entire system of beneficence was not centralized or subject to state control. It is this aspect that would prove crucial for non-Muslim millets to negotiate their differences within the Ottoman imperial legal and political culture. Founding a waqf meant endowing privately held property for charitable use in perpetuity for functions set out in its founding deed or charter (*vakfiye*; *waqfiya*) and according to the conditions specified therein. The waqf deed also set out the way in which the property would be administered and maintained. The charter was registered and authenticated by a local judge (*kadı*; *qadi*) and did not require further approval. The principles underlying the waqf, then, were self-sufficiency, perpetuity, autonomy, and beneficence. Among waqf founders were prominent sultans, sultanas, pashas, as well as much less prominent members of the Ottoman governing and merchant elite. More significantly, there were notable numbers of women and non-Muslim waqf founders, a fact that needs to be investigated in terms of their rights and duties.

We need to investigate the role waqfs played as beneficence institutions enabling millet subjects to govern themselves, their relations with the Ottoman imperial authorities, and their ties with Muslim and non-Muslim subjects. The subject is vast, but it may provide a glimpse into how various groups negotiated otherness and difference as well as insights into the rise of modern nationalism, which displaced the practice of governing through millets. The research I have summarized here is therefore a part of a broader investigation on 'oriental citizenship,' which interprets various social and political practices as citizenship (understood as a generalized otherness that enables negotiations of recognition, difference, and identity). I am thus investigating if, and to what extent, waqf can be considered a 'citizenship' practice in the classical age of the Ottoman Empire, with a focus on Istanbul.

Conclusion

It is possible to illustrate that while the Ottoman Empire was not an empire of associations or communes in the way Weber saw the foundations of occidental citizenship, both the waqf institution and the way in which various social groups were able to claim, negotiate, and exercise rights did indeed enable subjects to have a group-differentiated legal and political status. While the city's collective identity was not expressed in a commune or association, the waqf was clearly an urban institution. Moreover, waqfs possessed juristic personality in law, and various non-Muslim groups were able to develop autonomous, if not autocephalous, rights for self-government, possibly through these institutions. Yet, this argument itself runs the risk of orientalism by trying to demonstrate the presence of practices and institutions that were ostensibly absent in the orient. When we consider citizenship not as contract or status but as acts and practices that enable subjects to negotiate differences, we find that the waqf and millet were indeed sophisticated acts of citizenship. Thus, it would be wrong to assume that Ottoman citizenship only appeared in the nineteenth century, when Ottoman authorities began to allocate rights to 'minorities' and attempted to develop a universal Ottoman identity for affiliation and loyalty. When citizenship is not understood or translated as nationality, we find acts of Ottoman citizenship before the nineteenth century that require investigation. If these conclusions are plausible, it should also be possible to extend our investigations into the relationship between Islamic waqfs and citizenship.

Notes

1   I would like to thank Erkan Ercel, Bora Isyar, and Ebru Ustundag for their assistance during various phases of this research. I would also like to thank the Department of International Relations at Koç University, Istanbul, for hosting me in Fall 2003, when I undertook archival research on waqfs in the Basbakanlik Arsivi (BOA). I am grateful for the assistance I received from BOA staff. I am also grateful to Fuat Keyman at Koç University for his hospitality in 2003 and 2005. I cannot begin to express my gratitude for the assistance I received from various *sahaf*s (antiquarians) in Istanbul in tracking down numerous rare books on Ottoman waqfs. I would like to extend special thanks to Nedret İşli, and to Ayhan Aktar for introducing me to Nedret. I am also indebted to Murat Çizakça and Bahaeddin Yediyıldız for their guidance and assistance. The research that this is chapter is based on was supported by the Social Sciences and Humanities Research Council.

2   Isin and Nielsen, eds., *Acts of Citizenship*.

3   Baer, "The *Waqf* as a Prop"; Hathaway, "The *Waqf* in Islamic Tradition"; Hoexter, "*Waqf* Studies in the Twentieth Century."

4   Isin and Lefebvre, "'The Gift of Law.'"

5   Benhabib, *The Claims of Culture*; Benhabibibid, *The Rights of Others*.

6   Weber, "Citizenship," 315–37, 319.

7   Weber, "Citizenship," 320.

8   Weber, *Economy and Society*, 1227.

9   Weber, *Economy and Society*, 1227.
10   Weber, *Economy and Society*, 1228.
11   Weber, *Economy and Society*, 1233.
12   Weber, "Citizenship," 332.
13   Weber, "Citizenship," 320.
14   Weber, *The Religion of China*, 1917.
15   Weber, "Citizenship," 321.
16   Weber, "Citizenship," 321.
17   Weber, "Citizenship," 322–23.
18   Weber, *Agrarian Sociology*.
19   Weber, *Economy and Society*.
20   Käsler, *Max Weber*, 42.
21   Weber, *Economy and Society*, 1236.
22   Weber, *The Religion of India*, 33–35.
23   Weber, *Economy and Society*, 1237.
24   Weber, *Economy and Society*, 1238.
25   Weber, *Economy and Society*, 1238.
26   Weber, *Economy and Society*, 1239.
27   Weber, *Economy and Society*, 1241.
28   Weber, *Economy and Society*, 1242.
29   Weber, *Economy and Society*, 1244.
30   Black, *Guilds and Civil Society*; Frug, "The City as a Legal Concept."
31   Weber, *Economy and Society,* 1243.
32   Isin, *Cities without Citizens*.
33   I refer the reader to the bibliography for my work on this subject, in particular Isin, *Being Political*.
34   Isin, *Being Political*, 283–84.
35   Weber, *The Religion of China*; Weber, *The Religion of India*; Weber, *Ancient Judaism*.
36   Isin, *Being Political*, 22ff.
37   Ünsal, "Yurttaslik Zor Zanaat."
38   Aybay, "Teba-I Osmani'den."
39   Deringil, "'Legitimacy Structures"; Deringilibid, "'The Invention of Tradition"; Kadioglu, "'Milletinin Arayan Devlet."
40   Davison, *Reform in the Ottoman Empire*; Davison, *Essays in Ottoman and Turkish History*; Timur, *Osmanlı Kimliği*, 121–43.
41   Makdisi, "After 1860"; Timur, *Osmanlı Kimliği*.
42   Timur, *Osmanlı Kimliği*, 139–40.
43   Timur, *Osmanlı Kimliği*, 144–48.
44   Armağan, *Osmanlı'da Hoşgörü*.
45   Reppetto, "Millet System"; Stefanov, "Millet System."
46   See Venn, *Occidentalism*.
47   Isin and Isyar, "Türkiye'de Ulus-Devle."
48   Armağan, ed., *Osmanlı'da Hoşgörü*.
49   Ercan, *Osmanlı Yönetiminde*; Soykan, *Osmanlı İmparatorluğu'nd Gayrimüslimler*.
50   İnalcık, "Istanbul."
51   Braude and Lewis, eds., *Christians and Jews*.

52 Braude, "Foundation Myths"; Braude, "'Millet Sistemi'nin" I'lgin Tarihi"; Karpat, *An Inquiry;* Stefanov, "Millet System."
53 Çizakça, *A History;* Singer, *Constructing Ottoman Beneficence;* van Leeuwen, *Waqfs.*
54 Çizakça, *A History.*

Bibliography

Armağan, M., ed. *Osmanlı'da Hoşgörü: Birlikte Yaşama Sanatı.* Istanbul: Gazeteciler ve Yazarlar Vakfı Yayınları, 2000.

Aybay, R. "Teba-i Osmani'den T.C. Yurttaşı'na Geçisin Neresindeyiz?" in A. Ünsal, ed., *75 Yilda Tebaa'dan Yurttaş'a Doğru,* 37–42. Istanbul: Tarih Vakfi, 1998.

Baer, G. "The *Waqf* as a Prop for the Social System, 16th–20th Centuries." *Islamic Law and Society* 4 (1997): 264–97.

Benhabib, S. *The Claims of Culture: Equality and Diversity in the Global Era.* Princeton, NJ: Princeton University Press, 2002.

————. *The Rights of Others: Aliens, Residents and Citizens.* Cambridge: Cambridge University Press, 2004.

Black, A. *Guilds and Civil Society in European Political Thought from the Twelfth Century to the Present.* Ithaca, NY: Cornell University Press, 1984.

Braude, B. "Foundation Myths of the Millet System," in B. Braude and B. Lewis, eds., *Christians and Jews in the Ottoman Empire,* 69–88.

————. "Millet Sistemi'nin Ilgin Tarihi," in H.C. Güzel, ed., *Osmanlı'dan Günümüze Ermeni Sorunu,* 315–32. Ankara: Yeni Türkiye Yayınları, 2001.

Braude, B., and B. Lewis, eds. *Christians and Jews in the Ottoman Empire: The Functioning of a Plural Society.* New York: Holmes and Meier Publishers, 1980.

Çizakça, M. *A History of Philanthropic Foundations: The Islamic World from the Seventh Century to the Present.* Istanbul: Bogaziçi University Press, 2000.

Davison, R.H. *Essays in Ottoman and Turkish History, 1774–1923: The Impact of the West.* Modern Middle East Series 16. Austin: University of Texas Press, 1990.

————. *Reform in the Ottoman Empire, 1856–1876.* New York: Gordian Press, 1973.

Deringil, S. "The Invention of Tradition as Public Image in the Late Ottoman Empire, 1808 to 1908." *Comparative Studies in Society and History* 35, no. 1 (1993): 3–29.

————. "Legitimacy Structures in the Ottoman State—the Reign of Abdulhamid II (1876–1909)." *International Journal of Middle East Studies* 23, no. 3 (1991): 345–59.

Ercan, Y. *Osmanlı Yönetiminde Gayrimüslimler: Kuruluşundan Tanzimat'a Kadar Sosyal, Ekonomik Ve Hukuki Durumları.* Ankara: Turhan Yayınları, 2001.

Frug, G.E. "The City as a Legal Concept." *Harvard Law Review* 93 (April 1980): 1057.

Hathaway, J. "The *Waqf* in Islamic Tradition: A Source of Socio-Political Power." *International Journal of Middle East Studies* 30, no. 1 (1998): 121–23.

Hoexter, M. "*Waqf* Studies in the Twentieth Century: The State of the Art." *Journal of the Economic and Social History of the Orient* 41, no. 4 (1998): 474–95.

İnalcık, H. "Istanbul: An Islamic City." *Journal of Islamic Studies* 1 (1990): 1–23.

Isin, E.F. *Being Political: Genealogies of Citizenship.* Minneapolis: University of Minnesota Press, 2002.

————. *Cities without Citizens: Modernity of the City as a Corporation.* Montreal: Black Rose Books, 1992.

————. 2002. "Citizenship after Orientalism," in E.F. Isin and B.S. Turner, eds., *Handbook of Citizenship Studies.* London: Sage: 117–28.

————. "The Origins of Canadian Municipal Government," in J. Lightbody, ed., *Canadian Metropolitics: Governing Our Cities*, 51–91. Mississauga, Ont.: Copp Clark, 1995.

————. "Rethinking the Origins of Canadian Municipal Government." *Canadian Journal of Urban Research* 4, no. 1 (1995): 73–92.

————. "Ways of Being Political." *Distinktion: Tidsskrift For Samfundsteori* 4 (2002): 7–28.

————. "Who Is the New Citizen? Toward a Genealogy." *Citizenship Studies* 1, no. 1 (1997): 115–32.

Isin, E.F., and B. Isyar. 2005. "Türkiye'de Ulus-Devlet Ve Vatandaşlığın Doğuşu," in T. Tarhanlı and A. Kaya, eds., *Ab Üyesi Ülkelerde Ve Türkiye Gerçekliğinde Anayasal Vatandaşlık Ve Azınlıklar.* Istanbul: TESEV.

Isin, E.F., and A. Lefebvre. "The Gift of Law: Greek Euergetism and Ottoman *Waqf*." *European Journal of Social Theory* 8, no. 1 (2005): 5–23.

Isin, E.F., and G.M. Nielsen eds. *Acts of Citizenship.* London: Zed Books, 2008.

Isin, E.F., and B.S. Turner, eds. *Handbook of Citizenship Studies*. London: Sage, 2002.

Kadioglu, A. "Milletinin Arayan Devlet: Türk Milliyetçiliginin Açmazlari'," in A. Ünsal, ed., *75 Yilda Tebaa'dan Yurttas'a Dogru*, 201–11. Istanbul: Tarih Vakfi, 1998.

Karpat, K.H. *An Inquiry into the Social Foundations of Nationalism in the Ottoman State: From Social Estates to Classes, from Millets to Nations*. Research Monograph 39. Princeton, NJ: Princeton University, Center of International Studies, 1973.

Käsler, D. *Max Weber: An Introduction to His Life and Work*. Oxford: Blackwell, 1979.

Makdisi, U.S. "After 1860: Debating Religion, Reform, and Nationalism in the Ottoman Empire." *International Journal of Middle East Studies* 34 (2002): 601–17.

―――. "Ottoman Orientalism." *American Historical Review* 107, no. 3 (2002): 768–96.

Öztürk, N. *Türk Yenileşme Tarihi Çerçevesinde Vakıf Müessesesi*. Ankara: Türkiye Diyanet Vakfı, 1995.

Reppetto, T.A. "Millet System in Ottoman and American Empires." *Public Policy* 18, no. 5 (1970): 629–48.

Singer, A. *Constructing Ottoman Beneficence: An Imperial Soup Kitchen in Jerusalem*. SUNY Series in Near Eastern Studies. Albany: State University of New York Press, 2002.

Soykan, T.T. *Osmanlı İmparatorluğu'nd Gayrimüslimler: Klasik Dönem Osmanlı Hukukunda Gayrimüslimlerin Hukuki Statüsü*. Istanbul: Ütopya Kitabevi, 2000.

Stefanov, S. "Millet System in the Ottoman Empire: Example for Oppression or for Tolerance?" *Bulgarian Historical Review* 2–3 (1997): 138–42.

Timur, T. *Osmanlı Kimliği*. 2nd ed. Istanbul: Hil Yayınları, 1994.

Ünsal, A. "Yurttaslik Zor Zanaat," in A. Ünsal, ed., *75 Yilda Tebaa'dan Yurttas'a Dogru*, 1–36. Istanbul: Tarih Vakfi, 1998.

van Leeuwen, R. *Waqfs and Urban Structures: The Case of Ottoman Damascus*. Studies in Islamic Law and Society, vol. 11. Leiden: Brill, 1999.

Venn, C. *Occidentalism: Modernity and Subjectivity*. London: Sage, 2000.

Weber, M. *The Agrarian Sociology of Ancient Civilizations*. Translated by R.I. Frank. London: New Left Books, 1909.

―――. *Ancient Judaism*. Translated by H.H. Gerth and D. Martindale. New York: Free Press, 1919.

—. "Citizenship," in M. Weber, *General Economic History*, 315–37. London: Transaction Publishers, 1927.

—. *Economy and Society: An Outline of Interpretive Sociology*. Edited and translated by G. Roth and C. Wittich. 2 vols. Berkeley: University of California Press, 1978 [1921].

—. *The Religion of China*. Translated by H.H. Gerth. New York: Free Press, 1916.

—. *The Religion of India*. Translated by H.H. Gerth and D. Martindale. New York: Free Press, 1917.